942.08 Mon   18236

£1-10

1900

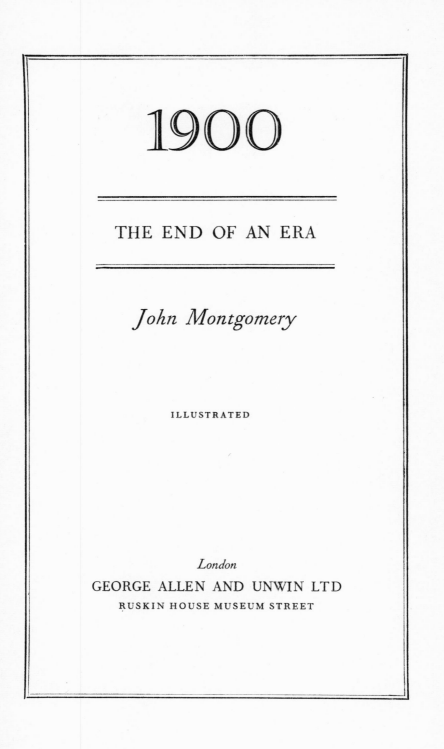

1900

THE END OF AN ERA

John Montgomery

ILLUSTRATED

London
GEORGE ALLEN AND UNWIN LTD
RUSKIN HOUSE MUSEUM STREET

To
Evelyn and Graham Montgomery

ACKNOWLEDGEMENTS

Permission was kindly granted for the reproduction of photographs as follows:

Radio Times Hulton Picture Library: 1, 2, 3, 5, 8, 9, 10, 11, 12, 13, 15, 20, 21, 22, 23, 24, 26.

Cadbury's: 25.

National Film Archive: 19.

The *Daily Mail*: 4.

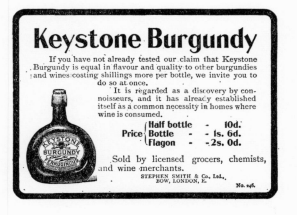

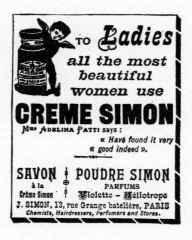

CONTENTS

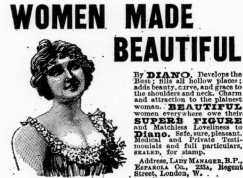

ILLUSTRATIONS

1

THE LAST YEAR

The year 1900 was the last of the great Victorian age; nothing would ever be quite the same again. With the coming of new discoveries and the intense rivalry between Britain and Germany, which was in fourteen years to find expression in the First Great World War, Victorianism and all that the term implied was soon to end. Yet Britain's colonial Empire was still expanding, and on January 4th the flag of the Royal Niger Company was formally lowered at Lagos and the Union Jack was hoisted over yet another sphere of British influence.

The old Queen was much loved. She was eighty-one in May 1900, her eyesight was failing and she was in poor health, but she had emerged triumphantly from the shadows of widowhood and she was now once again influencing the politics and prosperity of her dominions. Hardly anyone alive remembered a time when she was not representative of everything British, and Britain seemed the greatest power and force in the world. No monarch had so symbolized the hopes and achievements of her country since Queen Elizabeth the First. She walked slowly and weakly into the age of aeroplanes, motor cars, wireless telegraphy, the cinematograph, and a revolution in everyday living, while neither she nor the majority of her subjects realized the importance of the changes which were taking place around them.

The last few months of 1899 had brought war in South Africa. On January 1, 1900, the Queen sent personal New Year greetings to the various commands fighting against the Boers, expressing her deep and genuine interest in her soldiers. Later she gave orders that in future all Irish regiments in her army would wear sprigs of shamrock on St Patrick's Day, to commemorate the gallantry of her Irish soldiers. Visiting London from Windsor, she drove in state along the Embankment to the City, where she was received by the Lord Mayor and Corporation and was cheered by tremendous crowds. Next day she again drove through the streets of London, and in the evening a public demonstration took place outside Buckingham Palace, where, a tiny figure in black, she stood at the window and acknowledged the cheers of the crowds.

The political position of Britain in the first and last years of the nineteenth century was surprisingly similar. At both times she was heavily engaged in a futile war which was misjudged by her leaders, while at the close of the century, as at the beginning, she was without a strong Continental ally. Europe in 1900 was as hostile to Britain as it had been in 1801 on the signing of the Treaty of Luneville, although no European nation was actually in arms against her.[1]

Beyond Europe, however, Britain had built up great alliances in her colonial Empire, which had grown rich and powerful during the latter half of the century. As we shall see, when the old country fought against the Boers in South Africa it was the Canadians, Australians, New Zealanders, West Indians, and the semi-independent wealthy rulers of India who came forward with men and arms and money, unfettered by conditions and demands, to fight for Britain.

'Everyone who was born during the last few years of the Victorian age must cherish memories,' says H. V. Morton. 'We saw a new world developing before our eyes, its significance distinguished by touches of comedy or broad farce, so that we could not recognize the march of events. Neither did we recognize that into our hands had been given the awful heritage of a century of peace and splendour. Even when the 1914 War came we did not understand that it would shake the very foundations of the

[1] Lord Rosebery, however, thought that in 1898 the prestige of Britain stood higher than it had done since Waterloo. Even if this were true, the Boer War was to lower that prestige in the eyes of other nations.

world we knew, and shatter into bits the last vestige of our security. We thought the war had only to be won and that we should return again, victorious and singing, into the ease and comfort of the nineteenth century—for such, in reality, were the first years of the twentieth century. We have since learnt wisdom.'

It was a world of few controls, very low wages, little income tax, uncertain profits, thin markets, sharp class distinctions, appalling snobbery based on privilege and wealth, great vulgarity, and considerable unemployment. There were squalor and extreme poverty in the back streets, where the drab tenement houses were lit by gas or candles and where hot water was rare and hygiene was primitive; crime and drunkenness kept the magistrates busy from morning until night; and to many of her citizens Great Britain offered so poor a future that tens of thousands sought a new life year after year, in the United States, Canada, Australia, New Zealand and South Africa.

Yet the Victorian age which was closing had brought great discoveries and developments. Later generations were to owe much to the courage, impetuosity and daring with which the Victorians entered fresh fields of scholarship, science and art. As John Russell pointed out in the *Sunday Times*, the end of the century saw a period in which the possibilities of mechanized violence were beginning to find hideous expression; but it was also a period in which the hierarchy of everyday living was subtly overturned, and the day was glimpsed on which the good life, or a large part of it, would be available to everyone.

The struggle which had been continuing since the Reformation, the urge of the people to be set free and to enjoy the fruits of civilization, was finally to end at the close of the nineteenth century with the triumph of the British middle class. Once people were congregated into cities and towns the old authoritative squirearchy was dead. The new Victorian spirit was rooted in the middle class, but along the country lanes men and women still walked many miles to hiring fairs where they stood in line to await the will of employers. Domestic servants, carters in smocks, thatchers, cowmen, dairymaids and ploughboys still used the market places as their register office for employment. There were still sailors with earrings in their ears, holding their possessions in gay bandana handkerchiefs, ostlers in striped waistcoats, cheapjacks shouting their wares, a blacksmith in a leather apron, a blind man with his tin and dog.[1] England in 1900 was still to some extent an agricultural country, and the motorcar had not yet opened up the byways and lanes. But agriculture had for fifty years been on the decline and by 1900 there were many more people in cities than in the country.

During the century the British, by their industry, political sagacity, and the judicious use of military force, had created the nearest thing to a world government that man had yet known. This had operated on two levels—one *de jure*, the other *de facto*. In this last year of her reign Queen Victoria ruled over more human beings, and over more races speaking more languages and practising more religions, than any monarch had done before her. One in five of the world's population owed her allegiance; 25 per cent of the land surface of the earth lay under the Union Jack; Britain influenced the whole world; both North and South America and much of the Continent looked to London for capital banking, insurance, and shipping facilities; she was the world's greatest importer of food and raw materials, and in return she supplied every kind of manufactured goods. During the Queen's reign the population of the United Kingdom had doubled and its external trade had increased by 600 per cent, while over every ocean the white ensign and the red ensign proudly waved. The average Englishman considered that his word was his bond, while his country stood for trade, justice, law and order, the sanctity of contracts, the bearing of the white man's burden, the freedom of the individual, and parliamentary democracy.[2]

The years 1840–1900 had seen a period mainly of peace for Britain because no established state was capable of challenging her might, and the United States and Prussia were concerned with building up their economy. The American civil war, and the Prussian victories over Denmark, Austria-Hungary and France had not been conflicts which upset the peace of the world, and in

[1] Dion Clayton Calthrop, *English Dress*, London, 1934.
[2] Stephen King-Hall, *Our Own Times*, London, 1934.

1900 the prospect of a war between the great powers seemed to the average Briton to be extremely remote.

Yet the great conflict was only fourteen years off, and there was no room for complacency. This last year of the reign and of the century marked the close of an epoch in the country's home and foreign affairs alike, as the subsequent rise of the Labour party and the search for international alliances were to bear witness during the Edwardian era which was to follow. It was no less the end of an epoch in thought and feeling and a way of life. It had been a positive age, imaginative and daring in its great explorations and scientific developments, but it was gradually shading off into a period of doubts and difficulties, not less serious but more critical and ironical. In the minds of more and more educated people a belief in the assumption of natural science was gradually supplanting Christianity as orthodoxy. Even in the 'eighties it had seemed to the lady who was to become the socialist Mrs Sidney Webb that the mainspring of philanthropy was no longer the service of God, as taught by the churches, but instead the service of man.[1]

Throughout Victorian times Britain had held the supremacy of the sea, and on the whole she had used the might of her Navy on the side of peace, goodwill and freedom. The Victorians knew and cared little about the military or naval might of the other Continental powers. They knew more about their Empire cousins. Europe was the rich Englishman's playground, with the Alps, the Riviera, its picture galleries, its ancient cities and castles. Britons were islanders with a great overseas Empire, not Continentals. They were proud to be sailors in the tradition of Nelson, but service in the army was regarded in the middle and working classes as a low calling, except in time of war:

It's Tommy this and Tommy that, an' 'Chuck him out, the brute!'
But it's 'Saviour of 'is country' when the guns begin to shoot.

Except for the Crimean and Boer wars, there were no really serious or lengthy military or naval conflicts for Britain during the Victorian era, and there was no consistent foreign policy with

[1] Sir James Butler, *A History of England*, 1815–1939, Oxford, 1960.

a strong army and armaments attached to it. Indeed, foreign affairs were considered a matter for Liberal or Conservative politicians, not affecting the man in the street or likely to threaten Britain's existence.

Queen Victoria, Empress of India, had little opportunity to see for herself the many squalors of Britain. Her advisers accused the reformers of exaggeration or counted on the slums being decently draped in bunting and the children scrubbed clean when she visited them.[1] But she was too astute, even in her old age, to be deceived, and she was never hypocritical, as were many of her ministers. When she drove through a townscape too vast in its dreariness to be concealed, she was deeply shocked. Of the Black Country in 1852 she had written in her private journal:
'It is like another world. In the midst of so much wealth, there seems to be nothing but ruin. As far as the eye can reach, one sees nothing but chimneys, flaming furnaces, many deserted but not pulled down, with wretched cottages around them ... Add to this a thick and black atmosphere ... and you have but a faint impression of the life ... which a third of a million of my poor subjects are forced to lead. It makes me sad!'

In 1900 two important problems continued to confront the politicians at Westminster: the South African War in which at the end of 1899 the British had suffered serious reverses, and which we shall examine at length; and the question of Home Rule for Ireland, which continued year after year to be a thorn in the side of successive governments. At all times the problem had roused the fiercest passions. The Irish still continued to demand Home Rule, and many more men and women were to be murdered before the country's independence was finally achieved.

In the United States the year opened turbulently. A bitter election contest in Kentucky had brought the inhabitants of the state almost into armed conflict. Both the Republican and Democratic parties claimed to have won the state election of 1899. The Republican governor's use of troops on election day was loudly denounced by the Democrats as a case of flagrant intimida-

[1] Elizabeth Longford, *Victoria R.I.*, London, 1964.

tion; lawless mountaineers entered Louisville, the capital of Kentucky, and received arms from the state government. On the morning of January 30th, Senator William Goebel, the Democratic governor-elect, was struck down by a bullet in the Capitol grounds. The shot, fired from the window of a nearby executive building, proved fatal. The governor of Kentucky and his threatened associates then sought the protection of the Federal Government, and the state militia was called out, but the soldiers split into two factions. Having failed to obtain help from outside, Governor Taylor fled from Kentucky and was promptly indicted for murder.

The killing of Senator Goebel had turned public opinion against the faction held responsible for the crime. Retribution was visited on the Republican party in Kentucky when it ultimately lost almost all the points which had been gained in the 1899 election.[1]

And what of the last year of the century? Many people thought it was the first year of a new century. In New Jersey two young German Americans, William J. Witt and Anna Waddilove, stood before the Reverend Rufus Johnson of Holy Trinity Church and were promptly married at 12.01 a.m. on January 1, 1900. They had planned to be the first couple to be married in the twentieth century, but unfortunately they were a year too soon. As the newspapers carefully explained, the nineteenth century would end with the conclusion of year 1900, not the beginning of it. But the immigrants were not convinced, and nor were many other Americans, for in Germany had not the Kaiser ordered the new century to be saluted with a salute of thirty-three guns? Addressing his officers, His Imperial Majesty promised the rebirth of 'my navy', so that in the coming century Germany might at last win 'the place which it has not yet attained'.[2] In Britain many people wrote to *The Times* claiming that the start of 1900 was indeed the turn of the century. And, as if to prove it, the *New York Times* of December 21, 1899, devoted nearly four columns to a retrospective review of the nineteenth century, saying: 'We

[1] Edwin Emerson Jr., *A History of the 19th Century*, New York.
[2] Walter Lord, *The Good Years*, London, 1960.

step upon the threshold of 1900 which leads to the new century, facing a still brighter dawn of civilization.'

In *The Illustrated London News* for January 6th, Mr L. F. Austin tried to put the record right. 'Greeting to 1900,' he said, 'the last year of the nineteenth century, if you please, not the first of the twentieth! I hope that any readers who believe a century to consist of ninety-nine years will not take this address as too aggressive . . . yet crowned heads, I notice, side with the zeroists. There is the Kaiser, for instance, and the King of Sweden; and who am I that I should presume to differ from them? Nothing but the unreasoning habit of arithmetic, which will not allow a hundred to be ninety-nine, sustains me against this imperial and regal authority . . . judging from the letters in *The Times* the zero party is touched with fanaticism . . . one correspondent demands a short Act to make 1900 the first year of the twentieth century! The Bishop of London says that nothing is so suggestive of the need for humility as the "familiar spectacle of bodies of Englishmen desperately determined to have their own way by every means in their power". But how is the Bishop of London to bring to a sense of humiliation the man who wants the twentieth century proclaimed in a *short Act*? And those hasty crowned heads, however are they to be humbled?'

Britain's chief concern in the last year of the century was her failure to conquer the Boers in South Africa, and this was a source of satisfaction to most European countries, and to the United States. To the average American the Boer seemed like the traditional colonist, a free man fighting against oppression. Americans naturally looked back to the days when they had also struggled for independence. It was not unreasonable that they compared their own not distant traditions—Bunker Hill, Valley Forge, George Washington, Israel Putnam, Nathan Hale with the aspirations of Oom Paul Kruger, Cronje and De Wet.

America's mood in 1900 was for the underdog against the upper, a throw-back to the time when all true Americans had been underdogs, the rebels, when Britain was against freedom and independence. Understandably, Americans in 1900 sympathized with the Boers against the British. In the campaign of the Democrats against imperialism, Richard Croker, when asked for his definition of anti-imperialism, replied, 'My idea of anti-imperialism is opposition to the fashion of shooting everybody who doesn't speak English'. The Boers appeared to the Americans and to most Europeans as their kin, free men, economically independent. When the British finally announced that the Boers were conquered (although they were not), the American *Life* magazine said, 'A small boy with diamonds is no match for a large burglar with experience'.

Until 1900 the largest strain by far in the racial composition of the people of the United States had come from northern and western Europe—from Britain, Germany and Scandinavia. But the number of immigrants into America from these countries had gradually been diminishing, and at the same time large numbers of people had set out from the south and east of Europe, from Latin and Slavic lands, and from Hebrew centres, to seek their fortunes in what was still regarded as the new world. This tendency was to be checked in later years by the Immigration Restriction Acts of 1921 and 1924.

During the century the United States had adhered to a policy of splendid isolation, being occupied in developing her own economy and her vast resources, but when in 1898 the island of Cuba revolted against Spain, American popular feeling demanded us intervention on behalf of the rebel Cubans, and the country declared war on Spain. Three months of fighting brought decisive victory to the United States, which set up a Cuban Republic under its protection, and took over the Philippine Islands from the Spanish. Britain was surprised. Was the United States, with so many home problems to be solved, becoming imperialistic and looking for colonies?

The average American, reading his newspaper on Monday morning, New Year's Day 1900, might observe with some un-easiness that the headlines occupied themselves largely with imperialism—the Philippines, Cuba, Porto Rico, Guam, Aguin-aldo, the Igorrates, places which only three years earlier would have meant little. Annexation overseas was the principal issue in the presidential campaign of 1900. The Republicans called it expansion, the Democrats called it imperialism and militarism. Thus, the United States was split between being a great new world power or remaining independent and alone. It was in February, only a year earlier, that Rudyard Kipling had published his verse:

> Take up the White Man's burden
> Send forth the best ye breed . . .
> To wait in heavy harness,
> On fluttering folk and wild—
> Your new-caught sullen peoples
> Half devil and half child.

Mark Sullivan[1] pointed out later that the poem was taken as being addressed both to America in her expansion and to Britain in her attempt to master the Boers. Someone said of the verse that 'in winged words it circled the earth in a day and by repetition it became hackneyed in a week'. Someone else said it 'revealed a necessary but thankless task to be performed by the white race under the restraints of conscience'. But there were other points of view as the *New York Times* put it:

> Take up the White Man's burden;
> Send forth your sturdy sons,
> And load them down with whiskey
> And testaments and guns.
> Throw in a few diseases
> To spread in tropic climes,
> For there the healthy niggers
> Are quite behind the times.

Most Americans felt that the Philippines were beyond their reach and were vaguely Asiatic. Although the benevolent Mr Taft referred to the Philippino as a 'little brown brother', Robert F. Morrison in the Manila *Sunday Sun* expressed the United States view quite differently:

> I like the word fraternity, but still I draw the line;
> He *may* be a brother of William H. Taft,
> But he ain't no friend of mine.

[1] Mark Sullivan, *Our Times*, London, 1926.

Once the American administration had decided to take over the Philippines, it offered to pay for them. By the Treaty of Paris, signed in December 1898, the United States gave 20,000,000 dollars for the islands. Spain evacuated Cuba and also ceded Puerto Rico and the island of Guam in the Pacific. But the average American citizen's anti-imperialist feelings were so strong that the treaty was eventually ratified by only a two-vote margin in the Senate. And in October 1899 the anti-imperialists held a congress in Chicago at which they loudly denounced the attempt to subdue the Philippines as being 'open disloyalty to the distinctive principles of our government', quoting Abraham Lincoln's speech on slavery and despotism.

So widespread was American opinion against imperial expansion that in 1900 Jennings Bryan, the Democratic candidate for President, made it the leading issue of his election campaign. But the Republicans renominated William McKinley for President[1] and Theodore Roosevelt, the Governor of New York, for Vice-President, carefully avoiding the issue of imperialism, on which they were themselves divided. Adopting as their election slogan 'the full dinner pail', they claimed credit for the prosperity which the country had enjoyed during McKinley's previous administration and predicted a severe depression if the Democrats won. The result of the election was an even more decisive victory for the Republicans than that of 1896. The anti-imperialist Jennings Bryan did not even win in his home state of Nebraska.

There was no doubt that the United States was enjoying an unheard-of wave of prosperity and industrial expansion. The *Boston Herald* summed it up: 'If one could not have made money this past year, his case is hopeless'. From coast to coast, the country had never known such good, rich times. The Portland *Oregonian* called 1898 'the most prosperous year Oregon has ever known'.

In 1900 the United States was a nation of just under 76,000,000 people, with dependencies in the West Indies, off the coast of Asia, near the Arctic Ocean, and in the mid-Pacific, all acquired

---

[1] William McKinley (1897–1901), who was to be assassinated during his second term of office.

recently, except Alaska. It was in mineral resources and raw materials already one of the world's richest countries, producing more than half of all the cotton, corn, copper and oil, more than a third of all the steel, pig iron and silver, and substantially a third of its coal and gold. It was a nation whose white population of about 41,000,000 contained about 30 per cent of British stock, 31 per cent of German, 4 per cent of Swedish, 4 per cent Russian, 4 per cent Austrian, and 3 per cent Italian. For most of these people this vast country offered new freedoms, an absence of class or caste systems which could not be found in Europe, and an almost inspired belief in the future. Indeed, it was a great land of opportunity for anyone with initiative, and America was already becoming one of the world's largest producers and exporters.

At this time America was Britain's biggest single customer, buying in 1899 goods to the value of over £18,000,000 while the total exports of the United Kingdom amounted to £6 10s 5d per head of the population, and her imports cost £11 19s 2d per head.

In North America a series of appalling disasters made the year memorable. On April 27th a terrible fire destroyed three-fifths of the city of Hull, Ontario, and a large section of the city of Ottawa, on the opposite bank of the St Lawrence river, wiping out the leading industries of both cities, about 15,000 people being made homeless. A few days later, on May 1st, a violent explosion wrecked the coal mines in Utah, several hundred miners being suffocated by poisonous gases. Then, on June 30th, came one of the most disastrous fires ever known in the United States, involving great loss of life, at the Hoboken docks, opposite the city of New York.

The fire started among some bales of cotton lying at one of the piers, and it soon spread to other piers. Among the goods lying in the docks were barrels of oil, which quickly caught fire and exploded. Unfortunately it was a Saturday, the public visiting day to the vessels of the North German Lloyd Company, and the docks were filled with men, women and children anxious to see the officers and crews in port. The entire system of piers belonging to the company, stretching for a quarter of a mile, was destroyed. To prevent the fire spreading further, one of the main piers was blown up. The liners *Maine, Saale* and *Bremen* were towed out into the stream after they had caught fire, and they were later beached. The *Kaiser Wilhelm der Grosse* was scorched by the flames and was saved only by the prompt action of the officers and crew, the great vessel being tugged out into the river while sailors kept the fire under control with hoses. Nearly 300 lives were lost, dozens of people trying in vain to climb to safety through the portholes of the burning vessels. Many jumped into the water and were drowned, and many more were burned to death.

In September, Southern Texas was visited by a devastating cyclonic hurricane. In the town of Galveston alone some 6000 people were estimated to have been killed, and another 15,000 were made homeless, while property worth about 20,000,000 dollars was destroyed. The hurricane lasted from four o'clock in the evening of a Saturday until half-past four on Sunday morning, the town being shrouded in darkness. Men tied their wives and children together with ropes, the streets rapidly became flooded, and many large vessels were wrecked on the shore and were carried inland. A sloop was stranded in the centre of the city at its highest level, and another was berthed in a stable near the main hotel. The smell of the bodies under the fallen debris soon became so overpowering that bonfires were lit to dispose of thousands of corpses. Ninety negros were accused of looting and were shot. Meanwhile hundreds of bodies floated beneath the piers in the bay, and each tide brought scores of them ashore.

To fortify the area against a repetition of the disaster, enough sand from the Gulf of Mexico was pumped into the district to raise the level of Galveston by seven feet. A massive concrete sea wall was also built, and this was later fortified to protect the city against the severe storms of 1909 and 1915. Within five weeks of the September 1900 disaster, Galveston had returned to normal business.

In December 1900, Senator Hoar, the dean of the American senate, summed up the achievements and developments of the United States, pointing out that the surplus of this single year was more than seven times as much as the entire receipts of the government in 1800 and ten times as much as its entire expenses in that year:

'Today the United States is by far the richest country in the world. Its wealth exceeds that of the United Kingdom, which is the next in rank, by about 22,000,000,000 dollars. In 1800 our population was 5,308,483; now it is 76,304,799. The sixteen states have grown to forty-five, and our territory has expanded from 909,050 square miles to 3,846,595 square miles. At the opening of the Revolutionary War there were but forty newspapers. Today we have 20,806. The men who wrought this great work are gone—most of them. A few of their companions and helpers survive to behold the dawn of the new century . . . they seem to survive for a brief period only that the new century may clasp hands with the old, and that they may bring to the future the benediction of the past.'

The great Klondyke Gold Rush was still only two years old. In the summer of 1897 the arrival in San Francisco of several hundred successful gold prospectors from the Yukon in Canada had started an epidemic of gold fever which resulted in 1898 in the world's biggest gold rush along the valleys of the tributaries of the Klondyke and Yukon rivers. From Skagway, Alaska, about a quarter of a million gold-hunters, mostly inexperienced, had set out on a 500-mile trek through swamps and snow in search of quick fortunes. Only about 10 per cent of the travellers reached the promised land of Dawson City, founded in 1896 and already over-populated. In 1900 about 22,000,000 dollars worth of gold was found in this region, but ten years later the richest deposits would all be worked out.

In Britain prices were rising, but wages had risen very little in the 'nineties, except in certain industries such as coal and cotton. To compare the cost of living with today's scale is difficult because the value of the purchasing power of money had steadily declined. But even by modern standards some goods and services were comparatively cheap. In general, however, lower-class wages were so low that it was possible for families earning only a moderate income to keep at least one servant, who was paid very little. Thus, because labour was cheap, so were many of the essentials and luxuries of life.

In 1893 income tax was still only 7d in the £ and feelings were strong when a year later it rose to 8d. It was not until the Boer War that it became 1s and eventually 1s 3d. In 1899–1900 it produced over £18,600,000 for the Exchequer, and next year the higher rate brought in £25,300,000. Anyone with an income of less than £160 a year paid no tax, and this meant the majority of people.

In August 1900 the price of coal at the London Coal Exchange caused some misgivings. The price of Welsh coal at the pit had been advanced by 3s a ton, which meant that the consumer now had to pay from 37s to 41s a ton, depending on the quality. Coal firms were finding it cheaper to buy coal from the United States, whose output was for the first time greater than Britain's. The South Metropolitan Gas Company had ordered 4000 tons from a Philadelphia colliery, stating that the price was considerably lower than that of Durham coal. Not only was American coal reaching London, but it was also being sent to St Petersburg, Marseilles, Genoa, Venice, Naples and Barcelona, previously exclusively British markets.

At this time a well-dressed Englishman could buy six good white shirts for 30s post free, and in London's Regent Street his wife could buy a 'stylish three-quarter cape' for one-and-a-half guineas. Leading brands of champagne cost 48s for a dozen bottles, really good cigars cost 16s a hundred, there were half-penny horse-bus fares, popular cigarettes cost a penny for a packet of five, pipe tobacco cost threepence or fourpence an ounce, a glass of beer cost twopence—and was strong—and most evening newspapers and many dailies cost a halfpenny.

By modern standards, travelling in 1900 seems cheap. A return excursion ticket from Brighton to the Crystal Palace, leaving at 10.5 a.m. by London, Brighton and South Coast Railway, cost 3s 9d, or to London and back, 3s. The journey from Liverpool to New York by the White Star's new twin-screw liner *Oceanic* (17,274 tons) cost from £20 to £40 and upwards. On the *Majestic* or *Teutonic* (10,000 tons each) it was £10 to £35 and upwards. These were the saloon prices, the second saloon and third class fares being cheaper. The fare by the Bibby Line's steamers from Liverpool to Marseilles was eight guineas, and to Port Said it was £17. Furthermore, in those days a British passport, manufactured with a great deal more care and elegance than today, cost 2s, no matter how many people were named in it.

Housewives in 1900 were paying 1s, 1s 2d, 1s 4d or 1s 6d a pound for good tea, choicer varieties costing 1s 10d, 2s, 2s 4d, or 2s 10d a pound, coffee cost 8d, 10d and 1s a pound, and it was possible to furnish a house completely and adequately for £100. A flat just off Vincent Square, Westminster (four rooms and a bathroom, first floor) cost £4 18s monthly unfurnished. One on the ground floor with three rooms cost £3 10s monthly, inclusive of rates and heating. A cottage at Ponders End, redecorated, with 'a good garden, open situation, close to station', could be rented for 6s 6d a week. Good office accommodation in the city of London was advertised for £15, £25 and £40 a year.

The Hackney Furnishing Company, making its own goods and cutting out any middle man's profit and interest, did not require a deposit unless one wished to pay one, and offered free life insurance with its hire purchase arrangement. Carriage was free up to 300 miles, carpets and linoleum were laid free, and the business hours were from 9 a.m. to 9 p.m., including Saturdays, but on Thursdays the firm closed at 4 p.m. Here are their terms:

Value of goods	Charge per month
£10	6s.
£20	12s
£30	18s
£40	£1 6s
£50	£1 9s
£100	£2 15s
£200	£5 10s
£300	By special arrangement

In 1900 it cost a penny to send a letter (under 4 oz.) within any part of the United Kingdom, including the Orkneys, Shetlands,

Channel Islands, Isle of Man or the Scilly Islands. A parcel weighing 4 lb. cost 6d. For a shilling you could send an 11 lb. parcel. To send a postcard cost a halfpenny. Ten postcards, impressed with a halfpenny stamp, could be bought for 5½d, or a parcel of 240 for 11s. The cost of sending an inland telegram was 6d for the first twelve words and a halfpenny for each extra word. Telegram forms were of two kinds, one issued free, the other (A.1) embossed with a stamp, could be bought singly, or 'interleaved with carbonic paper', and was available in books of 20, price 10s 2d.

On payment of 2d to a 'railway servant', in addition to the usual 1d stamp, inland letters not exceeding 4 oz. could be forwarded by the next available train *or steamship* by those companies in agreement with the post office, to be collected at the station to which the letter was addressed. The letters were taken to the passenger station of the railway company; or for an extra 3d a messenger would take them to the station for you, so that they caught the next train.

In the area between Temple Bar, Charing Cross and the South-West of London there were no fewer than twelve postal deliveries daily. In the other districts there were only from six to eleven daily collections and deliveries.

In 1900 Sir John Bennett, watchmaker, of 65 Cheapside, London, was offering 'gentleman's gold keyless hunting or half-hunting lever watches for £15, or in silver for £6'. A rival firm, J. W. Benson Ltd. of 62 Ludgate Hill, offered English lever watches at £3 10s payable in five monthly instalments of 10s and a deposit of 20s with the order. Streeter & Co. of New Bond Street offered a solid silver tankard for £4 15s, a solid silver inkstand for £3 5s, four solid silver salt cellars and spoons in a morocco case for £3 5s, and a silver tea caddy (reproduction George III period) for £3 10s.

In the United States, prices were low and sales were high. A Chicago couple furnishing a home could buy a mahogany parlour table for $3. 95, a sofa for $9, and a brass-trimmed bed for $5. Food was no problem with the best corned beef selling at 8 cents a pound, provided one was working. In Denver, turtleneck sweaters cost 8 cents each, and a good quality suit could be bought for $10. 65. Wages might be modest by later standards but a man from Birmingham, Alabama, could celebrate New Year's Eve 1900 with six-year-old whiskey at $3. 20 for four quarts.[1]

The Omaha, Nebraska, *World-Herald* advertised 'sugar, 4c. a lb.; eggs, 14c. a dozen', the Williamsport, Pa., *Gazette & Bulletin* offered 'potatoes 35c. to 45c. a bushel, butter 24c. to 25c. a pound', the Dallas *News* offered 'top hogs 4 dollars. 14', wheat was 70c. a bushel, corn was 33c., Texas steers were '4 dollars. 25 a hundred' (a hundredweight). The Boston *Herald* invited 'Boarders wanted, turkey dinner, 20 cents; supper or breakfast, 15 cents'. In the Trenton, New Jersey, *Times* the United States Hotel quoted rates of 'one dollar per day; furnished rooms 50 cents—horse sheds for country shoppers'. In the Chicago *Tribune* Messrs Siegel, Cooper & Co. advertised 'Ladies muslin nightgowns, 19c.; 50-inch all-wool sponged and shrunk French cheviots, water and dust proof serges, all high-class fabrics, warranted for color and wear, 79c.' In the same newspaper women's shoes 'worth 3 dollars' were offered at one dollar, 95; with 'misses' and children's shoes, one dollar. 19'. In the Dacatur, Ills. *Review* was advertised, 'A good well-made corset in long or short style, all sizes; our price, 50 cents'. Gingham was 5 cents a yard; men's box-calf shoes were 2 dollars. 50; ten dollar overcoats were offered for six dollars. In the Los Angeles *Express* an advertisement said, 'Wanted, Jan. 8, lady cashier for store; salary 8 dollars a week; name 2 or 3 references'.

At the end of the century a British army private soldier still earned only a shilling a day, a traditional wage, out of which he was lucky, with compulsory stoppages, to receive eightpence or ninepence. In applying for a paternity summons against a private in the 3rd Battalion of the Royal Sussex Regiment stationed at Preston barracks, Brighton, the young woman concerned expressed her fears to the magistrate that the soldier would probably go off with his regiment to South Africa and leave her in the lurch. She said that up to three weeks previously he had been

[1] Walter Lord, *op. cit.*

1. Field Marshal Lord Roberts in 1895

2. Joseph Chamberlain in 1900

3. Lord Kitchener of Khartoum

paying her from 2s 6d to 3s a week. The magistrate now ordered him to pay 2s 6d a week.

Defendant:	Isn't that impossible, sir?
Magistrate:	No, it is not impossible.
Defendant:	Out of 8½d. a day?
Magistrate:	Pay half-a-crown a week.

2

WAR IN SOUTH AFRICA

The Second Boer War, or South African War, extended from 1899 to 1902, but 1900 was the critical year of the conflict. It was fought between Britain, with the Empire, and the two Dutch Boer republics in South Africa, the Transvaal and the Orange Free State, and it was a sequel to the First Boer War of 1880 to 1881.

In the spring of 1899 two questions to which the governments of Great Britain and the Dutch republics gave irreconcilable answers had become vitally important to both countries. Was the Transvaal a sovereign state or was she a subordinate of the British crown? Could the republic legally treat British settlers as aliens, or should it give them a share in governing the country? Britain held that the Transvaal was not a sovereign state, but the Boers violently disagreed, wishing to be free of imperialist domination. The spirit of independence which had made the Dutch settlers march into the hinterland from the Cape to be free of British control now found an outlet in internal dissension.

In 1877 Disraeli had annexed the Transvaal but had come into conflict with the Zulus and the Boers. Seven years later, after the Boer farmers had defeated British troops at Majuba Hill, Gladstone had acknowledged the failure and had signed a treaty recognizing the independence of the republic, but not the sovereignty. He gave the Transvaal (called the South African Republic or S.A.R.) independence in everything except, mainly, the right to make treaties with any country other than its sister Boer republic, the

Orange Free State. So illogical and contentious an arrangement could not possibly prove to be a final settlement, and a Boer agitation was soon on foot for its revision.

In Winston Churchill's opinion the Boers wished to shake off British control—which had never been properly defined—because they had 'an abiding fear and hatred of the movement that seeks to place the native on a level with the white man'. A mixture of Dutch and French Huguenots, they were tough, rough farmers who carried Bibles in their saddle-bags and rode with rifles in their hands. They were athletic and well-trained through frequent skirmishes with the native tribes and they were admirable horsemen. Some were youths who had almost been born in the saddle; others were bearded, kindly patriarchs who knew every fold in the terrain, and all were expert shots.

Britain's claim to suzerainty over the Boers had become important in view of the presence in the Transvaal of a large foreign (*Uitlander*) element, much of it of British descent, which had become attracted by the discovery of gold on the Rand. The Boers denied these Uitlanders the vote and other civil rights, and the Uitlanders strongly protested against this discrimination. The leading figures in the disputes which arose were Cecil John Rhodes, the Prime Minister of Cape Colony, and Stephanus Johannes Paulus Kruger, 'Uncle Paul'.

As a boy Kruger had taken part in the Great Trek, when the Dutch farmers had journeyed with their oxen and wagons and cattle far into the interior to establish settlements north of the rivers Orange and Vaal, and had fought fiercely against the native Zulu tribes. After serving as commandant of the Transvaal forces he was recognized as the leader of the new state and was elected president. His dream was that Boer influence should dominate the whole of South Africa.

Cecil Rhodes was English and was not only a visionary but also a brilliant businessman. He is generally considered, in South Africa today, to have been the man with the greatest influence of all the English-speaking people in the history of the continent. He was born in 1853 at Bishop's Stortford, and went at the age of seventeen to Natal, where his brother had a farm in the Umkomaas Valley. The farming venture was unsuccessful but the discovery of diamonds caused him in 1871 to move to Kimberley, where he ventured into mining. By the time he was twenty he had saved enough money to return to England to study at Oxford, but in 1873 he was forced by tubercular trouble to return to Kimberley. He was again in Oxford in 1876, at Oriel College, but a further breakdown sent him back to Kimberley. He never lost his love for classical learning, and finally took his degree in 1881, by which time he was wealthy and a member of parliament in Cape Town. In 1880 he founded the De Beers diamond mining company.

Rhodes was inspired with great political ambition for the Empire and for himself. He believed that Britons were the highest product of mankind and that they had a sacred mission to extend their influence and trade across the world. He also had a sincere regard for the Dutch-speaking Afrikaaner and in 1882 he helped to control Dutch freebooters on the Bechuanaland, Stellaland and Goshen frontiers. By 1890 he was Prime Minister of Cape Colony and was planning a Cape to Cairo railway. In England he was now regarded as one of the most important figures of the day, a great empire-builder who would forward British colonial interests. He helped to extend the Cape railway to Johannesburg through the Orange Free State, bought up large tracts of land outside Cape Town, planned a Cape to Cairo telegraph line, built up industries in South Africa, and poured enormous sums of money into the country which was later to be named Rhodesia in honour of his achievements.

When President Kruger refused to allow the Uitlanders the right to vote, Rhodes unfortunately identified himself in 1895 with the Jameson Raid, an illegal and abortive armed invasion of the Transvaal carried out by Dr L. S. Jameson with the object of protecting the Uitlanders and securing their representation in the colony. The failure of this ill-conceived attempt reflected gravely on Rhodes. When the raid turned out to be a fiasco, Kruger was in a stronger position than before and Rhodes's share in the raid made him so unpopular that he was forced to resign his position of Prime Minister in Cape Town. In Britain the Colonial Secretary, Joseph Chamberlain, found himself handicapped in supporting the claims of colonists who had placed themselves in a completely false position and could now expect little sympathy.

The political friction which the raid caused undoubtedly helped to make the South African war a certainty. Although in 1898 Rhodes resumed his position as managing director of the British South African Chartered Company, the coming conflict was to destroy his dreams of a great South African union. When war was declared in 1899 he was at Kimberley, but he took little active part in events, except for insisting, during the siege of the town, in making his own military arrangements for defence, in defiance of the Commander, Major-General Robert Kekewich.

The Uitlanders were not only Europeans. Many were Indians who had been introduced into South Africa because of a labour shortage in the sugar plantations of Natal. In the 1850s they had been paid only 10s a month, rising at the rate of a shilling per month for each year of work, with free rations and primitive housing, estimated to be worth another 8s a month. In time their modest standards of living and their ability to make money as shopkeepers and traders led to restrictive laws being imposed on them. Indians were forbidden to own land. In 1893 the barrister Mohandas Karamchand Gandhi arrived in Durban to appear for Indian clients in their fight against President Kruger's restrictions, and because of what he saw and the treatment he received he began his campaign for Indian rights. During the war he was to organize a corps of Indian stretcher-bearers and after the war he was to practise as an attorney in Johannesburg, where he would organize the famous passive-resistance movement, leading to his imprisonment, his settlement with General Smuts, the Minister of the Interior, and eventually to the Indian Relief Act of 1914. Having achieved most of his aims, Gandhi was to return to India to fight and win victory for his nationalist cause, only to be cruelly assassinated in January 1948.

Sir Alfred Milner was sent out as High Commissioner to negotiate with Kruger on the subject of the Uitlanders' rights, some 21,000 people having signed a petition asking Queen Victoria to intervene in the dispute which had arisen between Britain and the Transvaal, but after long negotiations Sir Alfred came to the conclusion that Kruger would make no concessions

of any value. It was clear that Kruger and his supporters were already preparing for war; stores of arms and ammunition were being secretly built up; European officers were drilling Boer troops. After the Jameson fiasco the German Emperor had sent

Kruger a telegram of congratulation. When the British War Office reinforced its military forces in the Cape, war seemed certain.

On October 9, 1899 the Boer leaders in the Transvaal government issued an ultimatum to Britain demanding that all British troops be withdrawn from their country's borders. The alternative was that the Boers would attack. The ultimatum was rejected and two days later the Boers invaded Cape Colony and Natal. The Orange Free State immediately made common cause with the Transvaal, thus widening the sphere of operations. Hostilities began on October 11th and at once the British forces were on the defensive. But at home very few people took the war seriously, and it was not until the famous 'Black Week' of reverses at the end of 1899 that the nation awoke to the importance of the situation. On the outbreak of war there were only 27,000 British troops in South Africa, widely dispersed, 11,000 of them in Cape Colony and 16,000 in Natal, but the Boers could put at least 45,000 men into the field, with 110 guns, mostly superior to the British.

In London the War Office entered the conflict with no intelligent plan appropriate to conditions on the South African veldt. It was nearly fifty years since the last major war, in the Crimea, but Britain's army and its methods and weapons had changed very little. It was bound to be a drawn-out campaign, with Britain experiencing all the disadvantages of long lines of communication and unfamiliarity with the country and the people whom she was fighting. As usual, the government and the War Office were unprepared to fight any war, anywhere. But most Britons, if they thought about it at all, believed that a small army would soon break the power of a few unruly farmers. The war began, as *The Times* observed, 'at tea time', a phrase which reflected the popular feeling, that it was unimportant and would soon be over.

For all its defects, Queen Victoria's army was not merely ornamental. No army of its time contained so high a percentage of officers and men who had seen active service. Only for one year in the reign—1862—had there not been fighting somewhere.

Until the recent introduction of khaki Britain's scarlet-tunicked soldiers had fought in India, the Crimea, New Zealand, Persia and Africa. But always, except with the Russians and very briefly the Boers in 1881, the enemy had been tribesmen crudely armed, knowing little of strategy, and using only elementary tactics. Against these primitive forces the collective volley or the British square had seldom failed. Provided the troops did not lack courage, which they seldom did, laurels and honours were easily won by the generals and senior officers. The temptation to adopt the same old methods in 1899 against a rabble of 'undisciplined farmers' was irresistible.[1]

Queen Victoria was at Balmoral on the outbreak of war, with General Sir Redvers Buller to explain to her what it would involve. He told her in his own 'blunt, straightforward way' that he did not think there would be 'much hard fighting'. The morality of the war, to be dissected so sternly by historians in later years, did not disturb the Queen; nor did the indignation of Germany and France. She rose, in this last formidable tragedy of her reign, to give her armies the encouragement they needed. She spread a map of South Africa out on a table near the window, and began her last bombardment of spurring memoranda to Whitehall. She left the quiet garden at Balmoral and drove through Ballater, to the barracks where her guard of Gordon Highlanders was drawn up, ready to sail for Africa. The Queen spoke to them, although she was so blind that she could barely see them. 'May God protect you! I am confident that you will always do your duty, and will ever maintain the high reputation of the Gordon Highlanders.' They cheered her, and then she drove home, as she later recorded in her journal, with 'a lump in her throat'.[2]

At first the army regarded the war almost as a simple Aldershot military exercise. When the Royal Horse Guards gave a 'send off supper' to the Cape Squadron, due to leave for South Africa, at Hyde Park barracks in November 1899, this was the menu:

[1] W. Baring Pemberton, *Battles of the Boer War*, London, 1962.
[2] Hector Bolitho, *The Reign of Queen Victoria*, London, 1949.

Oysters—Blue Points
Compo Soup
Toady in the Hole
Sandy Sole
Mafeking Mutton
Transvaal Turnips   Cape Sauce
Tinker 'Taters
Peace Pudding   Massa Ices
Dessert
(please do not throw shells under the table)
Boer Whines—Long Tom
Hollands-in-Skin
Orange Wine

No one believed there could be any serious opposition to the might of Britain's armies, trained in India and on barrack squares. Certainly there was nothing to fear from the rebel farmers. A glimpse of the cavalry, a flash of steel, the threat of artillery fire, and the Boers would quickly submit and be happy to live, as all sensible people surely desired, under the protection of the Union Jack.

From this dream, created by pride in great traditions, there was soon to be a painful awakening. Britain was to see the individual bravery of many of her sons made useless by years of public indifference to the art of war. At first an army corps was considered adequate, and in some quarters it was doubted if even that would be needed. The lessons of defeat at Laing's Nek and Majuba during the earlier, short Boer War, were already forgotten.

The Boers had excellent leaders in their Commander-in-Chief, General Joubert, and in Generals Pieter Cronje, Christian de Wet, and Louis Botha. They started on the offensive by crossing the frontier into Natal, which was to be defended by General Sir George White. At Talana Hill on October 20th and next day at Elandslaagte, the British troops repulsed the Boers, but White had only a small force and was unable to exploit the advantage he had gained. Then came a major disaster, when the Boers under

Joubert defeated Sir George White's forces, 37 British officers and 917 men being forced to surrender. Next, Sir George was invested in Ladysmith, where some powerful naval guns had been installed. Meanwhile the towns of Mafeking, where Colonel Baden-Powell was in command, and Kimberley, where Cecil Rhodes had established himself, were also besieged.

Early in November 1899 reinforcements sailed from England under command of General Sir Redvers Buller, and contingents were despatched from the colonies. Lord Methuen was sent to relieve Kimberley and after repulsing Boer attacks at Belmont and Graspan he crossed the Modder river and spent Sunday December 11, 1899 attacking the Boer trenches at Magersfontein. But here the enemy was firmly dug in, and a dawn frontal attack resulted in the sacrifice of some 650 officers and men, mostly of the Highland Brigade, including General 'Andy' Wauchope. Methuen's offensive failed to take the enemy positions, and his troops were forced at nightfall to fall back exhausted to the Modder river camp.

On the same day as the misfortune at Magersfontein, General Gatacre, who had been sent to the Orange Free State, misguidedly marched his troops into an impossible position at Stormberg and lost 700 men, 600 of whom were marched away to prison camps in Pretoria.

A third disaster marked the end of what came to be known in Britain as 'Black Week', when the newly-arrived General Buller, marching to relieve Ladysmith, crossed the river Tugela with 20,000 men, and was severely beaten by the Boers at Colenso. Among the dead was Lieutenant the Honorable F. H. S. Roberts, King's Royal Rifles, the only son of Field Marshal Lord Roberts.

'Will any of you volunteer to save the guns?' Buller had cried. Corporal Nurse, Gunner Young, and a few others responded, the desperate venture being led by three of the General's aides-de-camp, Congreve, Schofield and Roberts. Two gun teams were taken down, the horses galloping frantically through heavy enemy fire, and each time they succeeded in returning with a gun. But the loss was fearful. Roberts was mortally wounded. 'My first bullet went through my left sleeve and made the joint of my elbow bleed,' reported Congreve. 'Next a clod of earth caught me smack on the right arm, then my horse got one, then my left leg one, then my horse another, and that settled us.' Congreve crawled to join his comrades. Roberts insisted on being left where he fell, for fear of hampering the others. He died of his wounds and was awarded a posthumous Victoria Cross.

The army sent to South Africa was the best-equipped force ever to sail from Britain. The 1914 war would see a serious deterioration in the standard of equipment, but in 1899 and 1900 every soldier was issued with uniform and accoutrements which were superior to any in the world. In addition to cavalry, artillery, infantry, engineers, medical and transport units, there were a pontoon bridge unit, a balloon observation section, and several remount units. Only the rifles and artillery were inferior.

However strong the reinforcements seemed on paper and despite all the flag-waving at home, there could be little real confidence either in the War Office or in the generals commanding the army. There was no General Staff, nor was there, as Sir Charles Petrie has revealed, as late as 1901 in the War Office archives—with a single exception—any comprehensive statement of the military resources of any foreign country in the world, or the manner in which they might in the event of war be used against Britain. Furthermore, 50 per cent of the men who volunteered to join the army had to be turned down on medical grounds, usually because they were undernourished.

There was little doubt that in its early stages the war was conducted with extraordinary inefficiency. Addressing his constituents at Cinderford on January 11th, Sir Charles Dilke said that it was misleading to claim that Britain had three army corps in South Africa. The infantry might be there, but not the supporting cavalry and artillery. The Cabinet was responsible. By German or French standards there were only enough guns for one army corps. Later, on February 19th, it was admitted by Lord Lansdowne, the Secretary of State for War, that not a shilling of the £40,000 voted in 1899 for volunteer rifle ranges had been allotted.

Lord Rosebery, leader of the Liberal opposition, speaking at Chatham on January 23, 1900, said that the war was one of the most formidable in Britain's history—not only because of the number of troops which would be involved, but also because nearly all the rest of Europe was united against Britain.

The choice of General Sir Redvers Buller VC as General Sir George White's successor was unfortunate. Buller was a sixty-year-old Etonian who had seen service in China, Afghanistan, Egypt, the Sudan and Ireland, and had won his Victoria Cross fighting the Zulus. He was a brave man, and the public admired him as what was termed a 'hero'. In addition to being personally brave he was a jovial, pleasure-loving gentleman, who took great pains to care for the welfare and well-being of his troops. Buller did not eat until his men and horses had been fed. But he was unimaginative, and lacking in tactical ability, and was therefore of doubtful value as the commander of the British forces in the war. He had been a member of Sir Evelyn Wood's staff at the time of the disasters at Bronkhurst Hill and Majuba (1881) where the Boers had first shown their superiority, but he does not appear to have benefited from the experience.

Colenso cost some 1100 casualties, the action being later described as:

'One of the most unfortunate battles in which a British army has ever been engaged, and in none has there been a more deplorable tactical display. No proper reconnoitring of the ground, no certain information as to any ford by which to cross the river; no proper artillery preparation, no satisfactory targets for the artillery. . . . The lost guns were made a present to the enemy.[1]

Colenso was a serious set-back. 'At twelve o'clock,' wrote Arthur Conan Doyle later in his official history, *The Great Boer War*, 'all the troops upon the ground were retreating for the camp. There was nothing in the shape of rout or panic, and the withdrawal was as orderly as the advance; but the fact remained that we had lost 1200 men in killed, wounded and missing, and had gained absolutely nothing. We had not even had the satisfaction of knowing that we had inflicted as well as endured

[1] Gen. Sir Neville Lyttelton, *Eighty Years*, London, 1927.

punishment, for the enemy remained throughout the day so cleverly concealed that it is doubtful whether more than a hundred casualties occurred in their ranks. Once more it was shown how weak an arm is artillery against an enemy who lies in shelter.'

'The story is a record of gallant and determined fighting on the part of our men entirely thrown away owing to the badness of our guns,' reported the *Black and White Budget*. 'Colonel Long had to take his guns so near to the enemy (800 yards is the distance given) that they were put out of action almost immediately, and despite heroic efforts, in which Captain Schofield and Captain Congreve especially distinguished themselves, two batteries had to be abandoned. This rendered nugatory General Hart's successful attempt to cross the Tugela Bridge drift, and he had to retire with great loss, General Hilyard's attack being unable to retrieve the loss of the guns.'

In his official report on the Colenso battle, Buller later said that, but for Colonel Long's advance and the subsequent disaster to the artillery, the action might have been successful. 'A hard saying,' replied Arthur Conan Doyle, 'which throws perhaps too much responsibility upon the gallant but unfortunate gunner.' He concluded with the observation that Colenso taught the army nothing except that it had failed to grasp earlier lessons of warfare.

For six years Colonel Long remained the scapegoat for Buller's feeble tactics, but in 1906, largely due to the Boer General Botha's generous testimony, he was to be placed on the list of officers selected for rewards for distinguished conduct, and in 1914 he was to become an Inspector of Remounts. The evidence given before the Royal Commission on the South African War by Buller was later, at least on Colenso, utterly discreditable to the General, at once for the evasiveness and inaccuracy of his answers.[1]

A popular hero of the Colenso battle was fourteen-year-old James Dunn, a boy bugler in the Dublin Fusiliers. Although wounded in the arm and chest, he had swum the Tugela river and been helped back to camp by a soldier and a sailor. When he

[1] W. Baring Pemberton, *op. cit.*

recovered consciousness the boy discovered that he had lost his bugle. He was taken to Maritzburg two days later and was sent home on the steamship *Canada*. But his exploits had already been widely publicized in the British newspapers, and during his eighteen days in Netley Hospital he received many visitors, including the Queen's daughter, Princess Christian, whose son Prince Christian Victor was fighting in South Africa, where he was to die of enteric fever, aged thirty-three.

When the time came for Bugler Dunn to leave hospital, he and twenty of his comrades travelled by train to Portsmouth where nearly the whole town turned out to watch them march through the streets. As soon as the Netley train steamed into the station a roaring cheer broke out and crowds of people flocked forward to see the boy soldier who had captured the imagination of the nation. He jumped down on to the platform clutching a box of chocolates. Outside the station a crowd of several thousand was waiting, and the roadway to the town hall was lined five to ten deep. The boy was carried shoulder-high into the town hall, to the strains of 'Soldiers of the Queen'. It was not the first time in the war that a band boy had distinguished himself in action. At the battle of Elandslaagte, trumpeter Shurlock of the 5th Lancers had killed three Boers with his revolver.

No single defeat during the week of December 10–17, 1899 was of vital importance in itself, but the cumulative effect of 'Black Week' was very great. The total loss amounted to about three thousand men and twelve guns, while the indirect effects in the loss of prestige and the increased confidence of the Boers were considerable. It was admitted that Sir George White had made a tactical error in not destroying the river and railway bridges behind him during his retreat to Ladysmith, as this would have prevented the Boers from moving their big guns into Natal. With the bridges intact the enemy was now able to run trains direct to Pretoria. Meanwhile, General Gatacre was reported to have broken down when he heard of the losses suffered by his troops in his unsuccessful action at Stormberg.

To their surprise, the British found that, although they were fighting determined adversaries, the enemy was often magnanimous and frequently sentimental. No Boer liked to fight on a Sunday. Both sides respected the Red Cross and observed truces for stretcher and burial parties. Christmas Day in beleagured Ladysmith was celebrated by an entertainment for the children, with a Christmas tree, and no shots were fired. At the Modder Camp, Lord Methuen had established a market where goods were bartered between the soldiers and the Boer farmers, who brought in fresh milk and vegetables to exchange for tea and other army rations. Methuen also arranged cricket matches and athletic meetings, and on New Year's Day a 'grand series of races' was held for silver trophies which had been presented by loyalists in Cape Town.

The Boers frequently held their fire to allow the British troops to drink and wash in the muddy river Modder, and at Frere they heliographed to the British camp the message, 'Why is Roberts coming? What has Buller done?' to which the British could think of no more apt reply than 'How did you like our lyddite in the late battle?' to which the Boers replied 'Rats!'[1]

At Glencoe a wounded lance-corporal in the King's Royal Rifles was just going to be finished off at close range by 'an old fellow with a beard a foot long' when a younger Boer intervened, carried the wounded man off, propped him against a rock, and gave him some water. Then, in bad English, the Boer said, 'I save your life. Did you know?' The Englishman nodded. 'I save your life because you are like my brother,' said the Boer. Then he gave the lance-corporal a cigar and carried him on his back down the hill to the camp, where his comrades would find him.

From the beginning of the dispute the sympathy of most of the Continental powers was for the Boers. There was open satisfaction at the humiliating defeats which the Boers inflicted on the British. The Germans were especially delighted, for many of their officers had trained the rebel commandos. During a debate in the German parliament, Count von Bülow expressed the opinion of most of his countrymen:

'We severely deplore the outbreak of war between the South

[1] Lyddite: an artillery explosive, perfected by the School of Gunnery at Lydd, Kent, which had first been used against the Dervishes at Omdurman.

African Republic and England. We deplore the fact that such a war was possible between Christians, between white men, between members of the same great Germanic races. We also deplored the war because by it weighty German commercial and political interests were affected. Several thousands of German subjects had settled in South Africa, where they had founded factories and industrial and banking establishments; German capital invested in South Africa amounted to hundreds of millions of marks; the traffic between Germany and the South African coast was great, and from the commercial point of view we were interested to a high degree in the future of South Africa.'

The French press did not conceal its satisfaction at the military difficulties which Britain was encountering,[1] and in Britain itself a large number of people disapproved of the Conservative government's policy towards South Africa, and were dubbed 'Little Englanders'.

It was a critical day in December 1899 when Lord Roberts was asked to sail from England to take over command in South Africa. Frederick Sleigh Roberts, or 'Bobs' as he was affectionately called by the nation, was the son of an Irish general and the great-nephew of a bold sailor nicknamed the 'White Devil'. He dressed his little body with care and managed to overcome the disadvantages of being tiny and of having a blind eye. Suffering from heart and digestive trouble, he had kept a bottle of sherry by his bedside when he was at Woolwich, but he disapproved of drinking. He had joined the Indian army as an artillery officer and emerged from the Indian Mutiny aged twenty-six with seven mentions in despatches and the VC. For the next twenty years marriage and staff work in the Indian army absorbed him, relieved only by bloodless expeditions against the mad King Theodore of Abyssinia and the action to release the child Mary Winchester from an Assam tribe. Then fame came suddenly through the Viceroy's chance reading of a routine staff

[1] The Queen felt it her duty to cancel her usual spring holiday on the Riviera, and that year the Prince of Wales refrained from visiting Paris for the first time since 1883.

DAILY MAIL, SATURDAY, MAY 19, 1900.

RELIEF OF MAFEKING.

THE BESIEGERS CORDON BROKEN BY THE FLYING COLUMN.

HEAVY BOMBARDMENT AND FLIGHT OF THE BOERS.

THE UNKNOWN BRITISH FORCE TRIUMPHANTLY ENTERS THE TOWN.

UNPARALLELED SCENES OF REJOICING.

REJOICINGS ABROAD.

HOW THE NEWS WAS RECEIVED IN AMERICA.

AUSTRALIAN ENTHUSIASM.

LONDON'S ROAR OF JUBILATION.

WILD FRENZY THAT SURPASSES DESCRIPTION.

LORD MAYOR SPEAKS TO A VAST SHOUTING MULTITUDE.

TROUBADOUR SERENADES MRS. BADEN-POWELL.

RESISTANCE COLLAPSING.

PRESIDENT STEYN CONFERRING WITH PRESIDENT KRUGER.

PROBABLE PEACE PROPOSALS.

BOERS NOW SEEING THAT "THE GAME IS UP."

FATE OF THE MINES.

PROLONGED MEETING OF THE FORD EXECUTIVE.

THEY WILL NOT BE DESTROYED.

EASTERN FRONTIER.

NEWCASTLE TAKEN.

EXPERT BLOW UP LAING'S NEK TUNNEL.

LINDLEY CAPTURED.

FLIGHT OF PRESIDENT STEYN AND HIS OFFICIALS.

HOOPSTAD OCCUPIED.

4. The Relief of Mafeking, from the *Daily Mail*, May 19, 1900

5. Winston Spencer Churchill as a Boer War correspondent in 1899, wearing the uniform of the South African Light Horse

paper, and its author was singled out for command of the punitive column which marched on Kabul and Kandahar. 'Bobs' became a national hero and now at the age of sixty-seven he was a senior Field-Marshal.

'Lord Roberts,' said the *Illustrated London News*, 'whom the nation admired and the army adored, had the day before received the news of the death of his son from the wounds received in the attempt to save the guns at Colenso. Heartbroken, but clear-sighted and strong-willed, he answered at once the call of duty and within a week was on his way to the Cape.'

'Goodbye Bobs,' said the Prince of Wales at Waterloo station, 'and good luck to you'.

On December 18th, three days after the Colenso disaster, nine important measures were adopted by the government for the carrying on of the campaign. These were:

1 The command should be taken over in the field by Lord Roberts, with Lord Kitchener as his chief of staff.
2 The 7th Division (10,000 men) should embark for South Africa and an 8th Division should be formed in Britain as reserve.
3 The artillery should be reinforced.
4 Eleven militia battalions should embark.
5 A Corps of Volunteers should be sent out.
6 A Yeomanry mounted force should be sent out.
7 The remaining army reserves should be called up.
8 That volunteer mounted troops should be raised in South Africa.
9 That further contingents from the Empire should be welcomed.

It was calculated that from seventy to a hundred thousand men would thus be added to the South African armies by these measures, there being nearly a hundred thousand already out there. To support Roberts and Kitchener, plans were immediately made to send out sixteen field batteries, a number of militia battalions, twenty battalions of Imperial Yeomanry, and a new force of mounted infantry, while for each battalion in the line a company was formed from the volunteer battalions of its regimental district to serve as reinforcements. Australia, Canada and New Zealand supplemented their contingents, and the loyal colonists in the Cape and Natal increased their armed forces.

'Victory in South Africa is now assured,' said the *Morning Post*. But it was a long way off, and to Lord Roberts, sailing from Southampton in the *Dunnottar Castle* two days before Christmas, the task looked formidable.

After handing over the command of the Egyptian army to Sir Reginald Wingate, Lord Kitchener of Khartoum boarded the cruiser *HMS Isis* at Alexandria and joined Roberts at Gibraltar on December 27th. By the time they reached Cape Town on January 10, 1900 Roberts and his new Chief of Staff had evolved a plan to end the campaign.

The situation was grave. No real headway had been made against the Boers, and Buller's lack of ability as a commander in the field was now obvious. Ladysmith was still under siege, the Boers held the bridges across the Modder, Lord Methuen—still smarting from his defeat at Magersfontein—was waiting powerless at the Modder camp, organizing sports meetings. Mafeking, besieged by the Boers, still held out under Colonel Baden-Powell. But the British were hard-pressed.

When on February 8, 1900 Lord Roberts and his staff reached the main British camp on the Modder, there were some 37,000 men encamped there with 113 guns, 12,000 horses, and 22,000 transport and pack animals. Reinforcements and supplies had been pouring in to Cape Town by every ship from Britain, Australia, New Zealand and Canada. In advance of Roberts, Major-General Sir Hector Macdonald of the Gordons—'Fighting Mac' of Omdurman fame—had arrived to take over command of the Highland Brigade in place of 'Andy' Wauchope, who had been killed at Magersfontein. The troops were filled with a new hope; it looked as if the tide would turn.[1]

Unfortunately, Lord Roberts became ill with a feverish cold almost as soon as he arrived, and Kitchener took over temporary

[1] John Montgomery, *Toll for the Brave; the Tragedy of Hector Macdonald*, Max Parrish.

command. On February 17th he set up his headquarters on a hill south of the Modder, five miles from the position where the Boer commander Pieter Cronje and his forces were entrenched at Paardeberg. From this hill, known later as 'Kitchener's Kopje', he and his staff watched the Boers digging themselves into a massive laager, some 5000 men, women, children, horses and cattle. No doubt he recalled surveying the field of battle in the same way before Omdurman. But events were to prove rather different.

'Gentlemen!' announced Kitchener. 'It is now six-thirty. By ten-thirty we shall be in possession of that laager. I shall then load up French[2] and push him on to Bloemfontein with the cavalry.'

However, Kitchener's frontal attack on the Boer positions failed and, although Cronje remained surrounded, the British troops did not penetrate the Dutch lines. Far from taking possession of the laager, Kitchener was forced at 7.40 that evening to send Roberts a message: 'I hope tomorrow we shall be able to do something definite.' He did not mention that during the afternoon the Boers had developed an attack on their right flank, had inflicted heavy casualties on his army, and had maintained the initiative.

Kitchener's message roused Roberts, who rode out to take over command. Kitchener had never lost a battle, but he had also never fought against white men armed with modern weapons. When Roberts arrived he found Kitchener's Kopje in enemy hands, and some 1200 British casualties on the field, with hundreds of horses and mules killed by gunfire. The troops were weary, having made no progress, and their confidence was waning. The Highland Brigade under Hector Macdonald had marched for twenty miles before going into action, each man carrying his rifle, ammunition, equipment, greatcoat, cholera-belt, water-bottle, entrenching tool and folded waterproof sheet or blanket.

Cronje now sent a message to Roberts asking for twenty-four hours in which to bury his dead. It was a reasonable demand in a

[2] Lieutenant-General J. D. P. French. (See page 66.)

campaign in which there was little real hatred. All day his farmers had refrained from shooting the British stretcher-bearers and water parties and he had many women and children in his camp. But Roberts replied that if the Boers surrendered they would be able to carry out their burials peacefully. To this Cronje replied, 'Since you are so unmerciful as not to accord the truce asked for, nothing remains for me to do. You do as you wish.' This was interpreted by Roberts as a desire for surrender, so he sent an officer forward with a white flag, but it soon became clear that the Boers intended to stand firm.

'During my lifetime I shall never surrender,' Cronje proudly announced.

Kitchener now urged that a new attack should be mounted at dawn, but Roberts was unwilling to waste more lives on a frontal advance. He knew that the Boers, completely surrounded, must soon capitulate. And nine days after the start of the battle, on the day following the long-awaited relief of Ladysmith, Cronje surrendered.

It was on the anniversary of the disastrous skirmish on Majuba Hill in 1881, that the Boers, severely shaken by the continual heavy concentration of artillery fire which the British gunners had directed hour after hour on to their laager, finally gave up. Riding into the British lines on an old horse, Pieter Cronje wore a flat-topped slouch hat, an ancient green topcoat buttoned at the neck, and baggy trousers and worn shoes. He was accompanied by a nondescript collection of bearded and unshaven warrior-farmers, all ragged and dirty, but still proud. They were met by Field-Marshal Lord Roberts VC, wearing neat khaki drill, carrying his Kandahar sword, but no badges of rank. Cronje dismounted and walked towards the victor.

Roberts shook him warmly by the hand. 'I'm glad to see you,' he said, but at once realized that this might have been more happily phrased, and added, 'You made a gallant defence, sir.' Cronje did not reply, for he spoke no English. Roberts then invited the Dutch leader and his staff to eat with him. 'You have even taken away our Majuba Day,' said Cronje.

Although the British had snatched a victory, the Boer losses amounted to only 300 compared with the army's losses of 1262, including 24 officers and 379 men killed. The comparatively heavy casualties were due to Kitchener's headstrong policy of attacking the stronghold frontally with infantry and cavalry before Roberts assumed command.

'It is easy to be wise after the event,' reported Arthur Conan Doyle, 'but it does certainly appear that with our present knowledge the action at Paardberg was as unnecessary as it was expensive. The sun descended on Sunday February 18th upon a bloody field and crowded hospital tents, but also upon an unbroken circle of British troops still hemming in the desperate men who lurked among the willows and mimosa which drape the steep banks of the Modder.'

When news of the victory reached the Queen she dictated a letter to Kitchener:

Windsor Castle, February 23, 1900.

The Queen wishes to write a line to Lord Kitchener to say how she followed him and Lord Roberts everywhere, and how we have been cheered by news of the past ten days, and are hoping for more good news. She knows, however, that we must be patient and not expect things to go too fast.

The Queen saw Lady Roberts, who had heard from Lord Roberts what a help Lord Kitchener was to him.

The many losses grieve the Queen very much, but she knows they are unavoidable. She was sorry for poor General Macdonald, but hopes his wound is not really severe. Pray tell him so from her.

Pray say everything kind from the Queen to Lord Roberts, and believe that no one thinks more constantly or prays more fervently for the well-being of her dear, brave soldiers than she does.

Looting by soldiers was officially forbidden, but after the capture of Cronje's laager Lord Roberts—for some unexplained reason—allowed his men to take what they wanted from the Boer camp. Soldiers returned to quarters laden with clothes, blankets, kettles, cups and even umbrellas. The Duke of Wellington had allowed his soldiers four days of plundering after the storming of Badajoz, and Kitchener had taken treasures from

India for the decoration of his English home, but the latter's advice to 'loot like mad!' appears out of place in the conduct of this particular campaign.

Frederic Villiers, the correspondent of the *Illustrated London News*, thought that Mrs Cronje, a meek little lady, who later accompanied her husband into captivity on St Helena, looked not only bedraggled but also rather unshapely. But this was explained when a young officer ran up to him saying, 'Villiers, Villiers! I have the most charming loot in the camp!'

'What is it?' asked Villiers.

Holding a mysterious scroll above his head, the subaltern cried, 'Why, Mrs Cronje's corsets!' No doubt they went home on a troopship as a relic of the war, together with all the thousands of rifles, belts, revolvers, hats, antelope heads, skins and rugs which were to decorate the halls of Edwardian houses and can still be seen today, often unrecognized for what they are.

Subsequently, Cronje's clock turned up in a Covent Garden auction sale, where it was sold for £5. At the same auction his saddle, holsters, bridle and spurs fetched eight guineas.

After Cronje's surrender the Colonial Secretary Joseph Chamberlain announced the government's intention to annex the two Boer republics. There was no doubt that, in spite of some deadweight among the generals, the new command was getting things done, and even the worst of the generals was a hero to the people at home, who sang a music-hall song about a mythical infant with the unlikely surname Blobbs and several well-known, popular Christian names:

> The baby's name is Kitchener Carrington
> Methuen Kekewitch White
> Cronje Plumer Powell Majuba
> Gatacre Warren Colenso Kruger
> Capetown Mafeking French
> Kimberley Ladysmith Bobs
> Union Jack Fighting Mac
> Luddite Pretoria—Blobbs.

The sequence of events following 'Black Week' thrilled Britons at home and throughout the Empire:

Feb. 11   Lord Roberts begins advance from
          Modder River camp
Feb. 15   Relief of Kimberley
Feb. 27   Surrender of Cronje at Paardeberg
Feb. 28   Ladysmith relieved
Mar. 13   Roberts enters Bloemfontein
Mar. 17   Mafeking relieved
May 26   British annexation of Orange Free State
May 31   Roberts occupies Johannesburg

Buller's last, and as it turned out, successful attempt to relieve Ladysmith began on February 20th. He pushed three infantry brigades over the river, but three days of hard fighting followed, resulting in a check. Desperate attempts were made by the Inniskillings, the Connaught Rangers and the Dublin Fusiliers to dislodge the enemy from their entrenched positions, but on the 23rd and 24th it was all they could do to hold their own. Then Buller found another passage across the Langewatche Spruit, and developed a new attack which finally resulted on the 27th in the capture of Pieter's hill. This hill was approached by a precipitous ascent of 500 feet, but up this General Barton led the Dublin Fusiliers and two battalions of the Sixth Brigade, turning the enemy's left flank, while General Warren led the Fourth and Eleventh Brigades on to the enemy's main position. As evening fell the South Lancashire Regiment went forward to capture the enemy positions. Next day, Lord Dundonald, with the Natal Carbineers and a composite regiment, entered Ladysmith and relieved Sir George White's hard-pressed garrison.

'The game's afoot!' said the *Black and White Budget* of March 3rd. 'Kimberley relieved, Cronje in flight, Sir Redvers Buller within sight of Ladysmith, this is what the stir all along the line has resulted in. Lord Roberts has developed his plan and it has been an immediate success ... The moral effect of the dislodgment of Cronje from his Magersfontein strongholds will be enormous ... The great Boer hosts will flee back to their country like leaves before the wind. Once there it will be another matter. But then—we've Bobs! The news of Kimberley came as a welcome surprise, not only at home but also to the beleaguered city. It seemed too good to be true. "This is General French coming to the relief of Kimberley," signalled the relieving column. The besieged could not at first believe it. "What regiment are you?" they heliographed, fearing a Boer trick. They were soon put at their ease. The three cavalry brigades of General French, whom Lord Roberts had summoned from Colesberg, marched into the town ... Cronje fled, hoping to reach his base at Bloemfontein ... General Kelly-Kenny follows hotly on his heels.'

The Queen was still in bed on the morning of February 29th when her wardrobe maid entered the room with the news that a boy had arrived with a telegram which was to be given to the Queen immediately. It was from Buller, telling her that her subjects in Ladysmith were at last free. The Queen's joy was 'unbounded'. She later recorded in her journal that she 'let everybody in the castle know', and sent the news to her family. On March 13th Lord Roberts telegraphed, 'By the help of God and by the bravery of Her Majesty's soldiers, the troops under my command have taken possession of Bloemfontein.'

3

VICTORY IN SIGHT

In May, with the outcome of the war still not decided, public spirits were raised so high in Britain that newspapers began speculating on the reward that Lord Roberts would receive at the end of the campaign. A viscountcy was suggested, with a parliamentary grant of £100,000. General Sir Garnet Wolseley was now a viscount, and it was recalled that after the Ashantee War in 1874 he had been thanked by parliament and given £25,000. In 1898 Sir Herbert Kitchener had received a peerage and £30,000 for crushing the Khalifa in the Sudan. For his services in Afghanistan, Lord Roberts had been voted £12,000, or £1000 a year for life, and it was said that he had chosen the latter.[1]

May 15, 1900 was 'Mafeking Night', when the whole of Britain was plunged into jubilation. Anxiety for the safety of the Mafeking garrison had been acute, and earlier in the week it had almost seemed as if the heroic defence of Colonel Baden-Powell and his supporters during seven long weary months had been in vain. Mafeking, though not basically important in itself, had become a symbol of Queen and Empire and what was called the 'bulldog spirit'. It was after nine o'clock on Friday night that the telegram reached London, announcing the relief of the town by Colonels Mahon and Plumer. At first it seemed unbelievable; there had been so many rumours and false reports. Then, when the news spread, Britain went mad with excitement.

---

[1] In January 1901 the British Cabinet proposed to endow his new earldom with a grant of £50,000, but the Prince of Wales protested, and in July 1901 the House of Commons voted Lord Roberts £100,000.

'At 9.30 p.m. the Mansion House presented its usual evening appearance of respectable desertion,' reported the *Daily Mail* next day. 'The few passers-by did not even heed the empty bulletin board which so many had anxiously scanned during the day. The omnibuses went by west and east as usual, and only the two huge footmen, so familiar to London pageantry, stood by waiting and anxious to display the Baden-Powell picture that had been prepared for the great moment. Five minutes later the Lord Mayor received the news and the two footmen, in their desire to display "B-P." to the empty streets, nearly dropped it on the head of an unsuspecting passer-by. One of them shouted excitedly, "Mafeking is relieved!" A policeman below heard it, and he too shouted "Mafeking is relieved!" Instantly the cry was taken up on the omnibuses and the people came clambering down in hot haste to hear the news repeated over and over again. Most of them stopped still as if it were too good to be true. Others rushed off into the byways carrying the tidings farther and farther away and all the time the streets became thicker with people cheering, shouting and singing ... Within five minutes the historic home of the Lord Mayor was surrounded by a crowd of no fewer than 20,000 madmen, all yelling.'

By ten o'clock that night the news had been announced from the stage of every London theatre, and the suburbs and provinces were already roaring themselves hoarse with excitement. Few at first believed it when the news spread to Manchester, Birmingham, Liverpool, Glasgow and the other great cities. But as the tidings spread the people came pouring out of their houses in a state of wild abandon; flags were thrust out of windows, cheering men and boys ran up and down with bunting or handkerchiefs, the buses were taken over by young fellows and all rides were free, cheers rang out for the Queen, for 'Bobs', for 'B-P', and Major Lord Edward Cecil, but above all for 'B-P'. Crowds serenaded his mother's house; men climbed on top of cabs waving flags; street vendors, who suddenly appeared amongst the dense crowds in Trafalgar Square carrying Union Jacks and 'B-P' buttons, lost their stocks within a few minutes; by eleven o'clock London's traffic was at a standstill as groups of men and women

and children danced up and down the streets arm in arm; the *Evening News*, with a tricolour poster, was sold out directly it was put on the streets; whistles and hooters pierced the air; the band of the Endell Street Boys' Brigade marching down Shaftesbury Avenue became the centre of a great demonstration; girls

of eight or nine from the slums of Soho and Drury Lane drew up in lines in front of it and danced along the streets while people threw coins to them; the bars were filled with drinkers, who looked as if they would never go home.

At first the managers of most of the London theatres had feared to tell the audiences, dreading that the news would be contradicted. At the London Pavilion, the comedian Dan Leno was performing his blackboard trick when suddenly he flung the blackboard on the stage and began dancing a hornpipe on it. A shout went around, 'Mafeking is relieved!' and the theatre was suddenly turned into bedlam.

At the Alhambra in Leicester Square a *Daily Mail* reporter made the announcement, and the news was quickly thrown on to a screen by a projector. For a few moments cheers drowned everything else; then men began clambering on to the seats, some waving programmes, some handkerchiefs. A sudden hush fell and 'God Save the Queen' was sung with all the solemnity of a hymn in a meeting-house. 'After this,' said the reporter, 'there was a quarter of an hour of mad fits.'

At Daly's Theatre, Mr Huntley Wright forgot that he was a Japanese, embraced his leading lady, Miss Fanny Collingbourne, and danced wildly round the stage with her while the audience rose and cheered. At the Prince of Wales's Theatre, Mr Martin Harvey was reciting the line, 'At last you bring me good news!' when the play was interrupted for the announcement, and the audience rose and shouted and sang.

At the Avenue Theatre, Mr Charles Hawtrey stopped the show and asked the cast and audience to join him in singing the National Anthem. The Empire, Leicester Square, was the scene of a demonstration 'absolutely unequalled in its annals'. At the Shaftesbury the American cast behaved as if Mafeking were an American town. Meanwhile, thousands of railway engines all over the country were blowing their steam-whistles, and liners in the ports of Liverpool, Southampton, London, Glasgow and Cardiff were setting up a hooting that lasted for hours.

An American standing in the crush at Piccadilly Circus was reported to have said, 'Well, this beats Manila night in New

York all hollow. I thought that these Britishers were a soulless people, but blow me, if it ain't the worst I ever saw.'

In New York a tremendous crowd gathered in City Hall Park, where several Union Jacks were unfurled and bands played. In Montreal the news was posted at five in the evening, when all work was abandoned and French and English Canadians joined in acclaiming Colonel Baden-Powell's triumph. Later a torch-light procession marched through the city, led by the Highland cadets. In Quebec a torchlight procession was headed by the 8th Royal Rifles, and thousands of people roamed the streets singing and shouting. At Sydney the ships, all decked with flags and illuminated, sent up rockets which lighted up the whole city. German and Italian vessels in the harbour joined in, but not the French. The streets were almost impassable, bells pealed, bonfires blazed and the undergraduates of Sydney took over the city.

Next day, Saturday, there were official processions throughout Britain, parades, bands marching, the Church Cadet Corps and the Church Lads' Brigade and the Boys' Brigade out in force with police and fire brigades and tramways bands and civic dignitaries leading the way. It was a celebration which no man or woman or youngster who saw it would ever forget.

The *Brighton Gazette* reported: 'The Clarence Hotel was after midnight the scene of an enthusiastic muster. Led by visitors in the hotel, the crowd gave cheer after cheer for the generals and sang *God Save the Queen* and *Rule Britannia*. Earlier in the evening when the news first came there were many people in the hotel and the greatest enthusiasm prevailed. Amongst them was Mr John L. Toole, the aged actor, who when told that Mafeking was relieved, said, "And so am I".'

Lady Burne-Jones, the wife of the artist Sir Edward Burne-Jones, was at this time one of many who did not sympathize with the national cause, and she had for long been labelled 'pro-Boer'. This was unfortunate for her distinguished nephew Rudyard Kipling, the poet of imperialism, who lived opposite her across the green at Rottingdean. The climax came when the news of the relief of Mafeking arrived. Lady Burne-Jones was prepared for the great day. She had made a large linen banner, on which were proudly painted the words, 'We Have Killed And Also Taken Possession', and this she now displayed across the top windows of her home, North End House, so that all the village, and in particular her nephew Rudyard, could see and read it.

When war was declared the British field and horse artillery were armed with the so-called 15-pounder and 12-pounder gun respectively, and there were also a few batteries of the new 5-inch rifled howitzer. The guns, intended for direct fire, instead employed shrapnel shell, it being decided that this was the best weapon against infantry. The field artillery was well organized, mobile, and of excellent discipline, but quite insufficient in numbers. The field artillery material, the 5-inch howitzers excepted, was however sadly out of date. Most European armies had adopted new and improved field guns, and Britain lagged far behind. The Boer republics were much better off, sudden access of wealth from gold and diamonds giving them ready means of purchase. They did not need to replace existing guns, but bought the latest from Krupp, Nordenfelt, and Schneider. Thus they frequently had the advantage over the British field guns, until finally the latter were increased in overwhelming numbers.

The British infantry were equipped with the Lee-Enfield ·303 rifle, an accurate weapon which had replaced the earlier breech-loader and the later Martini-Enfield, but the Boers used either German or Spanish Mausers, the latter being a more advanced weapon than the Lee-Enfield. It was lighter, had a higher velocity, greater range and penetration, and a lower trajectory. As to rapidity of fire, when the magazine of the British rifle was emptied the weapon became for the time being a single loader, for there was no method of refilling the magazine except by inserting a single cartridge at a time. The Boers, on the other hand, employed a 'clip', which had been adopted by all the great powers except Britain. This contained five cartridges which could be loaded into the magazine in a single motion. Thus, the Boers could refill five times as rapidly as the British soldiers—a very important advantage at critical moments.

To make matters worse for the British, the Boers were better marksmen. Little had been done, despite the lesson of the 1880 war, either in musketry or tactics, to prepare the British soldier for the new conflict. The Boers were more thoroughly accustomed to the clear air, the local colouring, and the vast distances of their land. They were generally on the defensive, dug in deeply in carefully prepared positions with barbed wire to protect them, or ensconced in gullies or posted on rocky, broken kopjes covered with boulders. When the British attacked, the enemy knew all the range distances and picked them off individually. But the British soldier still stood up in the open, fired from the standing or kneeling position, marched in step as the pikemen had done centuries earlier, and behaved as if he were on the barrack square, at drill. By comparison with those of the Boers his trenches were mere rabbit scrapings; while the farmers fired accurately from the saddle, the British cavalry charged with lances, swords and revolvers.

Yet nothing could demoralize the British tommy, or his colonial cousins. With equipment weighing forty pounds he covered twenty marching miles a day, and then fought in the evening. The Guards marched forty miles before Bloemfontein, and the Queenslanders and Canadians who joined Plumer before the relief of Mafeking marched nearly as far. They sang as they marched, to keep their spirits up:

> Goodbye, Dolly, I must leave you,
> Though it breaks my heart to go . . .

As to courage, with all the odds against them they were often recklessly brave. If the professional senior soldiers did not appear to be endowed with clear vision, both they and the volunteers who flocked to the flag showed extraordinary spirit. The troops who were cut to pieces at Spion Kop in January, who were driven off Vaalkranz early in February, proved to be the men who went roaring over the Boer trenches in the last week of that same month.

When it had become clear that the regular troops would not be sufficient to provide an adequate army for the war, the Militia were called up. Some 40,000 men were permanently embodied, and a large number of battalions both infantry and garrison artillery, volunteered as complete units for field service. Over 15,000 militiamen went to South Africa.

The Yeomanry, though a very old force in Britain, had never before taken part in an overseas campaign. At the beginning of the war there were about 12,000 in Britain, divided into 38 corps and costing the country less than £70,000 a year. Their work was light—6 mounted parades, 6 dismounted drills, and 10 days' permanent duty during the period of training. Each Yeoman had to provide his own horse and was paid £3 10s a year for expenses. His grateful government issued him with horse equipment and uniform, and a Martini-Enfield or Martini-Metford carbine, which was about 2 lb. lighter than the infantry rifle but had no magazine. The musketry training was clearly inadequate. By 1900 the Yeomen were invited to go into camps of instruction, instead of undergoing ordinary training, for 28 days instead of 10, and the annual allowance was raised to £5.

In December 1899, after the serious reverses of 'Black Week', it was decided to call for new volunteers and to re-establish the Yeomen under the title of Imperial Yeomanry. Each man was to be taught to ride and shoot well, the new force being required to act as mounted infantry. The old carbines were hastily withdrawn, and the heavy service ·303 was issued with a bayonet, the cartridges being carried in a bandolier. £60 was to be provided for the purchase of a horse, £20 for outfit expenses, and a bounty was promised on discharge.

There were about 500 men in a Yeomanry battalion, each containing a staff, four companies of 121 rank and file, and machine-gun sections. Battalions took with them two Colt automatic guns mounted on Dundonald galloping carriages. Each company was named after the county or regiment where it was raised, but several patriotic gentlemen incorporated their names into their own companies. Thus there were The Duke of Cambridge's Own (one company), The Sharpshooters (four companies) and many others. The Sharpshooters were raised by Lord Dunraven and a committee of gentlemen interested in rifle-shooting, the Honorary Secretary being Mr Seton-Kerr, MP. The unit was unique because applicants had to possess a higher standard of shooting than the other Yeomen and were also allowed an extra outfit—pistol, field-glasses, and a life insurance policy. Paget's Horse (four companies), under Mr A. Paget and an influential committee, provided their own horses and outfits up to the date of their landing in South Africa. Then there were the famous Rough Riders, who were required to pass special riding tests, and Lord Lovat's Scouts, gillies and expert stalkers well-trained in field-craft drawn from the Lovat Highland estates, mounted on sturdy little ponies.

The whole of the Imperial Yeomanry was raised, equipped and organized between December 1899 and the end of March 1900, and consisted of twenty battalions with a total of 10,000 men. They first came under fire on April 5, 1900 in Lord Methuen's successful action at Tweifontein, near Boshoff, when the whole of a Boer raiding party, mostly Frenchmen, was killed or captured. The action was then described by a journalist as being 'a sporting affair from the first . . . the men from the Aylesbury country made a hunting business of it, and went ahead to be in at the death'. The Yeoman battalions in the engagement were the 10th (Lord Chesham's Bucks, Berks and Oxfordshire) and the 2nd (Colonel Younghusband's Yorkshire, and the Notts and Sherwood Foresters).

London's City Imperial Volunteers (CIV) formed a body by itself, comprising a battalion of infantry, some mounted infantry, and a battery of four field guns manned by volunteers from the Honourable Artillery Company. Its total strength was eventually 1600 men, the Council of the City of London voting £25,000 for completely equipping a corps of 1000 men within 21 days. So quickly were the CIV raised and equipped that on January 13, 1900 the first contingent sailed for South Africa, and by February 11th they were engaging the enemy at Jacobdal—7000 miles from London. The competition to be included in the ranks had been very keen, so that the CIVs were men of exceptional physique and intelligence. Their powers of endurance were proved when in pursuit of De Wet late in the campaign the battalion marched 224 miles in 24 days, including one day's halt, an average of about 17 miles a day.

By March 1900 no fewer than thirteen members of the Churchill family were involved in the war, twelve of them—including the head of the family, and one woman member—being in South Africa. 'Mr Winston Churchill has not merely bravery,' wrote J. M. Bulloch in *The Sphere*. 'He has brains too. Though he is just six and twenty he has seen a great deal of exciting service.' When war broke out he went off as correspondent of the *Morning Post*, and was captured and slightly wounded in the armoured train which was sent in November 1899 from Estcourt to reconnoitre. Taken to Pretoria, he escaped by scaling a prison wall, and after many adventures reached Durban. He then took a commission in the Imperial Light Horse. Meanwhile his mother, Lady Randolph Churchill, was looking after wounded on the hospital ship *Maine* at Durban, while her other son, John Churchill, had been wounded with the South African Light Horse. As for the head of the family, the Duke of Marlborough, he was a Captain in the Imperial Yeomanry, and the Duke of Roxburghe was a lieutenant in the Blues, as was the Hon. Dudley Marjoribanks.

Few of the generals in South Africa increased their reputations more than Lieutenant-General J. D. P. French.[1] When he went to the front nobody except the military experts had heard of him. Until the outbreak of hostilities the only fighting he had seen was in the Nile expedition of 1894–95. But as a cavalry commander he was largely responsible for the victory at Elandslaagte, he escaped in the last train out of beleagured Ladysmith, and harassed the enemy for weeks on the south border of the Orange Free State before achieving fame through his relief of Kimberley. He then led Lord Roberts' advance guard to Pretoria.

Conditions were tough at the Modder River camp. 'We have been treated like dogs since we started from England,' wrote a trooper with Lord Dundonald's brigade. 'We did not even receive a drink of beer or anything on Christmas Day, when we simply had salt pork and soup, with six oranges divided amongst eighteen of us. So you see, we are broken in to rough it a bit.'

[1] Afterwards Field-Marshal the Earl of Ypres, OM, GCB, KCMG, GCVO, KP, died May 22, 1925.

At home, patriotic people were raising money for war funds and knitting socks for soldiers. When Mrs Beerbohm Tree, wife of the famous actor, finished reciting Kipling's poem *The Absent-minded Beggar* to a packed audience at the Palace Theatre in London, she was showered with gold and silver coins, which littered the stage; cheques and gold poured into the Lord Mayor of London's fund and there was hardly a city or town in Britain which did not, early in 1900, start a war relief fund. Thus by January 13th 2,000,000 shillings had been collected by the *Daily Telegraph* for the widows and orphans of soldiers and sailors, without any deduction of expenses. Many other newspapers, including *The Scotsman*, ran similar funds. The *Daily Mail*'s 'Absent-Minded Beggar' Fund exceeded £100,000 by June. But the two London liberal morning papers took opposite sides in the conflict, the *Daily News* supporting the war, the *Daily Chronicle* opposing it.

There was, however, also a more sombre side of the story. The lessons which Florence Nightingale and her helpers had taught the army during the Crimea War had been quickly forgotten. Medical conditions were often appalling. During the campaign more British troops died of enteric fever than from enemy bullets. At home *The Sketch* and *Illustrated London News* carried the advertisement, 'Our soldiers in South Africa are issued with Bovril to prevent enteric fever'. But in addition they drank freely from muddy rivers like the Modder, fouled by dead horses and oxen.

Mr W. Burdett-Coutts, MP, who was sent out by *The Times* to report on the hospital and medical arrangements, denounced the hospital at Bloemfontein, where he saw typhoid patients without nurses, untrained soldiers acting as orderlies, and sometimes only two or three doctors to several hundred wounded men. Here there were soldiers huddled on blankets in bell-tents with thick clusters of flies crawling over their faces and hands.

'In many of these tents,' he wrote, 'there were ten typhoid cases lying closely packed together, the man in his "crisis" pressed against the man hastening to it.'

Major-General J. F. C. Fuller has described in *The Last of the*

Gentleman's Wars how as a wounded subaltern he was carried on a stretcher into Orange River Hospital, 'which consisted of one or two longish huts and a number of marquee tents. I was carried into a hut. There were no proper beds, only mattresses with bags of hay and blankets on them. The arrangements were primitive in the extreme, and the PMO, an elderly Major, even more primitive still. He asked me what was wrong, and I told him that I had dreadful pains in the abdomen and could keep nothing down. "Oh!" he replied. "You've got a twisted gut," and then left me.'

The Modder water was jokingly referred to by the troops as 'Boer Broth', but the battalion water carts filled up from it every evening at dusk. The Boers did not always trouble to throw their dead oxen into the river; it was easier to leave them where they lay. Rudyard Kipling wrote:

> The trek-ox when alive can haul
> Three-quarters of a ton per head,
> But he can shift you, camp and all,
> Once he is dead.

Early in December 1900 Lord Roberts returned home to take over his new appointment as Commander-in-Chief. Before leaving Cape Town he telegraphed to the Queen: 'I have just made over command of Your Majesty's Army in South Africa to Kitchener, in whose judgement, discretion, and valour I have the greatest confidence.'

During his ten months in South Africa, 'Bobs' had enhanced his reputation enormously. Arriving at the front at the beginning of February he had relieved Kimberley within a fortnight, captured Cronje, and was in Bloemfontein less than six months later. Then, after a halt of only six weeks, he had occupied Johannesburg and Pretoria. People in Britain imagined that victory had at last been won.

Later, Mr W. H. Knowles of Great Harwood revealed that when he thought the British flag would soon fly over Pretoria he had sent a cigar in an envelope addressed 'To the officer who hoists the Union Jack (when that happy event takes place), Pretoria,

South Africa.' Inside the envelope he had added a note, 'Thanks! Have a cigar.' This was faithfully delivered at the right moment to Lord Roberts, who passed it to his ADC. On June 7th the Duke of Westminster wrote to Mr Knowles from Government House, Pretoria:

Dear Sir,

I write to say that I was the officer who hoisted the Union Jack over Pretoria, in consequence of which I have received an excellent cigar which Lord Roberts gave to me, having been forwarded by you. I thank you again both for the cigar and congratulations

> and remain
> yours truly,
> *Westminster*
> (*ADC, HQ Staff*)

'There has been no rest,' 'Bobs' told his army as he left the Cape. 'No days off to recruit, no going into winter quarters as in other campaigns which have extended over a long period. For months together, in fierce heat, in biting cold, in pouring rain, you, my comrades, have marched and fought without halt and have bivouacked without shelter from the elements. You frequently have had to continue marching with your clothes in rags and your boots without soles, time being of such consequence that it was impossible for you to remain long enough in one place to refit. When not engaged in actual battle you have been continually shot at from behind kopjes by invisible enemies to whom every inch of the country was familiar, and who, from the peculiar nature of the country, were able to inflict severe punishment while perfectly safe themselves. You have forced your way through dense jungles, over precipitous mountains, through and over which with infinite manual labour you have had to drag heavy guns and ox-wagons. You have covered with almost incredible speed enormous distances, and that often on very short supplies of food. You have endured the sufferings inevitable in war to sick and wounded men from the base, without a murmur and even with cheerfulness.'

Gladys Laurie Pett, aged eleven, wrote these verses which summed up popular feeling:

> Lord Roberts is my hero,
> And a gallant one is he;
> A better, braver soldier
> Could never, never be.

> He sent old Kruger flying
> And set our prisoners free;
> A better, braver soldier
> Could never, never be.

> He marched proudly into Pretoria
> With the flag of our good Queen;
> A better, braver soldier
> Was never, never seen.

General Sir Redvers Buller was less fortunate. His reputation as a tactical general was at its lowest ebb in spite of his personal bravery and his genuine and ever apparent concern for the welfare of his troops. All this had in the past earned him the reputation of being the soldier's friend. Quite early in the campaign his colleagues had dubbed him 'Sir Reverse', and the nickname stuck.

On the fallacious assumption that his work in South Africa was completed, 'Bobs' was recalled to replace Field-Marshal Lord Wolseley as Commander-in-Chief. The Queen considered that Wolseley should be succeeded by her cousin the Duke of Connaught, but Lord Salisbury declined to support her recommendation and, as the Prince of Wales stood by the Prime Minister, Roberts was chosen.

On his way home through Natal 'Bobs' had cheerfully announced that the war was practically over, and referred to the remaining Boer forces as 'a few marauding bands'. But the conflict was by no means finished, and a thanksgiving service which had been planned in St Paul's Cathedral had to be hastily cancelled. Kitchener was still fighting the enemy, there were serious reverses and losses to come, blunder after blunder was yet to be committed, and the Tsar was to appeal for peace, calling it a war of extermination—unworthy of Britain. There were strong pro-Boer feelings in Britain, and Sir Henry Campbell-Bannerman

THE EMPIRE'S PART IN THE

TRANSVAAL WAR.

1899—1900.

In view of the approaching completion of hostilities, the Proprietors of

HAVE IN PREPARATION A

MAGNIFICENT RECORD OF THE WAR

Written by MR. SPENSER WILKINSON

(The Expert Authority on Military Matters).

The Number will also contain a description of the Exploits of Individual
Soldiers and of Regiments, Home and Colonial.
In addition there will be Special Photogravure Reproductions of Battle
Pictures by

MR. CATON WOODVILLE

and other well-known Artists, including our own Special Representatives
at the Front; the whole to form an absolutely

UNIQUE PICTORIAL RECORD OF THE CAMPAIGN.

*As the issue will be limited, and the price only 2s. 6d.;
we would most earnestly request our readers to book their orders
AT ONCE to obviate disappointment.*

Orders may be booked at any Booksellers or Newsagents, or direct
at the

OFFICE OF THE ILLUSTRATED LONDON NEWS, 198, STRAND.

spoke bitterly of the methods employed by the army in rounding up the Boers who continued to resist.

When Roberts handed over the command to Kitchener, he left his successor with the unenviable task of spending the next 18 months trying to hunt down the 25,000 men still serving in guerrilla bands in the field. President Kruger went into exile in Europe and was fêted in Paris, but the majority of the Boers escaped to cause further trouble. General Christian de Wet invaded Cape Colony and was effectively supported by other expeditions led by General J. B. M. Hertzog and General J. C. Smuts. The names of de Wet, Hertzog, J. H. Delarey, Smuts, Kemp, Louis Botha, Viljoen and Steyn were to be remembered by many a British tommy during the months to come.

Kitchener's method of subduing opposition was to use blockhouses for his garrisons, from which his cavalry and infantry swept the local countryside in a series of drives. But the guerrilla fighting continued, and even the internment of tens of thousands of Boer women and children and other non-combatants in what were called 'concentration camps' did not end hostilities, the system being inhumanely and badly administered. While the motive, to remove families from the firing zones, was intended to be a humanitarian one, allegations of callousness and neglect created intense bitterness. Camps were scattered through the Transvaal, Natal, and Orange Free State. The Liberal politicians in Britain, still resisting the government's policy and handling of the war, denounced the ill-treatment of 77,000 non-combatants as, in the words of their leader Sir Henry Campbell-Bannerman, 'methods of barbarism'. The annual death rate of children in the Transvaal was 585 per thousand, and in Orange Free State 629 per thousand. From July 1901 to February 1902 there were to be 17,627 deaths of women and children in the concentration camps. David Lloyd George, the Liberal member for Caernarvon, who had from the start resisted the war, predicted: 'At this rate within a few years there will not be child alive on the veldt, and when the Boer prisoners of war return . . . to look on the black embers of the house that has been burned to the ground, to hear from the lips of their wives how their children died in the disease-stricken camps—what then? A barrier of dead children's bodies will rise up between the British and the Boer races in South Africa. Herod of old tried such a thing as this. He sought to crush a little race by killing its young sons and daughters. He was not a success; and I would commend the story to Herod's modern imitator.'

After much opposition, Miss Emily Hobhouse, the English Quaker social worker and reformer, went out to South Africa to examine the conditions for herself. The reports which she sent back raised a national outcry in Britain, and through the appointment of 'ladies' committees' with influential backing, reforms were quickly made which brought the heavy mortality rate among women and children down to normal.

The Boers did not forget Miss Hobhouse. Although Kitchener described her as 'that damned woman', General Smuts later paid tribute to her, saying: 'Amid the sufferings of war she represented the eternal human, the eternal woman, the simple feelings of pity and comforting which the war spirit could not kill, and which in the end have led to the rebirth of the larger Africa.' When she died in 1926 she was given a state funeral by the South African government, and was buried at the foot of the Women and Children's memorial in Bloemfontein.

Although Kitchener proposed a meeting with the Boer leader, General Botha, to discuss a peace settlement, Botha refused the terms offered him. In January 1902 the Netherlands government offered to mediate, but the British refused. At last, after long discussions, peace was signed in Pretoria on May 31, 1902, leaving the Transvaal and Orange Free State as part of the Empire.

The war which Kipling had described as 'little more than a series of disorderly and ignoble scuffles by amateurs against amateurs' was at last over. Few Boers or Britons had wanted it, and time was to prove that it settled few arguments. But Britain's peace terms were hailed as magnanimous; no special taxes were to be imposed on the ex-enemy; Afrikaans was to be taught in the schools and used in the law-courts; and a gift of £3,000,000 was to go to the farmers to provide new homes. What is more, it did. These terms, General Botha was to say many years later, were the reason why South Africa stood by Britain in the 1914 conflict.

The war had lasted thirty-one months and some 448,725 men of all ranks had fought on the British side, of whom 52,414 were raised in South Africa and 30,000 came from other parts of the Empire. Exact figures of the Boer forces are hard to determine but the total is believed to have been about 60,000. Something like 3700 Boers were killed. The number who surrendered at the end of hostilities was 21,256.

British casualties were much heavier. 5774 men were killed, 2018 died of wounds, and no fewer than 13,350 died from disease. The campaign added £22,000,000 to the national debt, causing Britain's income tax to rise from eightpence in the pound to the unprecedented rate of 1s 3d.

In the year that peace was declared, Cecil Rhodes died. Among his last words were:

'You think you have beaten the Dutch! It is not so. The Dutch are not beaten. What is beaten is Krugerism, a corrupt and evil government, no more Dutch in essence than English. No, the Dutch are as vigorous and unconquered today as they have ever been; the country is still as much theirs as yours, and you will live and work with them hereafter as in the past.'

'We could always tell what you were going to do,' said a Boer prisoner at the end of the war. 'You would bombard our trenches for a time—anything from a couple of hours to a couple of days. Then your soldiers would march straight at us. It was very brave but *verdomd* foolish. For while your shells were bursting in our advanced trenches, we were not there'.

What had Britain learned from the war, and how did it benefit her armed forces? Little enough. More attention was henceforth paid to musketry and fieldcraft, and there were a few military reforms of a minor nature. But by 1914 most of the important lessons were forgotten. Indeed, only three years after the signing of peace in Pretoria, in July 1905, Lord Roberts was to stand up in the House of Lords and make this remarkable statement:

'I have no hesitation in stating that our armed forces, as a body, are as absolutely unfitted and unprepared for war as they were in 1899–1900.'

IMPERIALISM

The Prime Minister, the Marquis of Salisbury, who with his third government of 1895 had come to occupy a position of unrivalled authority in Britain and abroad, was generally regarded as the senior statesman of Europe. When Joseph Chamberlain became his Colonial Secretary it was Chamberlain who became the principal exponent of the imperial policy. It was Chamberlain who made use of public funds to build railways and harbours in Africa, granted money to shipping lines to aid the West Indies sugar market, found extra funds for Cyprus, waved the flag wherever he could, but at the same time helped to combat slavery, protect the Queen's subjects, and subdue the liquor traffic in tropical countries.

The poet of imperialism was Rudyard Kipling, who had indicated in his poem *Recessional* (1897) that Britons were charged with a sacred mission, to take civilization and the British way of life overseas:

> God of our fathers, known of old
> Lord of our far flung battle-line
> Beneath whose awful Hand we hold
> Dominion over palm and pine—
> Lord God of Hosts, be with us yet
> Lest we forget—lest we forget!

With Kipling, as with most of the great English moralists, duty was something more than a mere negative virtue. It was a mighty force, giving life, poetry and fire; his vision of the English was of a race finding its destiny in free surrender, self-training and self-

75

dedication to a divine purpose. In his hymn of the old Scots engineer McAndrew, published in 1896, he epitomized it as: 'Law, Order, Duty and Restraint, Obedience, Discipline'.[1] Thus Kipling was not only the poet of imperialism but also the teacher of conduct, with a militant faith in his country's destiny, which was a duty to bear 'the white man's burden'.

'It is this consciousness of the inherent superiority of the European which had won us India,' declared another imperial leader, Lord Kitchener. 'However well-educated or clever a native may be, and however brave he may have proved himself, I believe no rank we bestow on him can cause him to be considered the equal of a British officer'.

Commenting on this type of imperialism, George Bernard Shaw put into the mouth of Napoleon, in his play *The Man of Destiny*, the speech: 'Every Englishman is born with a certain miraculous power that makes him master of the world. When he wants a thing, he never tells himself that he wants it. He waits patiently until there comes into his mind, no one knows how, a burning conviction that it is his moral and religious duty to conquer those who possess the thing he wants. Then he becomes irresistible.'

'The Right Honourable Joseph Chamberlain, to whom Her Majesty has entrusted the care of her Colonies,' said the *Black and White Budget*, 'is the beloved of Birmingham, the loathed of the Little Englander, and the man whom Kruger fears above all others. He is over sixty, smokes a strong tobacco, never takes exercise, grows and wears orchids, and has done more to strengthen the supports of the British flagstaff than any other six of his colleagues in the cabinet. He can write a stinging despatch and he can pick a good servant—e.g. Sir Alfred Milner. And he is not above knowing a duchess.'

Joseph Chamberlain was born at Camberwell, London, in 1836. He was privately educated in a small school until the family moved to Highbury, after which the Chamberlain mansion in Birmingham was later named. At fourteen he went to University

[1] Arthur Bryant, *English Saga*, London, 1940.

College School and when he was eighteen—three years after the Great Exhibition—he moved to Birmingham to work for the business with which his father was connected, the screw firm of Nettlefold and Chamberlain. In those days few towns possessed public baths, libraries, schools of art, technical colleges, museums and art galleries, and the Birmingham of 1854–60 was not alone in having few of these. Looking back to those days in an interview in 1900, Mr Chamberlain recalled: 'The streets were badly paved, they were imperfectly lighted, they were only partially drained, but the footwalks were worse than the streets. You had to proceed either in several inches of mud, or in favoured localities you might go upon cobblestones, on which it was a penance to walk. The gas and water belonged to private monopolies. Gas was supplied at an average rate of about five shillings per thousand cubic feet. The water was supplied by the company on *three* days a week. On other days you either went without or you took advantage of the perambulating carts which went round the town and which supplied water from polluted wells at ten shillings for a thousand gallons. There were courts which were not paved, which were not drained, which were covered with pools of stagnant filth, and in which ash-pits and middens were in a state of indescribable nastiness. Birmingham, although it was no worse than any other of the great cities of the United Kingdom, was a town in which scarcely anything had been done either for the instruction or for the health or for the recreation or for the comfort or for the convenience of the artisan population.'

He was a reformer with a conscience. Entering the town council in 1869, he devoted himself to municipal work and was elected mayor in 1873, 1874, and 1875. Only two months after being first appointed he proposed to buy the gas works for the town, and there were only two votes against him and fifty-four in favour. By the end of the century the city was making a profit of about £50,000 a year from this enterprise. Next he suggested that Birmingham should run the water-works, and this was carried through. In his second year he proposed a city improvement scheme and the building of Corporation Street, a handsome thoroughfare to enrich the borough. When it was discovered that

77

there were no public funds for this, he himself gave £10,000 and then other townspeople supplemented it.

In June 1876 he entered parliament, uncontested, as one of the three members for Birmingham. Soon his silk hat, and his eye-glass and orchid were world famous. As President of the Board of Trade he was such a success that in 1895 he became Colonial Secretary, and eventually Britain's arch-imperialist.

'I believe in this race,' he said, 'the greatest governing race the world has ever seen; in this Anglo-Saxon race, so proud, tena-cious, self-confident and determined, this race which neither climate nor change can degenerate, which will infallibly be the predominant force of future history and universal civilization.'

Such sentiments had found their fulfilment in the careers of empire-builders like Cecil Rhodes, so that between 1880 and 1900 Britain had made vast increases in her overseas possessions, the Queen becoming the symbol of a vigorous, wealthy and powerful commonwealth based on trade and shipping. When in 1897 Victoria had celebrated her Diamond Jubilee she had been escorted in procession by 'a great band of imperial troops—Indian native levies, mounted riflemen from Australia, South Africa, and Canada, and coloured soldiers from the West Coast of Africa, Cyprus, Hong Kong and Borneo. Beacons burned on hill tops across Britain, and the festivities lasted a fortnight.'

This imperial concept of empire was strongly opposed in Britain by the radical section of the public, the 'Little Englanders' who were uninterested in the further extension of the Empire, preferring a policy of insular neutrality. Chamberlain stood for everything they opposed, for he was against Irish Home Rule, on which Gladstone had been defeated, he opposed free trade, and he wished to fight the Boer War to a finish.

As a prelude to the declaration of war in South Africa in 1899, he had said in the House of Commons: 'Our first object is to preserve our position as the paramount state in South Africa. It matters not whether we call ourselves suzerain or paramount, but it is an essential feature of our policy that the authority and influence of this country shall be predominant in South Africa.' His policy at the Colonial Office was to spend as much money as possible on the development of backward countries, while jealously guarding the inhabitants from exploitation by foreigners and financiers. The essential first step was to improve communications by building roads, railways and bridges; the eventual aim was to build up a great federation of empire whose commercial prosperity could be assured by a special tariff, a system of lower customs duties which would operate within the commonwealth of nations. This protectionist aim, however, was not to be realized because there was too much opposition. But Chamberlain succeeded in starting certain basic reforms that had far-reaching effects, and he undoubtedly improved the welfare and administration of many of the colonies by bringing them under central control.[1]

According to the estimates for 1900, Chamberlain's department was costing Britain about £67,000 a year, more than half of which went in salaries and about a tenth in telegrams. The principal colonies were self-supporting, but to help the smaller protectorates and dependencies the government allowed the Colonial Office about £880,000 a year, of which in 1900 some £250,000 went to Uganda alone. Altogether, Britain's Empire was costing her about £1,000,000 a year, not counting vast sums which had been lent in the past, Australia alone having borrowed £400,000,000, and Canada £100,000,000.

At the end of the century the Empire, excluding India and Egypt, was eighty times bigger than the United Kingdom, but on the other hand there were eight people in Great Britain for every five in what was called Greater Britain. The oldest colony was Newfoundland. The great landmark had been the middle of the century, when Britain was firmly established in Canada, South Africa, in the West Indies, the Pacific, and in India. By 1900 there were eleven self-governing colonies—Canada, New South Wales, Victoria, South Australia, Queensland, West Australia, Tasmania, New Zealand, the Cape, Natal, and Newfoundland. Their governors were sent out from Britain, but had little to do with the Colonial Office; they had their own parliaments, laws, armies, fleets, and other marks of sovereignty,

[1] Margaret M. Elliott, *British History Displayed*, Cambridge, 1955.

including debts. Where the Colonial Office exerted more direct
influence was in the smaller dependencies like British Guiana,
Malta (which also had a local government), Mauritius, the
Bahamas, Barbados, Bermuda, Jamaica, and the Leeward Islands.
There were also sixteen colonies under the direct control of the
Colonial Office: British North Guinea, Ceylon, the Falklands,
Fiji, Gambia, the Gold Coast, Grenada, Hong Kong, Lagos, St
Lucia, St Vincent, Seychelles, Sierra Leone, Trinidad, Tabago
and Turks's Island. Territories governed by the crown by Order
in Council included Basutoland, Gibraltar, Labuan, and St
Helena. Of Britain's army in 1900 rather more than 30,000 men
were stationed in the colonies, which also had effective forces of
about 100,000 men, Canada alone having nearly half of the total.

The wealth of the Empire was already immense; the colonial
countries had banking deposits worth over £200,000,000, while
their imports reached nearly £175,000,000 a year, with exports
slightly less. But more important than the financial position,
because most of these new countries possessed vast potential
wealth and natural resources, was the man-power problem.
Canada, Australia, New Zealand and South Africa needed many
more young men and women to help build up their industries,
agriculture, and their growing cities. During the century large
numbers of people had left Britain to seek fortunes and a new way
of life overseas—between ten and fifteen million, it is believed—
but the new lands desperately needed even more immigrants. In
the year 1880 alone some 166,000 Britons had gone to live in the
United States, and nearly 21,000 went to Canada. The Commonwealth of Australia (due to come into existence officially on
January 1, 1901) was incorporated by an Act of Parliament at
Westminster in 1900. It was a great new land of opportunity for
thousands of Britons. There was some possibility that New
Zealand would join in with the Australians, but in the end she
decided to remain independent.

In 1902 Lord Salisbury was to retire, and under the influence
of King Edward and the return in 1906 of the Liberals with an
overwhelming majority, Britain was to start seeking European
alliances. Which was to be the ally, France or Germany? Under

6. Shopping in Regent Street, London, 1900

7. High Holborn, London, Summer 1900

8. In 1900 bathing machines were still very much in evidence at Southsea, but mixed bathing was now tolerated

9. Off to Goodwood from Chichester, 1900

Chamberlain's guidance the first approach would be to Germany, but his proposal for a threefold alliance between Britain, Germany and Japan was unfortunately never to mature. Instead, Germany —now becoming the leading military power in Europe—would soon be regarded as the enemy. Only the treaty with Japan was to be signed, while on the Continent France was to be the ally and Germany the enemy.

By 1900 the British Empire in India extended over a territory larger than the whole of Europe, without Russia. The country was ruled by its own government in Calcutta, at whose head was the all-powerful Viceroy, the Rt. Hon. the Lord Curzon of Kedleston, PC, GMSI, GMIE, who had succeeded Lord Elgin in January 1899. His council, which completely controlled this vast area of seventy-eight languages, included only six native Indian leaders in the total of fourteen additional members who were responsible for making laws. These Indian members, moreover, were of the ruling class, whose legendary and fantastic wealth was eventually to be greatly reduced when the country finally gained independence.

There was no question of the Indian peoples ruling their own country, or having any share in the government. They had no chance, they were not considered, and they were not ready for it. The majority were completely illiterate and, because of language, caste and tribal barriers, India was not really a single country.

The rulers, wealthy feudal princes and rajahs, were encouraged and backed by the British, but only provided that they behaved themselves. 'Divide and rule' was the Imperial policy, separating Moslems from Hindus, district from district. Three great rulers were entitled to a salute of twenty-one guns, the most influential of the potentates being the Nizam of Hyderabad, who ruled some 12,000,000 people in an area of 82,698 square miles. His revenue in 1899 was about £3m a year. After him came the Maharaja of Mysore (whose wife the Maharani was personally entitled to a salute of nineteen guns) with about 5,000,000 subjects and a personal income of about £1,200,000 a year. The third of the great princes was the Maharaja of Baroda with nearly 3,000,000 subjects and a personal income of over £1m a year. There were eight other rulers entitled to salutes of nineteen guns, and their annual revenues added up to about £13m.

In India in 1900 the land revenue brought in over £18m a year, opium produced nearly £4m, salt £5m, stamps over £3m, postal services nearly £2m, and the state railways nearly £13m. The opium revenue was useful, poppy being grown in parts of Bengal and the north-west provinces and Oudh and in the central native states. The area of opium cultivation in the Ganges area in 1898–1899 was 564,000 acres. Opium-growing was a government monopoly. In the year ending March 31, 1899 nearly 40,000 chests of the drug were sold for export, mostly to China, realizing £2,776,000. Thus Britain was officially and actively concerned in the world's drug traffic.

To keep India under control there was an army of about 219,450 men, made up of 73,000 British troops, some 788 miscellaneous officers, and 145,627 native troops, including some of the finest fighting soldiers in the world.

This huge area continued to suffer not only because of its vast numbers of illiterates, but also from famine, especially if the monsoon failed, as it did in 1899–1900. Out of 95,970,162 Hindu males in 1891 no fewer than 85,868,770 were illiterate. But it was poverty and the threat of famine which most seriously affected the lives of the still rapidly-expanding population. To be able to read and write was unimportant when the struggle was really to survive, to find enough grain and rice to keep starvation at bay, to escape disease. This was the never-ending and constant preoccupation of millions of thin men, women and skeleton children. The tragic failure of the monsoon in 1899–1900 affected 85 million people, 6 million receiving relief work or famine relief— a bare minimum subsistence—at the time of the most severe pressure. Bombay, with its native states, the central provinces and Behar, and the native states of Hyderabad, Baroda and Rajputana, were the chief sufferers. Thousands of children were strangled at birth by parents who knew there was no future for them. The prolonged droughts which accompanied the great famine caused not only tremendous loss of human life through starvation, malnutrition and disease, but killed off millions of head of cattle. Even the most fertile tracts of Western India, which had not suffered from famine for half a century, were now seriously affected.

The Viceroy, Lord Curzon, made every effort to draw the attention of the rest of the world to the predicament. This was, he said, India's worst famine since Britain had ruled the country. It was spread over an area of 450,000 square miles. At a public meeting in Calcutta town hall he appealed for funds, the resources of the government being totally inadequate. In Britain, in the United States, Australia, Canada, New Zealand, South Africa, and in colonies wherever the Union Jack flew, efforts were immediately started to raise money. Hardly a mayor in an English, Scots or Welsh town did not start a fund. Britain's newspapers, responding to an appeal by the Lord Mayor of London, added their support. *Twopence, they said, would buy enough rice to keep an Indian man or woman alive for a day.* The twopences poured in, and the government of India did its poor best to buy and distribute food. But the task was beyond its powers. Many starving parents sold their children in order to buy food; no one will ever know how many people died, or how many committed suicide rather than face a slow death.

During the summer another, smaller tragedy took place in China, where from Peking came news of the murder by Chinese soldiers of Sugiyama, the chancellor of the Japanese legation. This was followed by the murder on June 20th of the German Ambassador, Baron von Ketteler. The murders touched off what came to be called the Boxer rebellion, started by the patriotic, nationalist and religious Boxer association, whose members sought to combat the influence of foreign powers and missionaries in China. The real name of the secret society of Boxers was I-ho Ch'uah. Hordes of Chinese fanatics, led by prominent members of I-ho Ch'uah and the Great Sword Society, fell upon Christians and foreigners in the province of Chi-li. A whole Chinese Catholic congregation was burned alive in a church; Chinese converts were murdered and their bodies were thrown into rivers; bands of Boxers, encouraged by soldiers, began to destroy the railways and telegraph lines around Peking, where the foreign colony considered themselves secure but where they were soon cut off from the outside world.

Christian refugees began pouring into Peking, and marines from foreign warships arrived to strengthen the garrison. The Boxers then surrounded the city, set fire to a missionary chapel, and began to burn down the Chinese Imperial Bank, while others stormed the Austrian legation. The Austrians fired at the mob, infuriating the crowds, who then started attacking other foreign buildings. An eye-witness reported that there were some 50,000 people shouting 'Kill the foreign devils! Kill, kill, kill!'

Meanwhile a large number of warships, mostly British and Russian, had assembled off Taku, and troops and sailors were landed. On June 10th, a relief force of about 2000 men of various nationalities left Tien-tsin for Peking under the command of the British Admiral Sir John Seymour, but the railways had been destroyed and the presence of large numbers of guerrilla troops made progress impossible. The warships therefore opened fire on the Taku forts and landed men to capture them. Only an American warship refused to take part in the action.

The shelling of the forts led to a general rising throughout China against foreign influence, and the legations were now the centres of action, the staffs and marines firing on the crowds. Fierce fighting took place, whole districts being burned to the ground, together with the great college of Hanlin and its priceless library. Finally an allied army of 12,000 Japanese, 3000 Russians, 3000 British, 2800 Americans and 1000 French marched on Peking, which they relieved in August, just in time to prevent the city's great Catholic cathedral from being blown up.

The Chinese Emperor and Dowager Empress, who had supported the Boxers, had fled together with the court and officials. Street fighting continued for several days, the palaces of the richest mandarins being looted and sacked. Many prominent Chinese citizens committed suicide. Finally, in the autumn, the Emperor signed a document agreeing to the demands of the occupying powers. These included the despatch of an Imperial Prince of China to Berlin to express regret for the murder of

Baron von Ketteler, the erection of a monument where he had died with inscriptions of regret in Chinese, German and Latin, and the punishment of guilty leaders to be designated by the allies. There were also to be reparations to Japan for the murder of the chancellor, Sukiyama, heavy money indemnities to the governments and individuals who had suffered loss, and finally the establishment of permanent Chinese guards outside all foreign legations and the destruction of all forts between Peking and the sea.

This victory by the great powers reaffirmed people's faith in what was still believed to be the natural imperial supremacy of the Occidental. 'History has repeated itself,' said *The Times*. 'Once more a small segment of the civilized world, cut off and surrounded by an Asiatic horde, has exhibited those high moral qualities the lack of which renders mere numbers powerless.' To the Americans and British, western supremacy really meant Anglo-American supremacy. In the United States the policy of 'assimilation'—more acceptable than the word imperialism—was at last an economic opportunity, and in many quarters the policy was held to be even a moral duty, God's will, and clearly the virile course to follow. As Princeton's young Woodrow Wilson observed, imperial expansion was 'the natural and wholesome impulse which comes with a consciousness of natural strength'.

In Germany, the Kaiser was already beginning to share the same imperial belief. President McKinley thought there was even more to the policy; it was in his opinion the least that America could do to help less fortunate peoples. On the question of annexing the Philippines he said he had prayed God for guidance, and it had suddenly come to him in the night: 'There was nothing left to do but to take them all and educate the Philippinos and uplift and Christianize them and by God's grace to do the very best we could by them as our fellow men for whom Christ also died.'[1]

These, as we shall see, were the sentiments of many other pious men of the century who wished wrongs to be righted poverty to

---

[1] Walter Lord, *op. cit.*

be overcome, and injustice to be defeated. But fortunately for the American people the President did not involve his country too deeply overseas. Indeed, he was not able to, the United States being at that time mainly concerned with putting its own house in order.

5

RICHES AND HIGH SOCIETY

The coming twentieth century was to see immense changes in outlook, social behaviour, class distinctions and standards of comfort. The life of the working man was to be greatly improved; transport would be easier and better; house-building would pay more attention to drainage and sanitation; many labour-saving devices were to be introduced, including the domestic use of gas and electricity for heating and cooking. But up to the outbreak of war in 1914 there would remain great contrasts in the way people lived. The rich in Britain were still very rich, the poor would still be very poor.

In 1900 there were a million domestic servants employed in British houses, mostly underpaid and often underfed, with their tin boxes up in the attics. Many were fearful of being told by the mistress of the house to 'pack your box and go', because there were plenty of other girls, usually from the country or from Ireland, ready to fill the vacancies. In 1898 Mrs Camilla Nicholls, after a trial lasting five days, was sentenced to seven years' penal servitude for having ill-treated and starved her servant, Jane Popejoy, to death. Often girls like this were paid five or six shillings a week, with keep.

Their masters and mistresses in the big town and country houses lived on quite a different scale. The old feudal order changed slowly; the footmen still wore livery, the country tenants remained 'loyal' and appreciative of Christmas bounty, the servants' halls in the great mansions were full of petty tyrants. There were still noblemen rich and eccentric enough to behave like the fifth Duke of Portland, who died in 1879 having built fantastic subterranean suites at Welbeck Abbey, including a carriage tunnel over a mile long dug under the park, which enabled him to drive home unseen. Visiting London, the Duke had travelled in a carriage with blinds drawn, which was loaded on to a railway truck. He had a chicken roasting on a spit at all times, in case he felt hungry, and at his death he left stables containing ninety-four horses, with nearly fifty grooms and stablemen to attend his funeral. In the grounds of Welbeck he had installed a skating rink, where his servants were ordered to take exercise.[1]

A young footman, Frederick John Gorst, who also worked in Buckingham Palace, has described what life was like below and above stairs at the turn of the century in the sixth Duke's reign at Welbeck Abbey.[2]

'When we served the Duke and Duchess of Portland at dinner there were always three men in attendance; two footmen and either the wine butler or the groom of the chambers. There was no butler on the staff because Mr Spedding was the chief steward or major-domo and unlike smaller establishments this great house required departmental heads and assistants.' The staff was divided and sub-divided into many categories:

Kitchens and Services

Steward
Wine butler
Under butler
Groom of the chambers
4 royal footmen
2 steward's room footmen
Master of the servants' hall
2 page boys
Head chef
Second chef
Head baker

[1] E. S. Turner, *What the Butler Saw*, London, 1962.
[2] Frederick John Gorst, *Of Carriages and Kings*, London, 1956.

Second baker
Head kitchen maid
2 under kitchen maids
Vegetable maids
3 scullery maids
Head stillroom maid
Hall porter
2 helpers (hall boys)
Kitchen porter
6 odd men

House and Personal Service

Head housekeeper
Duke's valet
Duchess's personal maid
Lady Victoria's personal maid
Head nursery governess
Tutor
French governess
Schoolroom footman
Nursery footman
14 housemaids

Mechanical Help in the Household

6 engineers (house and electric plant)
4 firemen (electric plant and steam heating)
Telephone clerk and assistant
Telegrapher
3 night watchmen

Stable

Head coachman
Second coachman
10 grooms
20 strappers and helpers

Garage

Head chauffeur
15 chauffeurs
15 footmen (2 men on the box at all times)
2 washers

Estate Management

Estate Manager (Duke's confidential clerk)
Secretary to the Duke

Chapel

Resident chaplain
Organist

Titchfield Library

Librarian
Clerk
Housemaids (for dusting)

Racing Stables

Stud groom
15 assistants

Gardens

6 house gardeners (subterranean greenhouses and
    house decorations)
30–40 gardeners
40–50 roadmen

Home Farm

Head farmer
15–20 men in vegetable gardens and orchards

Gymnasium

Head instructor
Japanese trainer

Golf Course

Head greensman
10 helpers

Laundry cottage

Head laundress
12 laundresses

Window cleaners

Head window cleaner
2 assistants

The Duke's principal servants at this time had their own houses where they lived with their families. All farmers, gardeners, stablemen and garage men had their own cottages. The estate consisted of about 100,000 acres, the Duke's income being several million pounds a year, mostly derived from coal mines. Within the borders of his estate he exercised an almost feudal power.

'All is vast, splendid, and utterly comfortless,' wrote the historian Augustus Hare after visiting Welbeck. But this was certainly not true of Knowsley, the seat of the Earls of Derby (a title created in 1485), where the household expenditure in the years before the First World War was seldom less than £50,000 a year. Neither was it true of Chatsworth, where the Duke and Duchess of Devonshire lived in great luxury and welcomed royal guests with blazing fireworks and an avenue lined with three hundred torchbearers. To greet the Kaiser at Lowther in 1895 the sporting fifth Earl of Lonsdale (a title created in 1807) had sent out Quorn servants in hunting pink, followed by a squadron of Yeomanry, two blue-coated outriders, a dark phaeton in which he himself rode, and nine other carriages, each drawn by two chestnuts and with footmen up behind. All of which befitted a nobleman whose north gate was eight miles from his south gate. Indeed, until 1914 the Earl was to maintain a private orchestra of twenty-four musicians, which he took abroad with him when he travelled.[1]

[1] Captain Lionel Dawson, R.N. *The Authorised Life of Hugh Lowther, Fifth Earl of Lonsdale*, London, 1946.

The rich, however, accepted their responsibilities as the traditional ruling class. Thus, in 1900, Lord Lonsdale offered the War Office the services of 208 officers and men for South Africa, with three Maxim guns, four ambulances, a detachment of trained nurses, and 280 carts from his estates.

Another great house, Kedleston Hall in Derbyshire, the home of the father of Lord Curzon, Viceroy of India, was set in a park of 1200 acres, which contained some of the finest oak trees in England and 400 head of deer. Another fabulously wealthy man, one of the richest in Britain, was the Duke of Westminster, whose vast estates covered large sections of London. From a simple knighthood the Grosvenor family had come, through a baronetcy, earldom and marquisate, to the supreme dignity of a dukedom in 1874. The family's Manor of Ebury included large parts of Belgravia, Grosvenor Square, and almost the whole of Mayfair, the wealthiest area of London.

Queen Victoria's court assisted the rise of the middle-classes, for although the Queen showed middle-class sympathies she combined the dignity and aloofness of a monarch. County and provincial towns, which had formerly had a rich society of their own, now became less socially important, county people going to London for their social intercourse. The Queen's and the Prince of Wales' friends were drawn not so much from the old aristocracy as from the middle-class, and in the Prince's case even from commerce and industry. The new rich could no longer be disregarded, even if they owned shops.

The Americans invaded Europe, married English people with titles, and bought up art treasures. Lady Randolph Churchill, Lady Harcourt, Lady Curzon, Lady Essex, Lady Craven and Mrs Arthur Paget were among the American society beauties who married English aristocrats. Of the so-called 'smart set' of the 'nineties, Lady St Helier wrote:

'Society now runs mad after anyone who can get himself talked of, and that not in the sole direction of great ability or distinction. To have a good cook, to be the smartest dressed woman, to give the most magnificent entertainments where a fortune is spent on flowers and decorations, to be the most-favoured guest of Royalty, or to have sailed as near to the wind of social disaster as is compatible with not being shipwrecked, are a few of the features which characterize some of the smartest people in London society. It must be admitted that these qualifications are not high or difficult to attain to, while the training ground is large and well studded with instructors.'

The social revolution was slowly undermining the great rich families, and many of them knew it. The Duke of Sutherland (a title created in 1833) could still afford to pin £1000 bank notes to his wife's pillow while she slept, but he foresaw the changes which were coming, and Stafford House was one of the first big London mansions to go, in the days when Devonshire House and the rest still seemed safe for ever. In 1899, Lord and Lady Warwick turned their estates into a limited liability company. Life interests in their Warwickshire, Essex, Leicestershire and Northampton estates and the leases of Clutton collieries, together with personal insurance policies, were registered under the title of Warwick Estates Limited, with a capital of £120,000. Thus they were the pioneers of a policy of turning estates into companies which was later to become accepted by most great landowners. The rich aristocracy sensed the prospect of becoming poorer rather than richer, and talk of money—once considered a vulgar subject—was now more universal. Strange names had found their way into the Court Guide: Zacharie, Zachner, Zingler, Zossenheim, Zotti, Zuccana, Zurcher and Zwilchenbart, while *Debrett's Peerage* now contained nearly 2000 pages, its growth in bulk being considerable every year. In 1864 it had run to only 400 pages. During 1900, 5 new peerages had been created, one life peer was granted a hereditary title, 2 received titles with special remainders, there were 9 new baronets, 13 privy councillors, 96 new knights, and 155 companions of members of orders.

When wealthy people died there were smaller death duties than there are now to rob the heirs of their inheritances. In 1899 and 1900 many rich landowners died. Baron Adolphe Charles de Rothschild, the Paris banker, left £2,357,979 in Britain alone;

Joseph Cowen, politician and newspaper-owner, left £491,826 gross; Thomas Henry Ismay, the Liverpool shipowner, left £1,297,881; Arthur Tooth, the Haymarket print-seller, left £104,165 net; John Arthur Ingham, the Halifax mill-owner, left £163,581; William Henry Horniman, the tea-merchant, left £180,642 net; Frederick Colman, of the mustard and starch family, left £604,956; Sir Henry Tate, first baronet, the London and Liverpool sugar-refiner, left £1,263,565 gross; Sir Henry Bruce Meux, the brewer, left £276,649 gross; Lord William Kensington, the fifth baron, killed at Bloemfontein, left £711,218 gross; but Vice-Admiral Colomb, the inventor of flashing signals, left only £4006, and Ralph Tuck, the art publisher and creator of millions of popular picture postcards, left £2636.

For the daughters of British upper-class families presentation at court was essential. 'It is an epoch in a woman's life not easily forgotten,' said *The Harmsworth Magazine* (May 1900). 'To a young girl it signifies a transition from girlhood to womanhood; from the obscurity of the schoolroom to the brilliancy of society life, in which at-homes, dinners, balls, garden parties, operas and theatres follow each other in a continuous whirl. The smile of her Queen has transformed the little homely grub into a gay butterfly.'

The Queen held her drawing-rooms and *levées* at Buckingham Palace, the state apartments there being more spacious than at St James's Palace, where they had formerly been held, but *levées* were still held at St James's by the Prince of Wales. Ladies and gentlemen wishing to be presented to the sovereign could do so only through an acquaintance who had already been presented. It was almost, to use a later phrase, a closed shop. A lady wishing to be presented had first to leave at the Lord Chamberlain's office, St James's, at least two clear days before the occasion, a card with her name written clearly on it, and another bearing the name of her sponsor. Until the 'nineties the honour of a presentation was undreamed of except for the wives and daughters of what were termed the 'upper ten', which included the higher ranks of the armed services. But time had now widened the list and converted the 'upper ten' into ten thousand. 'Even *trade* is not debarred,' reported Mr Harmsworth's correspondent, adding some useful advice on what to wear on the great day:

'For a debutante the dress *must* be white, but coloured flowers are permissible and shower bouquets have recently been much in favour. The bodice is cut in a round decolletage, showing the shoulders, and with short sleeves. If through ill-health a low bodice cannot be worn, special permission must be obtained from the Queen, through the Lord Chamberlain, to wear High Court dress, which means a bodice cut square or V shape, and filled in with either transparent or thick *white* material, and elbow sleeves to match. An unmarried lady wears in her hair *two white ostrich feathers*, and a married lady *three*, and these plumes must be so arranged as to stand high in front so that they can be *clearly* seen on approaching Her Majesty. *White* gloves must be worn.'

Cassell's *Etiquette of Good Society* explained what happened on such formidable occasions: 'On getting out of the carriage everything in the shape of a shawl or cloak is left behind. The train is carried over the left arm. When the lady's turn for presentation comes she proceeds to the Presence Chamber or Throne Room, and on entering it she lets down the train, which is instantly spread out by the lords-in-waiting with their wands. The card on which the lady's name is written is then handed to the Lord Chamberlain, who reads the name aloud to the Queen. The lady advances to the Queen, and when she arrives just before Her Majesty curtseys very low, so low as *almost* to kneel to the Queen, who, if the lady be a peeress or a peer's daughter, kisses her forehead; but, in the case of a commoner, Her Majesty holds out a hand to be kissed by the lady presented. The lady then rises, and making a curtsey to any member of the Royal Family who may be present, passes on, keeping her face towards the Queen, until she has passed out of the door appointed for those leaving the Presence Chamber.'

'In this year,' reported *The Illustrated London News* (March 24, 1900), 'so many of the eligible young men are in South Africa that wise mothers are as far as possible keeping their girls back for another and happier season. The Queen's presence at Court always increases the number of presentations. It is rather odd that it should do so, since the fair maidens have little hope of kissing her own royal hand. For many years past Her Majesty has not felt strong enough to remain to receive the stream of general company, and after seeing those who have the entrée, and perhaps a very few of the rest, she has retired from the throne room. Still, the bare possibility of making the eventful presentation bow to the great historic personality of Queen Victoria brings many girls to Court.'

While there were many indications that the class barriers were slowly being broken down, you were undoubtedly a 'lady' if you were presented at court, and all Englishwomen wished to be that:

'English ladies of the nineteenth century are not expected to milk cows and feed pigs, but if circumstances oblige them to do these or any other similar acts of labour, what we impress is that they would not necessarily cease to be "ladies" in the proper sense of the word. The constant use of the word "lady" and the term "lady friend" is also objectionable. It is to be presumed that all your female acquaintances are "ladies". A writer sarcastically observes: "There is scarce one *woman* to be met with; the sex consists almost entirely of *ladies*".'

At the end of the century the great country houses and mansions of England were occupied with frivolous 'Friday to Monday' weekends and a constant hunt for pleasure. At Sandringham, the residence of the Prince of Wales, nearly every type of bird that could be shot was carefully reared for slaughter, except grouse. From 10,000 to 12,000 pheasants were reared annually and the first shoot of the year was a notable social event at which about sixty beaters were employed, dressed in uniform and each carrying a flag. In the season of 1896–97, during the autumn of one year and the spring of the next, the Prince and his guests shot 13,958 pheasants, 3965 partridges, 836 hares, 6185 rabbits, 77 woodcock, 8 snipe, 52 teal, 271 wild duck, 18 pigeons, and 27 'various birds'. The birds had been carefully nourished for the slaughter. Hundreds of fowl were employed every year to complete the hatching-out of the many thousands of pheasants' .

10. Liverpool slum street scene in the 1890s

11. Liverpool slum families, about 1895

eggs in incubation and in rearing the young birds until they were plump enough to be turned loose in the covers and heavy enough not to be able to fly away when the shooting season drew near. The gunroom at Sandringham was the model for all the great country houses and estates in the United Kingdom, containing every type of sporting weapon, while the game larder could hold over 6000 head.

Even only moderately prosperous men and women were not efficient within their households, and they did not need to be. Their domestic chores and the care of the children in the nursery were attended to by servants. No upper-class and few middle-class families were without at least one domestic, and in homes where there was enough money the youngsters were packed off to boarding school at an early age, a practice which most foreigners thought barbaric.

England's public schools, many of which had been founded during the century for the education and segregation of the affluent middle-class, were open only to those who could afford them, wealth and influence buying education and the prospect of a career. Yet they somehow produced a breed which formed the backbone of the vast Empire, and served the professions and commerce well. Trade was breaking into the hallowed preserves of the professions, and professionalism was slowly elbowing its way into the world of the landed gentry.

Manners and habits were changing. The great Savoy Hotel, built by D'Oyley Carte in 1889 and managed by Cesar Ritz, had been the first of London's hotels in which ladies dined and supped out, and the first to boast an orchestra in its restaurant. The Carlton, built in 1889 with a palm court, remained exclusive because the Prince of Wales had first dined in public there. But most of London's luxury hotels were to be built after 1900 and they were to cater for a different society, including the *nouveau riche*.

Thus in 1900 London's latest luxury hotel was the Russell in Bloomsbury Square, described as 'a fine example of modern hotel building. It is well-proportioned, harmonious in design, and its red brick and terra-cotta, with tinges of yellow, are materials admirably suited to endorse the London atmosphere. The resources of the great establishment of Messrs Maple & Co., who have more experience in hotel equipment than any other firm in the world, have been drawn upon.'

At this time the Hotel Metropole in Brighton was advertised as 'the finest seaside hotel in Europe, with sumptuously furnished suites of private apartments facing the sea and high-class music by our own orchestra during luncheon and dinner in the spacious winter garden. Hot and cold sea water. Turkish and Russian baths.' Dinner, from 6 to 8.30 p.m., cost six shillings. Sixty years later there was no hot and cold sea water, and no Turkish or Russian baths.

In London the Criterion Restaurant in Piccadilly Circus was the centre of gay life for the prosperous; the rich patronized Claridges, the Savoy, or the Ritz; bohemians, writers and artists went to the Café Royal; actors and actresses dined out at Rule's in Maiden Lane when they could afford it; Gambrinus, in Regent Street, was a genuine German restaurant; many theatre folk went to the Pall Mall; families lunched at Frascatti's or the Holborn; foreigners liked the Monico; the man-about-town went to the Criterion bar. But standards were changing, and a significant indication of the altering social atmosphere was the tendency to eliminate the second-class on England's railways and the admission of all third-class passengers to amenities that the companies provided or would soon provide—upholstered carriages, express trains, lavatory and corridor coaches, restaurant cars, etc. The process had started with decisions reached by the Midland Railway between 1872 and 1875. The other lines protested but soon had to follow.[1]

[1] G. Kitson Clark, *The Making of Victorian England*, London, 1965.

6

POVERTY AND LOW SOCIETY

At the centre of Victorian family life was religion, particularly evangelicalism, based on the strict teaching of the Gospels and the study of the Bible, which was usually accepted literally and without dispute, although not by scientists, Darwinians, the new school of writers, or free-thinkers. The influence of churchmen, particularly nonconformists, was considerable, and the church, chapel or meeting-house motivated those who attended. In its broadest state this influenced the activities of high churchmen such as Gladstone and Lord Salisbury, the explorer David Livingstone, and Dr Alfred Nobel, the inventor of dynamite who nevertheless left most of his fortune in 1896 to provide prizes for people who were to benefit mankind. Even the scientist and agnostic T. H. Huxley (1825–95) showed a fervour and moral sense in his agnosticism, while it can be clearly seen in the imperialist concept of such men as Kipling, Charles Gordon, Rhodes and Kitchener, to name only a few. Indeed, it has been said that the Victorian empire-builders 'went among the natives carrying a bottle of gin in one hand and a Bible in the other'. Although perhaps exaggerated, the comment has an element of truth; trade and development were hand in hand with religion and reform. There was no doubt that most people had a firm belief in rewards and punishments yet to come in an after-life, and in divine responsibilities and a sense of duty in this life. Thus, President McKinley belonged to the Methodist communion, drawing inspiration from the connection and the fellowship, as he indicated when he wrote: 'My belief embraces the Divinity of

Christ and a recognition of Christianity as the mightiest factor in the world's civilization'.

In his study *England, 1870–1914*, R. C. K. Ensor has pointed out how strongly religious piety influenced the great middle classes:

'If one asks how nineteenth century English merchants earned the reputation of being the most honest in the world (a very real factor in the nineteenth century primacy of English trade), the answer is because hell and heaven seemed as certain to them as tomorrow's sunrise, and the Last Judgment as real as the week's balance sheet. This keen sense of moral accountancy had also much to do with the success of self-government in the political sense.'

Poverty and squalor existed in abundance not far beneath the surface of Victorian prosperity, and it is hardly surprising, therefore, to find many men and women who were prepared to devote part of their lives, and often the whole, to works of charity and reform and what might loosely be called 'good causes'. Just as Dickens had for an earlier generation drawn attention to the squalor and degradation in which large sections of his fellow-countrymen were enmeshed, so now there were others who were not willing that Britain, rightly or wrongly considered to be the greatest nation in the world, should continue year after year with the stigmas of extreme poverty, under-nourishment, disease and illiteracy still attached to large sections of her population. Thus, while there were many landowners and businessmen who neglected their tenants and properties, caring only for profits, there were others, although perhaps not enough, who genuinely cared for the less fortunate men, women and children around them. It was mainly the religious zealots who led the crusade for better houses and living conditions, free education, increased pay, medical attention, and fairer shares for the under-privileged, whether their particular form of religion was motivated by church, chapel, conscience, political platform, radicalism, a sense of duty, or simply the fear that in the next life they would have to account for their deeds. Whatever the reason, there were many good people anxious to put things right, while all around them was much that was wrong.

In 1899 London's infant mortality was 279 per 1000, while nearly half of the people of this and the other large cities and towns were living in appalling conditions of overcrowding and squalor due to low wages and lack of decent houses. In the

autumn of this year the Quaker industrialist and philanthropist Benjamin Seebohm Rowntree, with a team of investigators, carried out an extensive survey of living conditions among the poor of their native city of York. This covered 11,560 families living in 388 streets, a population of 46,754 centred on the older, poorer parts of the city. Among the questions on which the survey sought information were: What was the true measure of poverty in the city? How much of it was due to insufficiency of income and how much to improvidence? How many families were sunk in a poverty so acute that their members suffered from a chronic insufficiency of food and clothing? If physical deterioration

combined with a high death-rate ensued, was it possible to estimate such results with approximate accuracy? The survey, a unique experiment, was published in volume form in 1901.[1]

In the poorer slum areas of this city Mr Rowntree's team found many examples of life lived under the pressure of chronic want, the poverty of many families being so great that most of them would have been driven into the workhouse but for charity, either public or private. In many instances the amount of food they ate, and the quality, were totally inadequate, consisting largely of a dreary succession of bread, dripping and tea; bread and butter and tea; bacon, bread and coffee; with only a little butcher's meat and extras and very little variety.

A woman with a large family told Mr Rowntree's investigators of her struggles to live with her husband on 17s a week. Each week she put aside the rent money and then planned her budget as best she could. They could never buy a joint of meat, but occasionally she managed to afford sixpence for 'meat pieces'. At the birth of a child she employed a woman for a week to nurse her, paying her 5s and her board. As soon as she knew a child was coming she began saving coppers so that she would have 5s. During the time she was nursing her children she lived chiefly on bread and tea.

Out of 1295 people investigated, the team found that the immediate cause of poverty was the death or desertion of the wage-earner, or the inability to earn through illness or old age. When they came to overcrowding they found that this was due mainly to the sheer inability of tenants to pay higher rents. While 12 per cent of the working-class population of York was living in reasonably comfortable, sanitary houses, the remaining 88 per cent was existing in conditions that left much to be desired. 4705 people were living more than two to a room; in 164 of the houses examined there was only 1 water-tap to 2 houses; in 126 there was 1 tap to 3 houses; in 380 there was 1 tap to 4 houses; and in 170 there was 1 tap to 5. The courtyards were often filthy: 'The smell from these places is simply horrible in hot or wet weather' ... 'At the lower end of the yard a slaughter-house causes a bad

[1] B. Seebohm Rowntree, *Poverty: A Study of Town Life*, London, 1901.

stench at times' . . . 'One closet to four houses' . . . 'The ashpit is so full that refuse is being thrown into the yard' . . . 'There is one tap to six houses in this yard and one closet to four houses' . . . 'The house adjoining this yard is uninhabitable on account of bad smells' . . . 'Filthy unpaved yard' . . . 'The approach to this yard is through a narrow passage in which are two open drains from a slaughter-house; stench very bad'.

There were in 1899–1900 no fewer than 94 private slaughter-houses in York, most of them in densely populated, old parts of the city and often in narrow passages. To these the cattle and sheep were driven by hand or delivered in horse-drawn wagons. After they had been slaughtered, the blood was allowed to run into a common sewer, the grates of which were sometimes close to dwelling-houses. Not one of the 94 slaughter-houses was built in accordance with the local government board bye-laws.

The Rowntree survey showed that the health of the city was about the same as in the 33 largest towns in England and Wales, but was worse than the average standard of all the cities and towns, and also worse than the average of other towns of the same size. Until 1900 there was no medical officer of health giving his whole time to the work; as in most towns, the doctor appointed had a private practice, which kept him busy. In 1900 there were 244 cases of typhoid fever alone, with 38 deaths, which was hardly surprising considering the lack of sanitary conditions in the poorer districts, through which the River Foss ran. 'It often becomes more or less stagnant and unsavoury in the summer time, although its condition is not such as to poison the fish,' said the survey. In comparison, it is interesting to note that by 1908 many of the rivers and streams flowing through Britain's cities and towns were to be so polluted that no fish would live in them, some being little better than open sewers.

In 1900 an admirable series of investigations had just been carried out in America by the US Department of Agriculture to show how much, or how little, poor people in that country ate. When compared with Mr Rowntree's findings in York city the figures revealed that, while the food consumption of the well-paid artisans and of the servant-keeping classes in America appeared to be closely akin to that of similar sections in England, the labourers were much better fed in the United States:

Dietaries	Protein, per man per day in grams	Potential energy, per man per day, calories
25 families in poorest part of Philadelphia	109	3235
26 families in poorest part of Chicago	119	3425
12 labourers' families, New York City	101	2905
11 poor families, New York City	93	2915
14 poor families in York, England, wages under 26 shillings a week	89	2685
Standard requirements for men at moderate work (Atwater)	125	3500

The Rowntree investigation showed that the diet of labourers in York compared very unfavourably as regards nutritive value with the diet given to the inmates of Her Majesty's prisons and the local workhouses. The family of a labourer earning a total of 17s 6d a week was examined in detail. The household consisted of a father, mother, and five children; four boys aged 11, 9, 7 and 2 and a girl of 4. The father was an intelligent man, interested in social and labour problems. He was unable to earn a good wage because of a physical disability after a long illness. The mother was a bright, capable little woman and a good manager. As we shall see, she needed to be, for she had to fight against tremendous odds. She looked underfed and overworked, but was always cheerful and never complained. Johnnie, the eldest boy, was deformed and threatened with tuberculosis, but his health improved greatly as soon as extra food and fresh air were provided. Mrs R was conscientious in carrying out the doctor's directions, as far as means would allow, and the windows were open day and night. But the boy could not go to school, for as soon as he went into a room with other children he became ill and the cough and pain in his side returned. So he was growing up without any training, spending most of his time playing in the streets or sitting in a little chair outside the front door. The other children in the family also bore signs of privation.

The house, in a long row, contained four rooms and was clean. The street door opened into the living room. There were lace curtains in the window under which was a couch where Johnnie lay when too ill to go out to play. There was no easy-chair. A table covered with a tablecloth stood back against the wall, and on this was placed a fancy box or two and a few books. A table in the centre of the room, a few chairs and some framed photographs and pictures on the wall completed the furniture. The open grate with the oven was bright and polished. Mrs R baked her own bread, both wholemeal and white.

Mrs R bought some cheap fresh meat for the Sunday dinner, when the children had a tiny bit each. During the rest of the week the children did not have meat, but the cold meat left over from Sunday was saved for Mr R, who took his dinner to work. In cold weather the children often had pea soup for dinner or had to be content with bread, dripping and tea. The week's supplies were bought chiefly on Friday and Saturday. When anything extra was needed for the house, the family went short of food, the cost often being paid off in weekly instalments of a shilling or sixpence. Fortunately, the family was given a good many old clothes, which were carefully repaired and probably wore longer than cheap new ones. Mr R mended the children's boots himself in the evenings.

Mr R smoked and bought a weekly paper, but he could not afford to buy beer, although he was not a teetotaller. The family spent 5d a week on life insurance. This was the income and expenditure budget for these seven people during twenty-six weeks from April to September, in the summer of 1899:

Income	£	s	d
Wages, 26 weeks at 15s	19	10	0
Mrs R: charing, etc.	3	11	9
	23	1	9

Expenditure	£	s	d
Food, incl. beverages	13	13	$9\frac{1}{2}$
Rent	4	4	6
Coal, etc.	1	19	1
Oil and candles	0	1	$0\frac{1}{2}$
Soap, etc.	0	6	$1\frac{1}{2}$
Sundries	0	1	$2\frac{1}{2}$
Life insurance	0	10	10
Clothing	0	11	4
Boots	1	6	$0\frac{1}{2}$
Tobacco and matches	0	5	2
Stamps, stationery, papers	0	4	2
	£23	3	$3\frac{1}{2}$
Deficit	£0	1	$6\frac{1}{2}$

None of the children had been to the seaside or enjoyed a holiday, and they were unlikely to do so unless some charitable organization or a local school organized a day's outing. But this was the pattern of life for many hundreds of thousands of what General William Booth, the founder of the Salvation Army, had in 1890 called 'the sinking classes', and 'the multitudes who struggle and sink in the open-mouthed abyss'. They lived and died, Booth noted, 'in the midst of unparalleled wealth, and civilization, and philanthropy, of this professedly most Christian land'.

It is hardly surprising that one out of every three men—and some historians say half—of those who volunteered for service in the Boer War was turned down by the medical authorities because of ill-health. Yet many people still believe that the Victorian era was a golden age. 'I do believe this was a time when life had a great deal of beauty and charm. People were not in such a hurry to rush from one thing to another,' said Dame Irene Vanbrugh many years later. Beauty and charm! One cannot help wondering what happened to the boy Johnnie, on his couch under the window.

Mr Rowntree's survey showed that in few cases was poverty due to drink, although Britain's national drink bill was about 6s 10d a family, a high figure, something like one-sixth of the

total working-class income. The magistrates' courts in all the
cities and towns were full of drunks of all ages. Drunks under
twenty-one were frequent. Worse than the gin or beer drinkers
were the methylated-spirit imbibers, sipping the stuff at fourpence a pint bottle. They bought it in penny nips and diluted it,
a pennyworth then being equal in strength to two glasses of
whisky.

OVERCROWDING, 1900–1901

	Average number of persons per acre
ENGLAND	
South Shields	54·0
Plymouth	42·5
Manchester	42·1
Birmingham	41·1
Sunderland	39·2
Derby	30·7
Birkenhead	28·8
Nottingham	22·0
York	20·5
Norwich	14·7
Bradford	12·2
St Helens	11·6
Bolton	11·0
Huddersfield	8·1
Halifax	7·7
UNITED STATES	
Baltimore	21·0
New York	17·4
Pittsburg	17·0
Philadelphia	14·0
Chicago	13·8
San Francisco	13·8
Buffalo	12·0
Boston, Mass.	9·24
Washington	6·28

In York there were at this time eighteen clubs where alcohol was obtainable, 236 'on' licences which closed at eleven at night, and 102 'off' licences. As in most cities, there were also a few teetotal clubs, of which the largest was the Central Liberal Club, with over 400 members. Some of these clubs were in the poorer parts of the district, and were frequented mainly by Irish labourers. Entrance was jealously guarded but much drunkenness occurred. The members—unlike the publicans and proprietors of most of the gin palaces—were careful however not to allow anyone to leave the premises until he was sober enough to escape the risk of arrest. Members often remained in the club through the night, and even from Saturday until Monday. It was a completely all-male environment.

In all the cities and towns there were many vagrants, tramps, beggars and unfortunates moving from workhouse to work-house. York's 'Union' admitted 6877 men and women in the year 1899. On January 1, 1901 there were no fewer than seventy children there, theoretically forbidden to mix with the adult paupers, a rule which was difficult to enforce. The world of Dickens was not dead. The workhouse food consisted of bread and gruel at night and the same in the morning; but, as one tramp remarked, 'We don't mind wot they give us, becos we usually brings in meat and things wot we've got on the road'. The older people who could not move around the countryside were less fortunate.

Rowntree's conclusion was that for a family of father, mother and three children the minimum weekly expenditure upon which physical efficiency could be maintained was made up as follows:

Food	12s 9d
Rent	4s 0d
Clothes, light, fuel	4s 11d
	21s 8d

But he pointed out, the starkness of such a minimum standard of living, on the borderline of poverty, meant that such a family could never spend anything on a rail or bus fare, never go into the country except for a walk, never buy a halfpenny newspaper or a ticket for a popular concert, write no letters to absent children, never contribute to church, chapel or needy neighbour, and never attempt to save money or join a sick club or trade union. Further, the children could have no pocket money for dolls, marbles or sweets, the father must not smoke or drink, the mother could not buy pretty clothes for herself or the children. Only absolute necessities could be purchased for the maintenance of health and those must be of the plainest description. Finally, if a child fell ill it must be attended by the parish doctor; and if it died it would be buried by the parish. And, to ensure all this, the worker must never be absent from his work for a single day.[1]

Seebohm Rowntree had been born in York in July 1871. 'Merely to catalogue the contents of his files or the list of his engagements is to record the successive phases in the transformation of Liberalism, the assault on poverty and unemployment, the development of new views and practices in industry and the changing spiritual environment of our age,' says Professor Briggs in his biography.

The Rowntree family were interested particularly in the welfare of poor children, just as Anthony Ashley Cooper, the seventh Earl of Shaftesbury (1801–85), had been when he identified himself with the Ten-Hours Bill (1847), the Ragged School Union, reformatories, refuges, and other Christian organizations. At the same time Dr Barnardo (1845–1905) had opened his first home for destitute boys in 1866, in Stepney, with its merciful 'ever-open door' and his promise: 'No destitute child ever refused admission', written on a signboard outside the home. This was done after an eleven-year-old boy had unfortunately been refused admission because there was no room, and had been found dead from cold the next morning in a beer-barrel at Billingsgate. In the greatest and richest city in the world there had been no one willing to feed or clothe him or give him warmth.

Many of the reformers were Quakers, members of the Society of Friends. The exclusion of nonconformists from the universities tended to send them into industry and commerce, where they quickly came to observe the condition of the workers, and through

[1] Asa Briggs, *Seebohm Rowntree*, London, 1961.

the charitable efforts of their creed sought to improve the welfare of their employees and their families. Thus the Rowntrees of York and the Cadburys of Birmingham were among the pioneers in large social experiments, as were the Frys and also the Wills tobacco family of Bristol. Henry Overton Wills (1761–1826) had started the firm, and his descendants were to make large gifts to the University of Bristol and other educational foundations, as well as for the building and restoration of churches.

It was in 1900 that George Cadbury (1839–1922), a partner with his brother Richard in the chocolate and cocoa business, set up the Bournville Village Trust, a non-profit-making body controlled by twelve trustees. In 1897 the brothers had moved their factory from central Birmingham to a country district which they named Bournville. Here they bought space for expansion in hygenic surroundings, and created pleasant conditions for their employees. Here also George Cadbury saw an opportunity of providing better houses than those of other Birmingham workers. In 1895 he started building, and so formed the nucleus of the housing estate which he handed over to the trust in 1900. He renounced all financial interest in the estate, and its surplus income was to be devoted entirely to extension and improvement and to planning and building. His wishes were expressed in a deed which required that all houses were to be let at economic rents, and yet be within the reach of the working classes; that no house was to occupy more than a quarter of its site; and that at least one-tenth of the land, in addition to roads and gardens, was to be devoted to parks and recreation grounds.

In 1900 George Cadbury became the trust's first chairman, and later the City of Birmingham and the Society of Friends became trustees. On his death in 1922 his place was to be taken by his widow, Dame Elizabeth Cadbury, and in succession her sons George and Laurence were to become chairman. Within fifty years the estate was to cover over 1000 acres of open development in the south-west of Birmingham, a model garden city which was to influence the planning and building of similar estates in other districts. The first Bournville houses were modelled on the detached or semi-detached country cottage, in reaction to the dismal rows of 'tunnel-backs' still being built in many cities. In time, over 14,000 people were to be housed in the garden suburb, a far cry from the squalor and poverty which Seebohm Rowntree and his team had observed in York in the same year, 1900, when George Cadbury formed his trust.

Some people were by no means happy at the interest which the Liberals and churchmen displayed in matters of social reform. In opposition, Lord Salisbury had set the pattern in 1866 when he told the government:

'For myself, I will venture to make my confession of faith on the subject of the working classes. I feel there are two tendencies to avoid. I have heard much on the subject of the working classes in this House which I confess has filled me with feelings of some apprehension. It is the belief of many honourable Gentlemen opposite that the working classes are to be our future Sovereign, that they are to be the great power in the State, against which no other power will be able to stand; and it is with feelings of no small horror and disgust that I have heard from many honourable Gentlemen phrases which sound, I hope unduly, like adulation of the Sovereign they expect to rule for them.'

If you lived in Bournville you were lucky, but a poor man or woman in London or most of the big cities could find the problems of life almost insurmountable. 'Of course, in a place like London it would never do to leave the parks open all night,' said a writer in Cassell's *New Penny Magazine* (1899). 'From being the choicest spots in the metropolis they would rapidly become the least desirable. As it is, groups of tramps and other homeless people of both sexes are always at the gates before they open in the morning, anxious to get in.'

Joseph Ritson, a Primitive Methodist minister, an intense evangelist and an ardent social reformer, in 1892 considered the position of the agricultural labourer in relation to the land and landlords, 'one of the burning questions of the day'. The agricultural wage-earner was forced to 'slave all his days for what will barely keep body and soul together, with no better prospect at the end of his working days than the pauper's brand and two

PUBLIC HOUSES IN ENGLAND, 1901

Town	Population	'On' Licences	'Off' Licences
Northampton	87,021	295	224
Southampton	104,911	468	100
York	77,793	236	102
Manchester	543,969	2222	746
Bradford	279,809	618	513
Bolton	168,205	431	178
Plymouth	107,509	298	51
Liverpool	684,947	2042	144
Leeds	428,953	745	437
Newcastle	214,803	561	141
Bristol	328,842	1038	329
Birmingham	522,182	1600	567
Sheffield	380,717	1159	639
Nottingham	239,753	595	488

shillings a week'. As to the articles currently appearing in the *Daily News* on 'Life in Our Villages', he contended that a more appropriate title would have been 'Death in Our Villages'. They had revealed a 'condition of decay and death'. 'With the most beautiful natural surroundings—rustic cottages, flowery gardens, laden orchards, grassy slopes, and smiling meadows, bubbling springs and carolling larks, blue skies, and sweet fresh air-laden breezes, there is combined a condition of things that is a scandal to our civilization, to say nothing of our Christianity. The picturesque cottage covered with flowering creepers is in scores of instances a rotten, tumble-down place, damp, insanitary, and unwholesome, while the overcrowding is often as bad as in many of the slums of our great cities. ... Wealth accumulates but men decay. It may be true that the landlords and farmers have grown rich of late years but the aim of both is to accumulate wealth at the expense of the labourer. ... The life of a serf cannot be satisfactory to a man who has a soul in him.' Who could blame the labourers for emigrating or migrating to the towns? 'Is a sum of eleven shillings a week sufficient to maintain a family in decency? There are hundreds who, owing to not getting regular work, do not average even that small pittance. . . . A certain class of landlords whose policy has uniformly aimed at keeping the labourers down, will no doubt be of a different opinion, but neither fact nor argument will have any influence upon them.[1]

Discussing 'the practical Christian as social and political reformer', Ritson pointed out that, 'the working classes have not only awakened to a sense of their rights, but have secured many of them . . . In the North of England, which has really led this great social revolution, religious men, most of them associated with Primitive Methodism, have been the leaders who have given character to the movement.' Social reform he regarded as religious work, in which every Christian ought to be engaged. 'We have heard a great deal recently about rookeries and the dwellings of the poor. And not before time. . . . Not only in large cities but in country districts there is a wide field for reform. The condition of mining and agricultural populations, though vastly improved within the last generation in regard to their housing, is still far from satisfactory. . . . The Christian, whatever his position, may and ought to aim at the improvement of the social conditions of his fellows. Whatever is wrong, he should endeavour to right.'[2]

In another article, Ritson emphasized the contrasts of life; on the one hand 'the greatest wealth, the noblest buildings, the most abundant comfort and luxury, and the utmost refinement and grace'; on the other hand 'the most dreadful squalor, ignorance, depravity, poverty, and suffering . . . houses unfit for habitation . . . human abodes where all the laws of health and common decency are daily outraged'. Quoting from official sources, he pointed out that of the seven hundred families living in Marylebone, three-quarters were in single rooms. In another part of London 'two hundred and forty-six families' occupied 'two hundred and thirty-three rooms'. 'In London alone there are nearly fifty thousand families each occupying only a single room, and in most of them the conditions of health and morality are

---

[1] *Primitive Methodist Quarterly Review*, 1892.
[2] *Primitive Methodist Magazine*, 1894.

utterly absent.' 'In Tilney Court, St Luke's, nine members of a family, five of them being grown up, inhabited one room ten feet by eight. In Lion Row there was a room twelve feet by six, and only seven feet high, in which seven persons slept. In Summer Court, Holborn, there were two families in a room twelve feet by eight. At 9, Portpool Lane, there were six persons in a small back room. At 1, Halfmoon Court, in a three-roomed house, were found nineteen persons, eight adults and eleven children. ... At 3, Derry Street, the first floor front room was thirteen feet by twelve and nine feet high and was inhabited by a family of nine, who had only one bed.' In one of the rooms eight feet square 'walls and ceilings are black with the secretions of filth which have gathered upon them through long years of neglect. It is exuding through the cracks in the boards overhead; it is running down the walls; it is everywhere. What goes by the name of a window is half of it stuffed with rags or covered by board to keep out wind and rain; the rest is begrimed and obscured so that scarcely can light enter or anything be seen outside.'

Worse off than the overcrowded, thousands of Londoners were homeless. 'There are hundreds and hundreds who sleep every night in the parks, the trees being their only shelter. On summer nights hundreds sleep along the Embankment; in winter it is too exposed for them. Very many sleep on the bridges across the Thames. Indeed, it is a sight to cross London Bridge after midnight, and to look at the recesses filled with poor homeless ones in all attitudes, trying to snatch in sleep a few hours relief from life's misery. Where several families are in one house, the street door is left open, and in the morning seven or eight persons will be found in the passage or on the stairs.'

'The country was never so wealthy and never so poor as now, and with a result like this there must be something wrong somewhere,' said the *Primitive Methodist Magazine*. Quoting the case of a match-box company which paid its shareholders 22 per cent dividend and its workers $2\frac{1}{4}$d for 144 match-boxes, the editor asked, 'Is this righteous?' Many landlords had returned 15 or 20 per cent of the rent to their tenants, but they did not reduce the permanent rent. 'Is it right, then, to exact such rents? Sympathy with toilers,' he concluded, 'might take the practical shape of allowing them a fairer share in the proceeds of their toil.[1]

An account of Edward Street, Brighton, a typical back-street adjoining the main London road in a prosperous seaside holiday town, describes the place as 'an unsavoury locality', but 'very much maligned'. 'True that public houses abound, but if the outward and visible signs of bills and notices are worth anything, religious agencies do much more than abound. The walls and shop windows display a varied assortment of posters and hand-bills announcing religious services, tea fights, Sunday school celebrations, special sermons, and Salvation Army missions. Two preachers disposed the gospel and music at street corners, a religious choir sang in the open court at an assembly hall, the mission hall people invited the passers-by to step in for a short service, some people who pass for Salvation Army soldiers carried on in a small hall just off the street, and a coffee palace displayed its tempting wares in a blaze of plate glass and gas. *Could civilization want more?* It is a mistake to look for wretchedness and poverty in tumbledown, ill-smelling and objectionable streets. A tour of inspection through many three-storied well-built modern houses in some of the respectable districts where the working classes crowd three families into a house would reveal a picture of misery that Edward Street and its adjacent rookeries would blush to own.'

Nevertheless, the slum parts of the town, far from the industrial areas, were appalling. The Brighton Soup Charity met early in 1900 'to consider what steps should be taken for the relief of the poor by the distribution of soup or otherwise during the present winter'. Some £885 had been spent during the previous year on providing soup for old people and children. Meanwhile shop-robbery, drunkenness, drinking and fighting, assault, cruelty to animals, assaulting the police, stealing clothes, wounding, adulterating milk, wilful damage, petty pilfering, loitering and importuning—these were commonplace charges which magistrates heard daily.

[1] R. F. Wearmouth, *Methodism and the Struggle of the Working Classes 1850–1900*, Leicester.

In 1900 the very marked extremes of wealth and poverty greatly influenced the crime wave, but there were nearly always watchful servants in the big houses, and crimes were planned on a smaller scale than today. The number of indictable crimes in the year was only about 80,000 for the whole of England and Wales and some 1800 for London, about one-eighth of the number for 1959. Everyone except the professional criminal, who had abandoned normal standards, knew and felt that conviction for crime meant social downfall. In the middle and upper classes this was total, with very little hope of recovery except perhaps after emigrating to one of the colonies. In the working class there were more tolerance and understanding of human frailty, the conventions—although equally rigid—being less starkly upheld. But even so, respectable neighbours would not be on speaking terms with rowdy families in the same street. Respectability was the highest family ideal of the Victorian age, and this had a great influence both on the way crimes were committed and to some extent upon the type of crime. Middle-class families kept themselves to themselves, though a good deal of visiting went on. There was no television, no radio, no telephones except for the comparatively wealthy, and only the beginnings of a popular press. The secrecy of private life was very real and could lead to situations of horror and cruelty within the family circle that would be unimaginable in later years. Attacks by a husband and the ill-treatment of children were not considered respectable, and no one must know about them, but both were very common in working-class families.[1]

There is little doubt that the living conditions of the time bred crime. In 1867, only thirty-three years before our survey, there had been 2119 brothels in London and about 80,000 prostitutes, counting the amateurs, who were known as 'dolly-mops'. In the back-streets of the big cities the policemen patrolled in pairs.

In July 1900 London's ill-famed Newgate Prison, although not used after 1880 except for executions, was still standing. It was in 1892 that Dr Thomas Neill Cream had been hanged there after one of the most widely-reported murder trials of the century.

[1] Josephine Bell, *Crime in Our Time*, London, 1962.

He had undoubtedly murdered seven women and one man, and he was eventually executed for the killing of a prostitute named Matilda Clover. It is likely that he also killed several other prostitutes, for he seemed to prefer to select his victims from the London streets. It has since been accepted that he was a lunatic but, as at the time of his crimes he knew what he was doing and that it was wrong, he was not technically insane within the limits of the McNaghten Rules. It was stated that before his execution he boasted that he had killed other women. An interesting theory was advanced after his death, connecting him with the sensational Jack the Ripper murders of a number of London prostitutes in 1888. It was pointed out that the so-called Ripper murders (named because of the method of killing the victims with a knife) all coincided in time with the Dr Cream murders. Further, when Dr Cream went to Canada the Ripper murders ceased for a time; and when he was taken into custody and charged with poisoning his victims, the Jack the Ripper murders ceased altogether. The mystery of the identity of the Ripper remains unsolved.

The most sensational criminal case of 1900 was the trial of Herbert John Bennett for the murder of his wife on Great Yarmouth's South Beach. She had been strangled with a bootlace. Bennett, who was hanged on March 21, 1901, protested his innocence even as he was sentenced. At the trial, which was transferred from Norwich to the Old Bailey (then part of the Newgate Prison) because of the intense local animosity against the prisoner, a gold chain found in his lodgings was the pivot point of the prosecution's case. Witnesses swore that it was the same chain as Mrs Bennett had worn at Yarmouth shortly before her death. It happened that she had been photographed there by a local beach cameraman and the photograph showed her wearing a chain. But was it the chain which was found in Bennett's room? Edward Marshall Hall, who appeared for the defence, said no, but the chain in the photograph was so blurred that no one could be certain. On the fifth day of the trial Marshall Hall produced, without warning, a surprise witness, a man who said he had met Bennett on the evening of the murder near Eltham; an alibi which, had it been proved to the satisfaction of the jury, must have saved Bennett. But there was little doubt that the witness had invented his story, and Bennett preferred not to be put into the witness box to explain what he was doing at Eltham that evening. The jury took only thirty-five minutes to arrive at a verdict of 'guilty', but Marshall Hall, one of the greatest advocates of his day, always maintained that his client was innocent. Certainly the public's strong animosity against the prisoner, and perhaps even the jury's feelings, were influenced by the extraordinary bias of the popular press, which was apparent long before the trial began.

7

ROYALTY

Few women of her age could have endured the strain imposed on the Queen in her last year. She had felt acutely the humiliation of the South African defeats, but she had never shown herself more truly the mother of her subjects than in the dark days of the winter of 1899–1900. Despite failing health she went out amongst the public, knitted comforts for the troops, sent Christmas boxes and presents to the front, wrote long letters to newspapers and individuals, visited and consoled the wounded, and took an active interest in all the affairs of the nation.

On March 7th she went to London, and on the afternoons of 8th and 9th she drove for many miles through the streets to identify herself with the people. On the 22nd she visited the Herbert Hospital at Woolwich and talked to the wounded. The public was deeply touched. Lord Rosebery wrote to her on March 15th:

'I think the visit to London far more interesting and touching even than the Jubilees: it was more simple and spontaneous. It was as if a great wave of sympathy and devotion had passed over the capital. Your Majesty intimated as it were to London: "I will come among you and rejoice with you; as we have shared our anxieties and sorrows, we will share the common joys." Your Majesty does not much admire Queen Elizabeth, but the visit to London was in the Elizabethan spirit. There was, however, this difference, that with the pride that England felt in Elizabeth there was but little love. Now the nation glows with both.'[1]

[1] Sir J. A. Marriott, *Modern England*, London, 1934.

Although she was over eighty, the Queen decided in the spring to pay a state visit to Ireland instead of going on holiday to the South of France. It was her own idea and she completely disregarded the possibility that the Irish nationalists might demonstrate against her or perhaps even attempt assassination. During her long reign there had been several attempts, but she was now a very old lady and she wished to be at peace with the country which was sending so many of its soldiers to the war and for which she had done little during her reign.

When the idea was proposed to John Raymond, the leader of the Irish Nationalist Party, he guaranteed a safe visit for the monarch. In spite of her age and obvious feebleness, she planned an extensive programme. She had last visited Ireland over half a century before, when she had been accompanied by the Prince Consort and four of her children. This time she took with her her daughters Princess Christian and Princess Henry of Battenberg, together with a large entourage.

The Queen journeyed to Holyhead in the royal train which she used when visiting Scotland, and the voyage across the Irish Sea was made in the royal yacht *Victoria and Albert*. This was met in Dublin Bay by the channel fleet of warships, commanded by Vice-Admiral Sir Henry H. Rawson, and bedecked with flags and bunting. That night the fleet in the bay was illuminated with thousands of electric lights arranged along the ships' rigging, while searchlights swept the sky. A great cheer went up from the fleet when the *Victoria and Albert* and the accompanying yacht *Osborne* showed their outlines in coloured lights.

The streets in Dublin and Kingstown were crowded with sightseers, but the Queen dined quietly on board and went ashore next morning, to be greeted by the Lord Lieutenant and the Duke of Connaught, the Duchess of Connaught, Prince Arthur of Connaught, the Princesses Margaret and Victoria Patricia of Connaught, and the Countess Cadogan.

The city of Dublin had been transformed with elaborate decorations. There were about thirty miles of flags and thousands of yards of floral garlands and emblazoned shields. Nationalist feelings, never far beneath the surface, appeared to be temporarily forgotten, although there were few flags in back-streets and for several days before the visit the public houses and meeting places had been inspected by the police and a number of arrests had been made.

On entering the capital the Queen and her party were greeted by the City Marshal, Mr John Howard Parnell, who bore Dublin's keys on a silk cushion. With him was the Lord Mayor, who presented the keys to the Queen. The chain of office which he wore had been provided by King William III to replace the one which Charles II had given to the city but which had been carried off by partisans after the Battle of the Boyne.

The Queen replied to the address of welcome: 'I thank you heartily for the loyal welcome and good wishes which you have tendered to me on behalf of yourself and your fellow-citizens on my arrival in the ancient capital of my Irish dominions. I come to this fair country to seek change and rest and to revisit scenes which recall to my mind, among thoughts of the losses which years must bring, the heartiest recollections of the warm-hearted welcome given to my beloved husband and children. I am deeply gratified that I am able at this time to revisit the motherland of those brave sons who have recently borne themselves in defence of my Crown and Empire with cheerful valour as conspicuous as ever in their glorious past. I pray that the Almighty may ever bless and protect you in the high functions which you exercise for the benefit of your fellow-citizens.'

Elizabeth Longford, in her admirable biography *Victoria R.I.*, has pointed out that the Queen's decision to visit Ireland was influenced by her feeling of gratitude for the gallantry of the Irish soldiers in South Africa: 'She was suddenly consumed with longing to be loved by Ireland'. The city council had voted to present the address of welcome only if it did not mention loyalty to the crown. Nevertheless, the visit was a great personal triumph for the monarch, and the French satirical journal *Charivari* had no cause to publish a cartoon of British bayonets forcing the cheers from Irish throats:

> *Attention! Un, deux, trois;*
> Hip! Hip! Hip! Hurrah!

Victoria's twenty-two days in Ireland were entirely successful. She inspected her troops and then on Saturday, April 7th, she drove out to Phoenix Park to be greeted by 55,000 children who had assembled from all over the country to see her. On each side of the main road, which runs straight through the park, there was a mile of enclosures, the country schools on one side and the Dublin schools on the other. All the compounds were packed with youngsters, cheering lustily, as the old lady was driven slowly down the main road in her carriage. Two days later Princess Christian laid the foundation stone of the new nursing home attached to the city's hospital. Next day the Queen's family visited the St Joseph's children's hospital founded in 1872 in Temple Street.

'I am sorry to leave Ireland . . . I have had an extremely pleasant time,' said the Queen as she entered the royal train at Kingsbridge station to return to her yacht on April 26th. As a permanent record of her appreciation of her Irish army she had decreed that all Irish troops should wear a shamrock on St Patrick's Day. Further, she created the Irish Guards, re-forming a regiment originally raised as 'our regiment of foot guards in the Kingdom of Ireland', when Charles II had manned it with Irish Protestants from England. The new Irish Guards first appeared in action in South Africa as 'the Irish Guards section of the 1st Guards Mounted Infantry' and mustered only an officer, a lance-sergeant, corporal, drummer, and thirty guardsmen. Because Lord Roberts was their first colonel they were known as 'Bob's Own', although they were soon more popularly called 'The Micks'. The first Quartermaster, Mr Fowles, was appointed on May 24, 1900, at the Queen's last birthday parade. He had been a sergeant-major in the Grenadiers and as such he trooped the colour, although he had already been transferred to the Irish Guards.[1]

Albert, the Prince Consort, had wanted his son and heir Albert Edward to be like himself, and the Queen could think of no finer pattern on which to model the Prince's life, but the future King wished to be only himself. Despite the efforts of his tutors he had not secured a good education, and was inclined to

[1] Sir Harry Legge-Bourke, *The Queen's Guards*, London, 1965.

turn instead to the pursuit of pleasure and the enjoyment of other people's company. He was a complete extrovert and he could be friendly with anyone, being the centre of attraction wherever he went. Visiting Canada and the United States, he was lionized, being naturally popular on grounds of personality and charm and displaying a sense of democracy which the new world appreciated.

Except for a few months, he was Prince of Wales for sixty years. He had been born in 1841, and he would not succeed to the throne until January 1901. Many people viewed his life of pleasure with alarm as likely to sap the harmony, morality, sobriety and hard work which were held to be the foundation of Victorian middle-class life and national prosperity. The Prince lived a gay life of self-indulgence, very different from that of his mother and late father but almost identical with that of his grandfathers on both sides.

He had many lady friends—Mrs Langtry, the Countess of Warwick, Mrs Mary Cornwallis, Mrs Keppel, and others—and in 1869 he had been forced to give evidence in court in the famous Mordaunt divorce case, in which he was asked, 'Has there ever been any improper familiarity or criminal connection of any sort between yourself and Lady Mordaunt?' to which he replied, 'There has not'. Then, in 1890, he was called as a witness in the Tranby Croft case, in which Sir William Gordon-Cumming brought an action for slander against some society men who had alleged that he had cheated at baccarat.

However, the Prince had made a happy marriage in 1863 with Princess Alexandra of Schleswig-Holstein-Sonderburg-Glucksburg (1844–1925), the daughter of King Christian IX of Denmark. Although her father, whose private life was a scandal in Denmark, was not invited to the wedding, popular enthusiasm for the beautiful Princess was uninhibited and Alfred Tennyson, the Poet Laureate, had expressed the mood of the country when she arrived in England:

> Sea King's daughter from over the sea, Alexandra!
> Saxon and Norman and Dane are we,
> But all of Dane in our welcome of thee, Alexandra!

The Princess was more than the ideal partner for her husband; she became the idol of the British public, especially in London. During her long life she was the personification of devotion to duty and engaging charm, and she gave a great deal of her time to charitable causes.

During her Diamond Jubilee in 1897 the Queen had not been able to undertake so many functions as at the first Jubilee, and the burden of representation fell increasingly on the Prince and Princess. The chief permanent commemoration was the Hospital Fund started by the Prince, who was very active in its organization, and it was later named the King Edward Hospital Fund.

The Princess considered that, among the many good causes which were liberally provided for at the Jubilee,

'one class has been overlooked—namely, the poorest of the poor in the slums of London! Might I plead for these [she wrote to the Lord Mayor] that they also should have some share in the festivities of that blessed day, and so remember to the end of their lives that great and good Queen whose glorious reign has, by the blessing of God, been prolonged for sixty years?'

As a result of her letter 330,000 poor people consumed 700 tons of food in various public buildings. The Prince and Princess visited three of the centres—the People's Palace, the Central Halls in Holborn, and Clerkenwell. These dinners, arranged on her initiative and organized by Thomas Lipton, the grocer friend of the Prince, gave the Princess great satisfaction. Of more lasting benefit was the Alexandra Trust, a London charity which for many years provided a hot meal for only fourpence-halfpenny.

In contrast to her son's, the Queen's life had been comparatively blameless. She was strict and even severe in her insistence on obedience to the highest moral code among all those whom she could influence. Yet in her interest in her people and in her generous patronage of letters and arts there was no austerity. Indeed, she had always performed her duties faithfully and judiciously, although for some years after the death of her husband she had unfortunately withdrawn into seclusion and kept away from the public gaze. She was undoubtedly jealous of her son, and at times she showed active dislike. He was not allowed to take any part in affairs of state, although when he contrived to influence them the result was often satisfactory. Thus he had presided over the Royal Commission on the Housing of the Poor set up by Gladstone in 1884, while the Housing of the Working Classes Act of 1890, which embodied most of the recommendations of the commission, helped to stem, if it did not actually reverse, the growth of slum-dwellings.[1]

In June 1863 the Queen wrote: 'Oh, what will become of the poor country when I die! I forsee, if Bertie succeeds, nothing but misery, and he would do anything he was asked and spend his life in one whirl of amusements, as he does now. It makes me very sad and anxious.'

The Prince certainly enjoyed life to the full, but his qualities as a leader were considerable, as was to be evident when he ascended the throne. Meanwhile he opposed snobbery and social injustice and, although he was always conservative in his outlook, he nevertheless encouraged many reforms. He was never too important to talk and joke with the man in the street, so that the common people, calling him 'Teddy', admired him, seeing in their Prince some reflection of what they themselves would like to be.

Like his great-uncle, George IV, he was an excellent mimic, and he liked to tell amusing stories. He was very good company—cheerful, easy-going, kind-hearted, vastly tolerant and entirely without racial or social prejudice. But he was also careful to maintain the respect due to his position, and more especially to that of his wife, and those who failed to know where to draw the line did so at their peril. He did not mind a certain amount of familiarity, and would at times tolerate an amazing degree of it, but it was always necessary for him to set the pace. Although he had a keen sense of humour, he hated having any of his friends ridiculed. To be his friend one must not be 'stuffy' but one could not be impudent; one must be amusing, and always intensely conscious of the royal dignity.[2]

[1] Sir Arthur Bryant, *English Saga*, London, 1940.
[2] Michael Harrison, *Rosa*, London, 1962.

'Lord' George Sanger, one of the most colourful of the circus showmen of late Victorian times, who took his travelling circus into nearly every large centre in Britain, has described how he was exhibiting at Astley's, his London theatre in the Westminster Bridge Road, 'the only white elephant ever seen in the western world'. The Prince was curious about this animal and went to see it, admiring the beautiful creature with its milk-white skin.

'Sanger,' he said, 'is this really one of the sacred White elephants?'

The showman replied, 'Well, your Royal Highness, a showman is entitled to practise a little deception on the crowd, but I should never think of deceiving my future king. As you see, it is certainly a white elephant, but only because we give him a coat of whitewash twice a day.'

The Prince roared with laughter, and later sent Sanger a heavy gold ring which he had brought from India. It was in the vulgar, ostentatious taste which exactly suited the circus owner, and it was obviously carefully chosen for him, being set with seven large diamonds and three hundred and sixty-five brilliants.[1] By such thoughtful acts of kindness the Prince endeared himself to the people, and his mother was no less generous. After seeing a performance of Sanger's travelling circus at Balmoral in 1898 she sent the showman a personal letter and a bracelet for his wife, and next year the whole circus procession was paraded, at her request, in the courtyard of Windsor Castle, where the old lady sat in her carriage watching the animals and acts pass in front of her. The Queen liked the colourful spectacle so much that she asked for the whole parade to be repeated. Then she invited Sanger to be presented to her and he was led to the royal carriage.

'So you are Mr Sanger?'

'Yes, Your Majesty.'

'*Lord* George Sanger, I believe?'

'Yes, if Your Majesty pleases.'

'It is very amusing, and I gather you have borne the title very honourably.'

[1] 'Lord' George Sanger, *Seventy Years a Showman*, London, 1966.

When the interview was over the Queen reminded her private secretary, Sir Arthur Bigge, 'Sir Arthur, be sure you remunerate Mr Sanger!' But the showman refused a cheque, and a few days later he received instead a massive silver cigar-box bearing the inscription:

Mr. George Sanger

V.R.I.

Windsor Castle, 17th July 1899

The last years of the reign saw several attempts to kill royalty. The Queen had been threatened and attacked several times in her lifetime. Now, when she was in Ireland, an attempt was made to kill the Prince of Wales at the Gar du Nord in Brussels, where he and the Princess had stopped on their way to Copenhagen.

Just as the train was leaving the station a youth of fifteen named Sipido jumped on to the footboard of the carriage and fired a revolver four times. Two bullets failed to fire, but two others passed close to the Prince. The train was immediately stopped, and when the crowd on the platform seized the boy the Prince called aloud to them not to harm him. Then the train moved out, and Sipido was taken away by the police.

At his trial, which was held three months later, the boy was revealed to be a member of a socialist society, many of whose members were strongly anti-British. He had been present at a pro-Boer meeting which had been addressed by Dr Leyds, President Kruger's agent in Europe, and he had left it feeling that it was his duty to kill the heir to the British throne who was 'an accomplice of Chamberlain in killing the Boers'. The court, however, acquitted Sipido on the grounds that he was 'irresponsible', and he was committed to the charge of his father.

'Fortunately, anarchists are bad shots,' wrote the Prince. 'The dagger is far more to be feared than the pistol.' Princess Alexandra, who had felt the bullets whizzing close to her, 'bore everything with the greatest courage and fortitude'. One of the bullets was found in the upholstery of the carriage, and it was later sent to the Prince, who kept it as a souvenir on his desk.

In August, a month after Sipido's trial, an attempt was made

127

to kill the Shah of Persia as he left the Palais des Souverains in Paris, when a man jumped on to the footstep of his carriage and levelled a pistol at his breast. The Grand Vizier immediately knocked the pistol out of the man's hand before he could fire.

On July 29, 1900 the world was shocked by the assassination of King Humbert I of Italy. Spending a summer holiday at Monza, he was returning after dark from the distribution of prizes at an athletic club when he was fired at while entering his carriage. The assassin was a Tuscan named Bresci, who had returned to Italy from the United States, where it was believed that he had been chosen by anarchists to murder the King. The first shot pierced the King's heart, and he died before he reached the palace.

A passionate soldier, who had distinguished himself on the battlefields of Solferino, Villafranca and Custozza, Humbert had defended himself bravely during a previous attempt on his life in Naples in 1878, and had then showed generosity in commuting the death sentence passed on his assassin. The King had been anxious to reinforce the Triple Alliance (Austria, Italy and Germany) with a similar Anglo-Italian *entente*. A constitutional monarch, he had earned the title of 'the good'. He was succeeded by his son Victor Emmanuel III, who abdicated in 1946.

The Prince of Wales' two favourite outdoor amusements were horse-racing and yachting, which greatly endeared him to the public. Racing was the sport of kings and commoners, having been made popular by James I. The Prince had been elected a member of the Jockey Club in 1875, but it was not until 1880 that one of his horses won a military hunt cup. Then, in 1895, he was victorious in six major events out of seven, winning the Manchester Cup, the Gold Vase at Ascot, and the Goodwood Cup. During his three years of racing, his horse Persimmon won nearly £35,000 for his owner; in 1895 he carried off the Coventry Stakes at Ascot and the Richmond Stakes at Goodwood; in 1896 he won the Derby in the record time of 2 minutes, 42 seconds, as well as the St Leger and the Jockey Club Stakes; and in 1897 he won the Ascot Gold Cup and the Eclipse Stakes.

12. Poor children in London in the so-called 'gay nineties'

13. Newcastle-on-Tyne slum street scene

14. Princess Alexandra

1900 was a particularly good year for the royal stable, the Prince's horse Diamond Jubilee (born 1897 and the brother of Persimmon) winning the Two Thousand Guineas, the Derby, and the St Leger, thus ranking among the ten horses to have won all three classic races.

The Prince was not alone in his love of yachting. In 1888 there were about 3000 private luxury vessels owned by wealthy Englishmen, and over 2000 of these were under canvas. The Prince loved to sail at Cowes, and the Kaiser's ambition was to beat him in the races there. This open hostility between the Prince and his nephew, the ambitious Emperor of Germany, whose power was growing greater every year, was undoubtedly influenced by Princess Alexandra's strong anti-German feelings, and this contributed to the rivalry between the two nations which was not, at least at the beginning, of the Kaiser's choosing. Was not the Prince the acknowledged leader of men's fashions, and what was the Kaiser doing dressing himself up in magnificent military uniforms? The hostility was intense.

To many thoughtful minds it appeared improbable that the Prince would ever succeed to the throne; his mother would surely outlive him. Some thought that the old Queen should abdicate in his favour; others hoped for a republic. But the vast majority, expecially in this closing year of the reign, accepted Victoria as an institution and were moved by her return to duty and her preoccupation with national affairs and interests, especially the progress of the war.

When the Prince eventually ascended the throne, late in life and set in his ways, Britain was not going to be disappointed with him. On his accession he was to reject the formal speech prepared for him and to speak without notes, his voice broken by emotion, declaring that it would be his constant endeavour always to walk in the footsteps of his beloved mother. 'In undertaking the heavy load which now devolves upon me,' he was to say, 'I am fully determined to be a constitutional sovereign in the strictest sense of the word and, as long as there is breath in my body, to work for the good and amelioration of my people.'

In March 1901, a few weeks after the death of the Queen, the author Arthur Conan Doyle (to be knighted in June 1902) was to be presented to the new King. His description of the occasion, in a letter to his mother, is interesting because Conan Doyle was a shrewd observer of people and events, as he had proved by his valuable war reports from South Africa.

'He asked that I should be placed next to him,' he wrote. 'He proved an able, clearheaded, positive man, rather inclined to be noisy, very alert, and energetic. He won't be a dummy king. He will live to be about seventy, I should say.'[1]

[1] Pierre Nordon, *Sir Arthur Conan Doyle Centenary* 1859–1959, London, 1959.

8

NEW WOMEN, NEW MEN

The leaders of the growing feminine revolution against male supremacy were by 1900 known as the New Women. Many now earned a living in professions, commerce and in callings hitherto denied them. Yet the majority of women in the late Victorian years continued to lack interest in emancipation; woman was naturally weak, her place was in the home, it was her lot to suffer in silence and to leave the running of the world to men. Her Majesty wrote to Theodore Martin:

'The Queen is most anxious to enlist everyone who can speak or write in checking this mad, wicked folly of "women's rights", *with all its attendant horrors*, on which her poor feeble sex is bent, forgetting every sense of womanly feeling and propriety. . . . It is a subject which makes the Queen so furious that she cannot contain herself. Woman would become the most hateful, heartless and disgusting of human beings were she allowed to unsex herself; and where would be the protection which man was intended to give the weaker sex?'

Thus, Victoria symbolized the innate conservatism of a nation which had—as had other countries—permitted feminine emancipation to move forward only with slow, leaden steps. Indeed, she represented the constant disapproval of any fashions in dress or change in manners which suggested an escape from the servitude of sex and feminine service. But she was not alone. In 1892 Gladstone had said of female suffrage, 'As this is not a party question, nor a class question, so neither is it a sex question.

I have no fear lest the woman should encroach upon the power of the man. The fear I have is, lest we should invite her unwittingly to trespass upon the delicacy, the purity, the refinement, the elevation of her own nature, which are the present sources of its power.' Earlier, the *Saturday Review* had suggested that 'throughout the civilized world the English parliament would

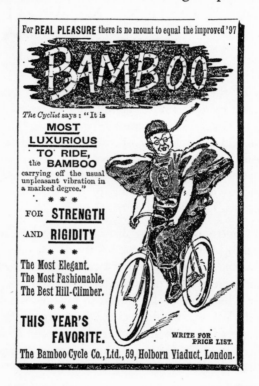

For **REAL PLEASURE** there is no mount to equal the improved '97

BAMBOO

The Cyclist says : "It is
**MOST
LUXURIOUS**
TO RIDE,
the **BAMBOO**
carrying off the usual
unpleasant vibration in
a marked degree."

* * *

FOR **STRENGTH**
AND **RIGIDITY**

* * *

The Most Elegant.
The Most Fashionable,
The Best Hill-Climber.

* * *

**THIS YEAR'S
FAVORITE.**

WRITE FOR
PRICE LIST.

The Bamboo Cycle Co., Ltd., 59, Holborn Viaduct, London.

lose in consideration if even one woman sat in it. The world has been so ordered that when things are at their best, men govern with wisdom and women obey with wisdom.'

In spite of opposition, the New Woman had access to many careers previously open only to men, and to higher education. She patronized the popular teashops which had been introduced in 1880, was openly but discreetly using make-up, and even smoked cigarettes. The Prince of Wales had made the cigarette popular among men, and now women took up the habit. A whole-page photograph in *The Sphere* showed the popular and beautiful actress Ellaline Terriss enveloped in cigarette smoke with an open box marked *giants* at her feet.

At formal balls and less formal dances women now whirled around the room in the increasingly vigorous waltz, polka, barn dance and lancers. The 1900 New Woman was also athletic; she swam bravely (clad in a voluminous bathing skirt), skated, played golf, badminton, lawn tennis, cricket, and even football. A British Ladies' Football Club had been founded in 1895. Women also went motoring, dressed in veiled hats and heavy furs. Games were usually played in ankle-length skirts of serge or grey flannel, shirt blouses and sailor hats, but at this time men wore knickerbockers for many sports. For cycling, women had for a time worn the long trousers made popular by the American Mrs Bloomer.

To be a governess or a paid companion usually led nowhere. Even domestic servants were starting to rebel. 'The present condition of friction between mistress and maid is one totally destructive to domestic peace,' noted *The Sphere* (April 21, 1900). 'Home is rapidly becoming the place that one seeks only when it is impossible to go elsewhere. The servant who takes interest in her work seems no longer to exist, and in return for high wages we get but superficial service. Where is the maid to be found who takes pride in the brilliance of the glass used upon the table or remembers of her own initiative to darn the damask? Every sort of contrivance now lessens labour—carpet sweepers, knife machines, bathrooms, lifts—in spite of these the life of a housewife is one long wrestle and failure to establish order.'

Increasingly, education was available. The North London Collegiate School for Girls, founded in 1850 by Miss Buss, and Cheltenham College, with Miss Beale as headmistress from 1858, had admirably set the pattern. Girton College had been founded at Hitchen in 1869 and moved to Cambridge with Miss Emily Davies as mistress in 1873. Newnham opened two years later. In 1879 Lady Margaret Hall and Somerville Hall (later College) had been established at Oxford. London University, which had admitted women students as early as 1867, had by 1878 allowed them to take degrees. But women's suffrage, which had started soon after the middle of the century, was to bring few real results until the coming of the twentieth century, and women would not be allowed to vote in Britain until 1918.

Meanwhile the outward segregation of the sexes and the taboo on their mutual relationships ensured that in what was termed 'polite society' men and women should never be alone together, unchaperoned, unless they were engaged, and not always then. In private there was a good deal of natural laxity in all classes, but there was always a pretence of respectability, divorce was considered scandalous, sex was not mentioned, and there was considerable hypocrisy.

In the United States woman's suffrage had by 1900 made only a small beginning in four thinly-populated Western States. A woman governor or congressman was considered ludicrous. America's newspapers contained no mention of women smoking, women doctors were regarded mainly with ridicule and, while a woman might be forced to earn a humble living, through circumstances beyond her control, as a governess, stenographer,[1] nanny, or servant, men continued—as in Britain—to rule the roost. How ridiculous, they said, it was for women to dress up in Mrs Bloomer's 'pantalots', long full trousers tied at the ankles, and go out cycling. Victorians had been shocked when they were introduced, and Mrs Bloomer had been accused of attempting to wreck the sanctity of home life, the music-hall comedians singing lustily about the new fashion. 'Well, what do you see? Eh, boys?' shouted Marie Lloyd. And in 1895 Basil Hood ridiculed them in the musical comedy *Gentleman Joe*:

> My eye! Here's a lady bicyclist!
> Look at her! Look at her! Look at her! Look at her!
> Hi! Hi! Hi!
> She's put her petticoats up the spout,
> And now she has to go without;
> She hopes her mother won't find out,

[1] What was called 'the first lady typewriter' had appeared in England in 1897.

And thinks they won't be missed.
Oh! My! Hi! Hi!
Keep your eye on the lady bi—
The lady bicyclist!

In 1899 a court case was brought by Lady Harburton, who
had been refused entry to a hotel because she was wearing
bloomers or, as they were more politely called, 'rationals'. After
the case she predicted: 'I admit that it is probably certain that
women will never ordinarily wear knickerbockers. But mark this
—short skirts for walking gear will be a boon that ought to be
easily attained and, once attained, cherished like Magna Charta
in the British constitution.'

In December 1900 the first lady barrister took the oath in
Paris. 'Welcome, bar maid,' said *Punch*. It was proposed that the
New Woman, according to the type proposed in *The Revolt of
the Daughters*, should be known as *The Revolting Woman*.
Nevertheless, women continued to protest against convention
and they made such revolutionary sorties as dining out together
without gentlemen, and meeting other women in pursuit of
enjoyment totally unconnected with relatives, church or charity.
In 1896 the Duchess de Clermont Tennorre had shocked London
society by smoking a cigarette at a dinner-table in the Savoy
Hotel, but it is interesting, in view of Lady Harburton's prediction
about knickerbockers and short skirts, that as late as 1967—the
year of the mini-skirt—there was to be a fuss when a lady wore
culottes when dining at the Savoy.

Women clerks, domestic servants and factory girls still worked
for appallingly long hours, and 'distressed gentlefolk' fared worse.
In 1900 *Punch* quoted an advertisement from the *Irish Times*:
'Wanted, a distressed lady, to mind and attend elderly lady and
make herself useful about house. Salary £7 to £8 a year to
suitable person.' But *Punch* shared the opinion of the popular
novelist 'Ouida' that the New Woman was 'an unmitigated bore':

There is a New Woman, and what do you think?
She lives upon nothing but foolscap and ink!
But, though foolscap and ink form the whole of her diet,
This nagging New Woman can never be quiet!

Women's dresses of the period suggested an odd blend of freedom and restraint, and this mental conflict, according to the fashion historian Dr Willett Cunnington, 'found expression in a taste for discordant colours; yellow trimmed with pink and green, violently contrasting in material and colour with the rest of the gown; a pink skirt and a black bodice. Often bodice and skirt seemed hardly on speaking terms.' The favourite colour of the age was undoubtedly yellow, and it is perhaps symbolic that the magazine which was creating the biggest stir among advanced people was *The Yellow Book*. New movements were everywhere in the ascendant. In manners, morals, and everything else the nineteenth century was clearly drawing to a close.[1]

Even the New Woman displayed an unwillingness to abandon the advantages obtained from 'clinging femininity'. While Paris fashions remained essentially feminine, London's achieved a curious compromise; the top half of a day dress would be frilly and flouncy while the lower half was plain. The South African war had established drab khaki as a fashionable colour, and in 1900 khaki hats, blouses and cloth, mostly with red trimmings, were to be seen in all the women's dress shops and drapers. Furthermore, fashionable garments in cheap form were now widespread, many ready-made clothes coming from Germany. Lace was used lavishly, lingerie was extravagantly embroidered, and it was boldly stated that the object of the tea-gown was its 'mystery and endless frou-frou of lace'.

By day women wore bodices with high necks, the collar being held up by silk-covered wires instead of the old whalebones. Boleros were almost universal for day gowns, accentuating the small waists. Eton bodices, resembling Eton jackets, were worn outside the skirts. Sleeves were often pleated at the shoulder. The skirt was usually made with a foundation, with the front touching the ground and the back four inches longer. Tea gowns, walking gowns, afternoon dresses and evening dresses all had their own styles. 'Bathing gowns in red and navy serge are remarkably pretty this year'; but these had skirts reaching to the knee. Some had knickers and very short basques to the tunics; others were

[1] James Laver, *Costume*, London, 1963.

ugly combination garments. Mixed bathing was beginning to come into fashion.

For full evening dress the bodice was cut low, either square or round, with lace bertha or chiffon fichu. The skirt, immensely full around the feet, was usually of a flimsy material over silk or

satin, the edge flounced or scalloped. Hats and toques were small, and black was a fashionable colour. For tailor-mades, the hat was often 'Trilby' shaped, with an upstanding feather. Hats were trimmed with feathers, birds, ribbons, and buckles. Feminine accessories included large muffs, gloves, parasols, gold and silver chain purses, ostrich-feather fans, and high pearl and diamond dog-collars, bracelets and brooches. Every year, 25,000 bird of

paradise skins were sold in London.[1] A solution to the vexing problem of skirts that blew up in a high wind or when the woman was bicycling was discovered in 1896 when it was announced that 'Princess Maud is having her skirts weighed with shot'. *The Graphic* in 1899 noted the popularity of fur toques for winter wear, and a year later remarked on a boat-shaped hat of Panama straw trimmed with rosettes of white tulle and two quills.

Women wore their hair done up in a bun high on top of the head. At the same time the front hair was sometimes drawn up from the forehead to form what was called a 'Pompadour front'. Pads of hair and wire called 'Pompadours' were inserted under the hair. Hatpins and hairpins were in vogue. The New Woman was certainly not under-dressed.

The 'nineties witnessed the revival of the male dandy, the fashionable novels of the period abounding in them, although it was a different kind of dandyism from that of the Regency period. Slim, elegant, pommaded, moustached young men served as the background for these books, but were not the reason for their existence. In the foreground was the artist, often dandified and aristocratic but essentially a creature of the romantic, aesthetic movement. There was a novelist in Marie Corelli's *The Sorrows of Satan*, a tenor in Ouida's *Moths*, a painter in George du Maurier's *Trilby*, a man of letters as an actor in W. J. Locke's *Stella Maris*. In his 1909 novel *Ann Veronica*, H. G. Wells was to tell of a New Woman who takes a biologist as her lover, only to be rewarded at the end by marrying the gentleman, who has somehow been transformed in the story into a successful playwright.

To amuse and gratify the New Woman many novelists created a new kind of masculine foil which combined the aesthete, the decadent, and the dandy. More playthings than heroes, these characters were often 'kept men'. In E. F. Benson's novel *Mammon and Co.* (1899) Ted Comber's effeminacy was briskly summed up by a more virile fellow: 'He ain't a man ... he

[1] C. Willett Cunnington, *English Women's Clothing in the Nineteenth Century*, London, 1956.

doesn't shoot, ride or play games . . . he sits on chairs and looks beautiful.' Worse, Mr Comber favoured scent, did embroidery, played the mandolin, and was interested in making women's clothes; yet he was not obviously homosexual, and the fast young wife of the novel who desired him was eventually seduced and made pregnant by him.

London society, said Oscar Wilde, was 'entirely made up of

REVIVAL IN FASHION.

SHEPHERD'S PLAID TROUSERS

will be greatly worn this season.

Messrs. THOMPSON BROS. have an immense variety of patterns in the above styles, and are prepared to supply these really high-class goods at 7/6 to measure, West End cut and style guaranteed. Patterns and rules of self-measurement forwarded post free to any address.

7/6

**THOMPSON BROS., TAILORS, Ltd.,
3, Oxford Street, London, W.**
(Corner of Charing Cross Road.)

dowdies and dandies. . . . The men are all dowdies and the women are all dandies.' As Arthur Waugh wrote in *The Yellow Book*, 'It may be, indeed, that we ourselves are beginning to appreciate that the new era of letters is not so much decadent as vulgar.' Indeed, it was an age of considerable vulgarity, as the music-halls, the legitimate theatre, female and male fashions, decoration, architecture, art and advertising clearly showed. During the Edwardian era this vulgarity was to become even more pronounced, but it was to be excused with the strange expression 'honest vulgarity'.

In London's city and 'up west' there were silk hats, bowlers, and plenty of whiskers under the gas-lights, where soldiers out walking wore pill-box hats and tight trousers and red tunics, and the clip-clop of horses drawing 'buses and hansoms could be heard along the streets. Even the clerk earning thirty shillings a week sported a top hat, while the working men wore tightly-brimmed bowlers and choker collars.

Men wished to show who and what they were by their clothes. The gay young spark, the lawyer, the divine, the coal-heaver, the actor, all wore uniforms; a man's trade could almost be told by his tie and boots. While the nation took a real interest in vulgarity it persuaded itself that it was really concerned with art and progress. It was new, highly varnished, glossy, and youthful. It embraced both the Royal Albert Hall and Evans's Music Hall and the Coal Hole in the Strand. It called 'bus conductors 'cads' and got uproariously drunk, but also made a great fuss about the word 'gentleman', and regularly attended church wearing decorous black. In clothes and manners it could be at one and the same time smug and dissolute, but above all it was essentially vulgar— and amazingly great.[1]

Men had their hair cut short with a side-parting, often it was plastered down with macassar oil. Long-haired men were condemned as 'poets' or 'musicians' or 'actors'. Moustaches were often heavy. A man wore gloves in town, and red-silk handkerchiefs were fashionable with evening dress, being thrust into the bosom of the waistcoat. Walking sticks were also popular, the 'shepherd's crook' and the light 'whangee' being in vogue. A watch in the waistcoat pocket with a gold 'Albert' chain,[2] passing through a chain-hole in the waistcoat, was for day-wear; with evening dress, gentlemen wore slim watches, often of gun metal, in their vest pockets. No jewellery beyond a tie-pin and perhaps a signet ring was permissible. The use of perfumes indicated the dandy or 'bounder'. But, on the other hand, in 1894, the corset was 'worn by thousands of men',[3] and *papier-poudre*, wafer

[1] Dion Clayton Calthrop, *English Dress*, London, 1934.
[2] Named after the Prince Consort.
[3] C. W. and Phillis Cunnington, *Handbook of English Costume in the Nineteenth Century*, London, 1967.

booklets of paper impregnated with powder and rouge, were bought and used by both women and men.

'New overcoats may come and go, but the Raglan goes on for ever,' said *The Sphere* (February 17, 1900). 'The reason for its continued popularity is in its usefulness more than its style, for surely no man with ambition to be considered sane can really think very highly of a character of shoulder-cutting that suggests, in the average figure, a bottle of champagne, and in the unduly slight figure, a bottle of hock.' So famous had London's tailoring industry become that all the world admired English suits, in spite of Lord Shaftesbury's statement at the Royal Academy dinner of 1899 that the dress worn by English gentlemen for the past fifty years had been 'the ugliest ever worn'. In this year the height of the fashionable collar had risen to about three inches ('certainly more than the average man can wear with comfort,' said the *Tailor and Cutter*), the most elegant overcoat being the single-breasted Chesterfield, closely followed by the Albert top frock coat, the Newmarket top frock coat, the close-fitting Inverness with cape, the Ulster, the Covert coat for riding, the Reefer, the Raglan, and the Talma overcoat, which allowed men to walk with their hands in their trouser pockets.

In America a man when 'dressed up' wore a Derby hat, a woollen suit of dark colour, the coat padded at the shoulders, collars and cuffs stiffly laundered, and the shirt held together at the bosom with studs. The 'dude' or 'dandy' wore garters to hold up his socks. There was little difference between summer and winter suits, the second-best doing service on week-days all the year round, the Sunday suit being worn once a week, good weather or bad. The overcoats were usually of substantial, heavy broadcloth, Merton or Kersey, designed to last for years. The mail-order catalogues of Sears, Roebuck, and their rivals were selling emblems which depicted the customer's trade; the blacksmith hung a gold anvil or horseshoe from his watch-chain; the bartender sported a jewelled beer-keg; the sailor a miniature anchor or compass; the railroad engineer a small locomotive; the conductor a caboose. Heavy, thick, gold watches—sometimes called 'turnips'—were an indication of prosperity, and of the essential vulgarity of the age, which America shared with Britain.[1]

This vulgarity affected architecture, furnishing and decoration. William G. Fitzgerald (in the *Strand Magazine*, September 1896) described how mounted trophies from India and Africa were incorporated into English homes; the Prince of Wales had a stuffed bear, which he had shot in Russia, set up as a dumb waiter with paws outstretched to hold a tray of drinks and sweetmeats; elephants' feet were hollowed out and made into liquor stands; eagles' claws were mounted in silver and displayed in drawing-room cabinets; a baby giraffe, shot by a bold adventurer in British East Africa, was made into a chair; a young Ceylon elephant became a hall porter's seat; antlers, stag-heads, tiger-rugs, leopards' heads, even stuffed monkeys, were used to prove that the English were superior in prowess not only to all other races, but also to the animals. The New Woman—wanting education—and the New Man, both were essentially vulgar in their tastes.

[1] Mark Sullivan, *op. cit.*

9

THE CONQUEST OF THE AIR

In 1897 the first attempt to reach the North Pole by aerial balloon had been made by three Swedish explorers—Salomon August Andree, Nils Strindberg, and Knut Frankel, but a heavy deposit of ice formed on their balloon and forced it down, and the three men later died of cold and exposure. Their adventure drew attention to the great progress which men of all nations were making in their attempt to conquer the air, although there were still many people who shared the pious opinion expressed when Mr Percy S. Pilcher, of Market Harborough, was killed in 1899 in his pioneer flying machine: 'If God meant us to fly he would have given us wings.'

Ballooning was to become an accepted sport during the Edwardian age. In 1900 the leading British exponents of the art were the brothers Spencer, whose father and grandfather had both been aeronauts, having been pioneers with Charles Green, the man who first used coal gas for inflating balloons. Mr Green had given the grandfather, Edward Spencer, a barometer which he had used in 200 balloon ascents. Previous to Mr Green's discovery balloons had been inflated either with hot air or with pure hydrogen gas. With the introduction of coal gas, ascents with large parties in a balloon car had become quite common, and the summit of Mr Green's fame had been reached when, with two colleagues—one named Monk Mason and the other an MP named Holland—his balloon had stayed aloft for eighteen hours, making the journey from Old Vauxhall Gardens, London, to Nassau in Germany in a day.

There were three Spencer brothers, and their balloon ascents and parachute descents at the Crystal Palace and at various exhibitions and galas through the summer seasons were a feature of the 'nineties. Percival, the eldest, had also soared above Egypt, India, China and Japan; Stanley had sailed over France, Germany, Canada, the United States, West Indies, Cuba, Brazil, the Cape, India and China; and Arthur had ballooned over Australia.

'When you drop on the roof of a house,' said Arthur, 'let go of your parachute at once and cling to the first thing you can lay your hands on. You see, as soon as you land on anything that takes your weight from the parachute it instantly closes and is no more use in supporting you. By keeping hold of it you are only robbing yourself of the hands you require for clutching the nearest chimney-pot.'

'Of course,' suggested Percival, 'the best place to drop into is a meadow. But I don't mind a tree at all, it's far better than a house. You swish through the foliage until you strike solid, then all you have to do is grasp the branches that are round you, and there you are all right.'

Visiting Calcutta, Percival made an ascent before a huge crowd, including the Viceroy, but a fresh wind carried him away towards the Sunderbunds where he was lost for three days, and given up for dead. The *Indian Mirror* announced, 'Seldom has Calcutta been thrown into a state of greater excitement and consternation than during the last two or three days, and the unwitnessed tragic end of Mr Spencer, the unfortunate young aeronaut, has filled society, both European and native, with intense gloom. Wherever one goes he hears nothing but a burst of grief for the brave Englishman who, from a mistaken sense of honour, literally gave a sacrifice of his body to the winds.'

Percival Spencer had ascended without a parachute, and had gone up helpless into the clouds on a mere sling. 'There were a quarter of a million people assembled to see me go,' he said later, when he returned to be greeted by a civic reception in Calcutta's town hall. 'The Viceroy was there, and his staff, and native princes of the greatest influence. I had been announced to make an ascent, and had already disappointed the crowd. Well, it was just a quarter

15. The Prince of Wales leads in his horse Persimmon after winning the 1896 Derby at Epsom

16, 17, 18. Stage beauties—Lily Elsie, Irene Vanbrugh, Zena and Phyllis Dare

to six, and at six it would become promptly dark. There was thus no time to lose, for if that enormous concourse of people had been disappointed a second time there would have been a riot, and native opinion of the Englishman and what he could do would have suffered a severe reduction. I *had* to go up, and the only way was to lighten the balloon. So I detached the parachute, which made a difference of 28 lb. The balloon, I was pleased to find, shot up to a great height, and my spirits shot up too as I left the heated air of India and entered the cool refreshing air above.'

In London *The Times* reported, 'By this feat Mr Spencer has illustrated once more how, above all other people, an Englishman will rise a hero in an emergency.'

Besides making their own balloons, the Spencers exported them to the Chinese, Dutch and Russian governments. At home they maintained a permanent fleet of twenty-four balloons, and on an August Bank Holiday they were all in use in public parks, at carnivals and fairs, or to celebrate some notable event. There was the *Majestic*, with a capacity of 100,000 cubic feet, the *City of York*, the *Wulfruna*, the *City of London* and the *Empress of India*. To man them the brothers employed a staff of aeronauts who, like them, enjoyed the pleasure of soaring through the air and ignoring the perils.

Aviation had come into its own in 1870, although very few people appreciated the fact. When Prussia had invaded France and besieged Paris, balloons had been used to send out messages. A number of expert balloonists were in Paris at the time, including Gaston Tissandier, Eugene Godard (who had made some 800 flights), de Fonville, Nadar, Mangin, and Jules Durouf. Although there were only six balloons in the city, all the aviators wished to ascend. On September 23, 1870 Durouf went up with a load of despatches, landing safely sixty miles outside Paris after a three-hour flight. Balloons were then built in the city, and out of 64 ascents no fewer than 57 got safely through, carrying 155 crew and passengers, with cargo and mail weighing about 9 tons. The last flight, on January 28, 1871, had carried the news of the surrender of Paris to the Germans.[1]

[1] Basil Clarke, *The History of Airships*, London, 1961.

Thus the siege of Paris had ushered in the age of aviation. On August 9, 1884 a dirigible airship made her maiden flight from Chalais Meudon. Designed and built by Charles Renard and A. C. Krebs, she was named *La France*. The envelope was made of Chinese silk, the car was constructed of bamboo trellis-work, and the airship, 170 feet long, was fitted with a Gramme electric motor of eight horse power, which with batteries weighed only 210 pounds per horse power. This dirigible could travel at over twelve mph and on her maiden voyage she not only covered about five miles but completed a circular flight, returning to her mooring.

France and Germany could claim to have created the airship. In Paris the pioneer Alberto Santos-Dumont, a Brazilian, made history by flying round the Eiffel Tower. He built several airships, and in 1906 he was to become the first man in Europe to fly in a heavier-than-air machine. To win a bet, Santos-Dumont flew above the street where he lived in the centre of Paris, made his airship descend, tethered it to a lamp-post, went indoors for a drink, and then flew off again. But perhaps the greatest of the pioneers was Count Ferdinand von Zeppelin, who completed the assembly of his first airship, the L.Z.1 in the spring of 1900 and made his first flight in it on July 2nd, with five people on board.

The L.Z.1 arose from a floating hanger on the Lake of Constance near Friedrichshafen, Germany. It was 420 feet long and 38 feet in diameter. Count Zeppelin was a retired army officer who, while serving as a balloon observer with the Union forces during the American civil war, had conceived the idea of placing a number of balloons in line with a streamlined structure which could be propelled and steered. Although there were structural weaknesses in the L.Z.1, the design and this first flight in 1900 proved that Zeppelin's theory was correct. Speeds of nearly 20 mph were soon reached.

In about 1890 there had been a revival of the ancient idea that man could fly with artificial wings, this time using the natural action of gliding and soaring on air currents. A year later the German aviator Otto Lilienthal started gliding from an artificial mound near Berlin, frequently accomplishing flights of a hundred yards. In the United States, Octave Chanute was engaged on similar experiments, as was Percy S. Pilcher in Britain. Both Lilienthal and Pilcher considered adding engines to their gliders. Other early experiments were made by Clement Ader in France, and Professor S. P. Langley in the United States. But the most important pioneer work being carried out at this time was the development of first the gliding and then the powered airplane by the brothers Wilbur and Orville Wright of Dayton, Ohio, who started their experiments with gliders in 1896 and, after nearly a thousand gliding flights at Kitty Hawk on the coast of North Carolina, began in 1900 to build a series of biplane gliders so that at the end of 1902 they were to have a biplane with a total area of 305 square feet and a weight of 250–260 lb., including the pilot, who lay stretched flat on the lower plane. This was later to be the famous Wright patent No. 821,383 (filed March 23, 1903). The brothers had only to install a light modified eight to ten horse power motor-car engine and to strengthen their glider to carry the extra weight, and the machine would be ready for its historic initial test on December 17, 1903; an event which was to mark the beginning of a new chapter in the history and progress of man, who was at last to conquer the air.

But Mr H. G. Wells was sceptical: 'I do not think it at all probable that aeronautics will ever come into play as a serious modification of transport and communication.' As for the submarine, which was in 1900 well past the development stage, he balked at the invention: 'I must confess that my imagination, in spite even of spurring, refuses to see any sort of submarine doing anything but suffocate its crew and founder at sea.'

10

LITERATURE AND JOURNALISM

The major works of the great Victorian novelists still influenced the public's thoughts and reading at the turn of the century and would continue to do so. Six of them were closely linked, forming almost a literary circle, for William Thackeray (1811–61) had known Charles Dickens (1812–70), and Dickens was a great friend of George Eliot (1819–80), while Anthony Trollope (1815–82) was proposed by Thackeray for membership of the Garrick Club, and George Meredith (1828–1909) contributed to the magazine which Dickens edited and was also a friend of Robert Louis Stevenson (1850–94).

There had been no time in history when so many talented writers were competing, the novel having developed in the eighteenth and nineteenth centuries to become the staple reading diet of the average man and woman. There were riches to be gained from writing fiction, yet from his first four novels Trollope said he made little: 'As regards remuneration for the time, stone-breaking would have done better.'

It was a golden age for literature, and although some great poets of the century were dead before the Queen's accession— Keats, Shelley, Byron, Coleridge—other writers flourished in mid-Victorian times. Wordsworth had died in 1850, Dickens in 1870, and John Stuart Mill in 1873, but Tennyson worked until 1892, Browning until 1889, and Matthew Arnold until 1888.

Among the great novelists still claiming attention was Trollope, whose *Barchester Towers* had been published in 1857 and who continued writing until his death in 1882. George Meredith was still at work in 1900, but Thomas Hardy[1] wrote no more novels after *Jude the Obscure* (1895). Robert Louis Stevenson had died in 1894, but at the end of the century many new names were attracting attention: H. G. Wells, George Bernard Shaw (one of those who started the revolt against Victorianism), Robert Bridges, W. B. Yeats, and A. E. Houseman, whose poem *A Shropshire Lad* was published in 1896. Aldous Huxley was not born until 1894, and T. S. Eliot four years later.

When John Ruskin died on January 20, 1900 aged eighty-one at his home at Brantwood near Coniston it was an event of great importance, for few writers of his time had so deeply influenced literature and art. He was born in Hunter Street, Brunswick Square, London, son of a travelling wine merchant who took him on long excursions; and a deeply religious mother who hoped the boy might be a clergyman. But it was probably his father's interest in art which influenced his choice of career. With him young Ruskin is said to have travelled around the great houses of England soliciting orders for wine, and so the boy was introduced to the art galleries and private collections of paintings which his father admired.

From Herne Hill, then a village on the outskirts of London, the family moved when Ruskin was twenty to Denmark Hill near Dulwich, where he came under the influence of the Dulwich Art Gallery, whose pictures affected his thoughts on art all his life. He was already taking drawing lessons from the water-colourist, Copley Fielding. In 1836 he went up to Christ Church, Oxford, but he studied little and his social life was hampered by the presence of his mother in nearby lodgings. He won the Newdigate Prize for Poetry in 1839 and because of a generous allowance from his father—who was, like Edward Burne-Jones's father, reasonably prosperous—he was able to travel abroad and write.

In 1843 Ruskin published the first volume of a book called *Modern Painters*, which was announced as being 'by a graduate of Oxford'. The work immediately thrilled the intellectual world,

[1] Leonard Woolf has described Hardy as 'the last great writer of the nineteenth century'.

for Ruskin believed that art was a heritage of the people and that industry without art was brutality. He introduced Italian art to British readers. A second volume appeared in 1846, and two more followed some ten years later. The fifth volume, completing the series, was published in 1860. More than anyone else, Ruskin may be said to have influenced the ideas on art of the Victorian intelligentsia, and the Pre-Raphaelites, in particular, owed much to his defence of them.

Dante Gabriel Rossetti, William Holman Hunt and John Everett Millais founded this new aesthetic school in 1848 with the aim of returning to art forms which had existed in Europe before the time of Raphael Santi (1483–1520). The Pre-Raphaelite Brotherhood first published its doctrines in January 1850 in a periodical called *The Germ: Thoughts towards Nature in Poetry, Literature and Art* and although the movement was short-lived (but not as short-lived as *The Germ*, of which only four numbers appeared) its influence was widespread.

Rossetti's attempt to decorate the Union Debating Hall at Oxford with frescoes, although unsuccessful, was the beginning of a revival of interest in the decorative arts, and William Morris, who helped him on this project, later founded the firm of Morris, Marshall, Faulkner and Co. with the object of revitalizing design and producing objects of use and beauty. Poet, craftsman and socialist, Morris was greatly influenced by Ruskin's battles against commercial ugliness, and in 1877 he founded the Society for the Preservation of Ancient Buildings, which still exists. Edward Burne-Jones, Rossetti's other helper, became a well-known artist, but he was hardly a great painter, although in the words of the author and critic Martin Armstrong he was 'a great decorator, a great handicraftsman, and within the narrow limits of his mood a great illustrator'.

In 1876 a rebellious figure, George Bernard Shaw, had arrived in London from Dublin to become a journalist. He wrote for the *Pall Mall Gazette, The World, Public Opinion,* and *The Star,* and contributed dramatic criticism to the *Saturday Review*. His first play, *Widowers' Houses* (begun with William Archer) was produced in 1892, but it was not until after 1900 that the full impact of his lively, unorthodox wit and great dramatic skill were to become accepted through his subsequent plays.

In 1898, the year that Burne-Jones died, his contemporary Lewis Carroll (the Rev. Charles Lutwidge Dodgson) also died. A master of comic verse and imaginative nonsense, he had written *Alice's Adventures in Wonderland* (1865), *Through the Looking Glass* (1871) and *The Hunting of the Snark* (1876). He may be bracketed with Edward Lear (1812–88), a shy, retiring gentleman who had lived chiefly in Italy, painting, sketching, and writing travel and humorous pieces. As a comic poet Lear developed the limerick, an epigrammatic verse form from the eighteenth century, as well as longer forms. He wrote his limericks to amuse the grandchildren of his patron, the Earl of Derby, and published them in his *Book of Nonsense* (1846). Late Victorian children and the generations that followed were brought up with Carroll's brilliant humour and quaint creatures, and Lear's delightful 'pobble' who was reconciled to his lack of toes, and 'the Dong with the luminous nose' who loved and lost his 'Jumbly Girl', and all the other absurd but credible creatures of dream worlds, often highly comic, which were to enrich the thoughts of adults and youngsters.

In 1900 the artist James McNeill Whistler was within three years of his death. An exquisite painter and etcher who revealed the beauty of London's river to the world, he had a strong influence on interior decoration. Born in 1834 at Lowell, Massachusetts, where there is now a Whistler memorial museum, he had been taken when nine to St Petersburg, where his father was employed on railroad construction. Back in America, in 1851, he went to West Point military academy but he was discharged in 1884 and soon travelled to Paris to study art in the studio of Charles Gleyre. In 1860 the Royal Academy in London accepted his painting *At the Piano* which had been rejected a year earlier by the French salon. Similarly in 1865 his *Little White Maid*, also rejected by the salon, was hung in London.

Whistler's famous picture of his mother, painted in 1871, was his last submission to the Royal Academy. But his reputation depended not entirely on painting and etchings and design. He was notorious for his wit, his malicious tongue, and his direct and devastating personal comments about his contemporaries, which gained him many foes, as he revealed in his collection of letters with comments, *The Gentle Art of Making Enemies* (1890). In 1878 the libel action following Ruskin's comment that one of Whistler's 'nocturnes' was 'a pot of paint flung in the public's face' brought Whistler again to the public eye, but its result combined with other debts, was to leave him bankrupt. From 1886 he was president of the Royal Society of British Artists, which during his two years of office set a new high standard for quality. It was in 1891 that the portrait of his mother was bought by the city of Paris for the Louvre, after which his growing reputation in France led him to return there. He was to die in Cheyne Walk, Chelsea, in 1903.

A writer with a strong influence on the changing social scene at this time was Robert Blatchford, who had been born at Maidstone in 1851, the son of theatrical parents. He had been trained as a brushmaker but joined the army and later worked on the staff of the *Sunday Chronicle*. In 1891 he founded and edited the weekly journal *The Clarion*, to encourage socialism and free thought. His book *Merrie England*, published at sixpence in 1894, sold many thousands of copies.

In January 1900 the venerable novelist R. D. Blackmore died, renowned for his novel *Lorna Doone* (1869), and at the same time the death was announced in beleagured Ladysmith of the *Daily Mail* war correspondent G. W. Steevens, a victim at the age of thirty of the typhoid epidemic which ravaged the battle areas.

In the Latin quarter of Paris there died on November 30th a gentleman calling himself 'Sebastian Melmoth'. He was in fact the Irish author and dramatist Oscar Wilde, who since his sensational criminal prosecution and conviction in 1895 had been imprisoned and then led a sad, secluded, outcast life abroad. Nearly all his friends had deserted him, his publishers withdrew his books, stage managements cut short the run of his plays or took his name off the playbills, his name was either whispered or made the subject of obscene jokes. It was to be several years before his witty comedies *Lady Windermere's Fan*, *A Woman of*

No Importance, An Ideal Husband and *The Importance of Being Earnest* were again to claim the recognition they deserved.

Shortly before this, in August, the brilliant German philosopher Fredrich Wilhelm Nietzsche died. Born in 1844, he had in his youth been greatly influenced by Schopenhauer, and Wagner was his friend. His German 'superman' philosophy was eloquently expressed in his many writings, which included *Thus spake Zarathustra, Beyond Good and Evil* and *The Will to Power*. The Danish critic Georg Brandes said of him, 'During the last ten years of the nineteenth century, Nietzsche has been the opposing pole to Tolstoy. His morality is aristocratic, while Tolstoy's morality is popular; it is individualistic while Tolstoy's is evangelical; it demands the self-exaltation of the individual, while Tolstoy holds for the necessity of individual self-sacrifice.' Nietzsche was noted for his prose style. It had been his ambition, he said, 'to say in ten sentences what others say in a book, or, rather, what others fail to say in a book'.

With the death of Stephen Crane in June 1900 at the early age of thirty, American literature lost an important author. His best-known novel, *The Red Badge of Courage*, had been written when he was twenty-five. An American of Americans, he had heard as a child tales of the Civil War which excited his imagination, of men fighting under Grant and Sherman, of brother killing brother and father shooting son. Yet when he wrote *The Red Badge of Courage* he had not seen a shot fired in anger. Subsequently he became a correspondent for the *New York Journal* and the *Westminster Gazette* during the Graeco-Turkish war of 1897, but his health was poor. In the United States' Cuban campaign he described the sound of bullets whizzing over his head as being like the low whistles of a small bird. He had wanted to see the fighting in South Africa, but fevers caught in Crete, Santiago and Havana prevented this, and his last year was spent writing boys' stories for *Harper's Magazine*.

A remarkable career ended in February 1900 with the death of Joseph Cowen, the owner of the *Newcastle Chronicle*. There had been a time, said the *Daily Telegraph*, when Mr Cowen could have attained almost any political position he fancied. He had immense wealth, strong and popular convictions, and he was one of the finest orators of his generation. Not only did he control a great and influential newspaper, but he was idolized in the north-east of England. At one time he was next to John Bright as the favourite speaker in the House of Commons. His father had entered Newcastle as a pedlar and had become extremely wealthy, rising to be mayor of the city and to be knighted by the Queen. Yet Joseph Cowen left parliament when he was still under middle-age, and spent the rest of his years outside the stream of political life, content to control his newspaper and to take an active interest in local affairs and charities.

The abolition of the newspaper tax in 1870, which followed the repeal of duties on papers in 1855, had led to a boom in English newspapers. Most of them were at first modelled on *The Times*, catering for the upper and middle classes, and until the coming of Alfred Harmsworth they were aimed almost exclusively at male readers. The literary and political journals, such as *The Spectator*, the *Saturday Review* and the *Fortnightly Review* were read by few women. Until about 1886 England's press was dignified, responsible, intelligent, and often dull. But when W. T. Stead became editor of the *Pall Mall Gazette* in 1883 (until 1889) journalism started to become more sensational and commercial, with a wider appeal to the masses.

The pioneer in the development of popular newspapers for the family, instead of merely for civil servants or officers sitting in clubs in St James's Street, was Alfred Harmsworth, who went to work in 1885 when he was twenty for the magazine owner George Newnes, and who in 1888, with his brother Cecil, started a rival to Newnes' weekly periodical *Tit-Bits* which the brothers called *Answers to Correspondents*. Success came to this venture when the Harmsworths offered a prize of a pound a week for life for guessing the value of the gold held by the Bank of England on a given day.

In association with his brother Harold (later Lord Rothermere) Harmsworth built up a lucrative empire of family magazines and comic papers. *Answers* soon sold 250,000 copies a week, and other journals were quickly added to the list, including the schoolboy *Comic Cuts*. By 1892 *Answers* was selling 1,009,067 copies a week, and could claim the largest circulation in the world for a penny periodical. '1900 is a long way off,' said the press magnate in that year, 'but given good health and strength I would not be at all surprised if our weekly sale reaches from ten to fifteen million copies a week', a figure, however, never attained.

In 1894 the Harmsworths bought the London *Evening News*, still selling at a halfpenny. Then in May 1896 they launched the halfpenny *Daily Mail*, which averaged 202,000 copies a day during its first twelve months and by 1899 was selling 543,000 copies, more than twice the number sold by any other English daily paper. 'We've struck a gold mine!' said Alfred, who had shrewdly appreciated that women could be persuaded to buy newspapers if the contents were made attractive to them. 'The *Daily Mail* appears to be a most interesting experiment to which I give my heartiest good wishes,' telegraphed Mr Gladstone. 'Written by office boys for office boys,' said Lord Salisbury. But the public, especially the great middle class, liked the presentation of the Harmsworth papers, which told the news in lively, short paragraphs. Until the end of the century and for several more years the *Daily Mail* was unique, and its original impact on the world of journalism is still apparent today.

In an effort to steal some of the *Daily Mail's* circulation C. Arthur Pearson started a new halfpenny paper in 1900 which he called the *Daily Express*, but it did not really succeed until 1913, when it came under the control of the Canadian Max Aitken, Lord Beaverbrook. During its first days it published exclusive messages from the Kaiser, the Czar, and the King of Sweden and Norway. It also claimed to be first with the news of the devastation of Ottawa by fire, the Prince of Wales' proposed visit to Paris, the Queen's forthcoming visit to Ireland, the resignation from parliament of Sir Henry Stanley, MP, the former explorer, and the great forest fires in America. The average sale was about 300,000 copies a day. In June 1900 Arthur Pearson announced that Rudyard Kipling, who had just returned from seeing Lord Roberts in Bloemfontein, would write a series of war stories for the paper.

'It will contain every day a special feature for women,' said the *Daily Express* preliminary announcements. 'Matters which are mysteries to the mere male, such as fashions, cookery, home management, and the care of children, will be here dealt with by the greatest living authorities. . . . The mechanical arrangements of the *Daily Express* are completed for an edition of *one million* and no more. Many millions of intending purchasers will be disappointed. Be one of the lucky million.'

Meanwhile *The Times Weekly Edition* continued to be published on Fridays at twopence, having been enlarged at the beginning of 1900. A year's subscription cost eleven shillings, or thirteen shillings abroad, the paper providing all the news of the week, a parliamentary summary, naval and military intelligence, musical, dramatic and sporting news, law reports and stock exchange news, together with a serial story 'by a well known and popular writer'.

The mass-circulation magazines gave considerable space both to serial and short stories, publishers like Newnes, Pearson and the Harmsworths employing the best story-tellers and inviting leading commercial artists to illustrate their work. The 'nineties were the years of Sherlock Holmes's initial popularity. The first of Arthur Conan Doyle's adventures in detection, *A Study in Scarlet*, appeared in *Beeton's Christmas Annual* for 1887. The second, *The Sign of Four*, was commissioned for *Lippincott's Magazine* at a small dinner-party at which Oscar Wilde was also present, and at which Wilde undertook to write *The Picture of Dorian Gray*. Conan Doyle's story appeared in 1890 (entitled in America *The Sign of the Four*, as it still is). But it was in the George Newnes' recently established *Strand Magazine* that Holmes, in July 1891, began to gain his world public. The first six stories were so successful that Newnes invited Conan Doyle to write six more. Soon Holmes was earning a fortune for his creator, becoming one of the most famous characters in literature who never existed. Desmond McCarthy later considered him to be the most representative Englishman of the end of the nineteenth century.

A modest rival to Sherlock Holmes was Raffles, the gentleman 'amateur cracksman', a hero devised by E. W. Hornung (1866–1921), who had married Conan Doyle's sister. A. J. Raffles was an elegant, sporting thief who lived in bachelor chambers in Albany, Piccadilly, played cricket for the MCC, smoked Sullivan's cigarettes, and possessed in his friend 'Bunny' the counterpart to Holmes' biographer Dr Watson. It was in 1899 that the first volume, *Raffles, the Amateur Cracksman*, attracted the public's attention. But in 1901 Hornung decided to kill his hero, and patriotically ended his life with a Boer bullet on the South African veldt in *The Knees of the Gods*.

Meanwhile the short stories in *The Sphere* were by such popular writers as W. Pett Ridge, 'Ouida', E. Nesbit, Jerome K. Jerome, A. E. W. Mason, Marie Corelli, 'Q' (Sir Arthur Quiller-Couch), Mrs Andrew Dean, Robert Buchanan, Edward H. Cooper and F. Marion Crawford. The artists were no less talented and included T. Walter Wilson, Sidney Paget, Bernard Partridge, J. Finnemore, A. Pearse, W. B. Wollen, and Cecil Aldin. Stories in *The Graphic*, another popular illustrated weekly, were by Hall Caine, Rudyard Kipling, and H. Rider Haggard, while Sir Wemyss Reid and Frank Barret contributed serials to Cassell's *New Penny Magazine*.

In 1900 the Scottish poet and critic Robert Buchanan (who had in 1871 attacked Rossetti in his piece 'The Fleshly School of Poetry' turned his guns on the Poet of the Empire in a short essay entitled 'The Voice of the "The Hooligan": A Discussion of Kiplingism'.

'Our fashionable society is admittedly so rotten,' he wrote, 'root and branch, that not even the Queen's commanding influence can impart to it the faintest suggestion of purity, or even decency. As for our popular literature, it has been in many of its manifestations long past praying for; it has run to seed in fiction of the baser sort, seldom or never, with all its cleverness, touching the quick of human conscience; but its most extraordinary feature at this moment is the exaltation to a position of almost unexampled popularity of a writer who in his single person adumbrates, I think, all that is most deplorable, all that is most retrograde and savage, in the restless and uninstructed Hooliganism of the time.'

Buchanan attributed Kipling's success to the 'utter apathy of general readers, too idle and uninstructed to study works of any length or demand any contribution of serious thought', and to 'the rapid growth in every direction of the military or militant spirit, of the Primrose League, of aggression abroad, and indifference at home to all religious ideals—in a word, of Greater Englandism, or Imperialism'.

Kipling's muse, said this severe critic, alternated between two extremes—'the lowest cockney vulgarity and the height of what Americans called "high-falutin" '. He called Kipling's piece *Belts* 'horrible savagery—the apotheosis of the soldier who uses his belt in drunken fury to assault civilians in the street':

> But it was: 'Belts, belts, belts, an' that's one for you!'
> An' it was: 'Belts, belts, belts, an' that's done for you!'
> O buckle an' tongue
> Was the song that we sung
> From Harrison's down to the Park!

In most of Kipling's army verses Mr Buchanan could find 'no glimpse anywhere of sober and self-respecting human beings— only a wild carnival of drunken, bragging, boasting hooligans in red coats and seamen's jackets, shrieking to the sound of the banjo and applauding the English flag'. Mr Kipling's poems transported him to 'the region of low drinking-dens and gin-palaces, of dirty dissipation and drunken brawls; and the voice we hear is always the voice of a soldier whose God is a cockney "Gawd", and who is ignorant of the aspirate in either heaven or hell. Are there no Scotchmen in the ranks, no Highlanders, no men from Dublin or Tipperary, no Lancashire or Yorkshire men, no Welshmen, and no men of any kind who speak the Queen's English?'

Meanwhile a new art form, *Art Nouveau*, appeared in Europe and America in the 1890s, and would continue to find patrons in art and industry until the 1920s. There has recently been a considerable revival of interest in it. It was mainly a style of decoration using flat patterns of writhing flowers and leaves, based on natural plants rather than a formalized type of decoration. Cast-iron lilies, copper tendrils, jewelled embroidery, and furniture with heart-shaped holes, were popular.

Many *Art Nouveau* products, with their wilful asymmetry and their swirling convolvulus, certainly did not pay much attention to fitness for purpose. It is significant that some of the critics of the day actually praised them for not being 'afflicted with that distressing naïveté and "simplicity" which is the rather easy goal of a certain class of decorators'.[1]

The movement in Britain owed something to the works of William Morris and Aubrey Beardsley (1872–98), art editor of *The Yellow Book* and a brilliant decorative artist. But Beardsley's illustrations for Oscar Wilde's *Salome* were generally considered not only *avant-garde* but obscene as well.

W. H. Smith's bookstalls had first appeared on railway stations in 1848, and the comparatively cheap fiction which they supplied was immensely popular. This, with the carefully selected books in the libraries run by this famous firm, and by Charles Mudie, who began his project in 1842, and by Boots, founded at the turn of the century led to a great boom in fiction. The shilling or florin paperback or hard-back volume, often with a bright cover, dominated the bookstalls. In 1840 Charlotte Brontë had regretted that she had not existed fifty or sixty years before, when the *Ladies' Magazine* was flourishing. By the end of the century, after the era of important women writers like the Brontës, Mrs Elizabeth Gaskell and George Eliot, the popular lady novelists were in full swing, led by Miss M. E. Braddon (1837–1915), Marie Corelli (1855–1924), Ouida (1839–1908), Mrs Humphrey Ward (1851–1920) and Charlotte Yonge (1823–1901).

Marie Corelli (Minnie Mackay) chose her pseudonym with a musical career in mind, and fondly and frequently professed to be the offspring of an Italian countess, but was in fact the daughter of the English second wife of Dr Charles Mackay, a well-known journalist and composer. Her first novel, *A Romance of Two Worlds*, proved an enormous success in 1886, and *Barabbas* (1893) and *The Sorrows of Satan* (1895) made her the best-seller of her

[1] James Laver, *Victoriana*, London, 1966.

time. Her first published piece was a magazine article about the oyster-shell grotto at Margate, which she ingenuously called 'one of the world's wonders'. Her romances were equally wonderful, although by modern standards they appear turgid, sensational, and artless. Yet Miss Corelli and her many rivals held the recipe for popularity. 'I attribute my good fortune to the simple fact that I have always tried to write straight from my own heart to the hearts of others,' she said. Her immense public was said to include the Prince of Wales, Lord Tennyson, Dean Farrar, Mr Asquith, and Lord Haldane. 'You are the only woman writer of *genius* we have,' said the Prince, who read little fiction.

Her stories provided superb material for the type of Victorian public which wanted to read fiction, and enjoyed the sensational, but felt uneasy in doing so unless it had an appearance of religious and moral propaganda. Miss Corelli, who found no halo too large for her, was described as a prophet of 'good things to come in this filthy and materialistic generation', and *The Sorrows of Satan* reached its forty-second edition within five years.

The 'nineties were the heyday of the popular novelist. *Punch* depicted the 'fair authoress' of *Passionate Pauline* gazing fondly at her plain, elderly reflection in the glass and writing:

'I look into the glass, reader, and what do I see? I see a pair of laughing, *espiègle*, forget-me-not blue eyes, saucy and defiant; a *mutine* little rose-bud of a mouth, with its ever-mocking *moue*; a tiny shell-like ear, trying to play hide-and-seek in a tangled maze of rebellious russet gold; while, from underneath the satin folds of a *rose-thé* dressing gown, a dainty foot peeps coyly forth in its exquisitely-pointed gold Morocco slipper . . .' etc. etc.

There was plenty of choice and variety on the bookstalls and in the libraries in 1900. The well-known publisher T. Fisher Unwin of Paternoster Square, London, EC, was offering Scott's Waverley novels at a shilling each and *The Story of the Nations*, standard histories of all the leading countries, in fifty-five volumes, at five shillings each. Unwin's Green Cloth Library presented the novels of well-known authors at six shillings. Macmillan's at this time were doing well with Lord Roberts's autobiography, *Forty-One Years in India*, with illustrations and maps, selling at ten shillings, while Professor Friedrich Rätzel's *The History of Mankind*, with coloured plates and maps in three volumes, was sold at twelve shillings a volume, or in thirty parts at a shilling each. Mr William Heinemann, at 21 Bedford Street, WC, offered *A Little Tour in France* by Henry James, with 12 photogravure plates, 32 full-page engravings, and 40 other illustrations, for ten shillings, while *Characters of Romance*, a portfolio of sixteen pastels in colour by William Nicholson, could be bought for two quineas. From Chatto and Windus, Sir William Besant's *London*, with 125 illustrations, or *Westminster*, with 120, cost 7s 6d each. Besant's *Jerusalem*, also 7s 6d, was now in its fourth edition.

Messrs Longmans fiction list included *Savrola*, a tale of the revolution in Laurania, by Winston Spencer Churchill at six shillings; Arthur Conan Doyle's *Micah Clarke*, *The Captain of the Polestar*, *The Refugees* and *The Stark Munro Letters*, all at three and sixpence each; Bret Harte's *In the Carquinez Woods*; and the works of such varied writers as William Morris, Stanley J. Weyman, L. B. Walford, S. Levett-Yeats, E. Nesbit (Mrs Hubert Bland), Dean F. W. Farrar, H. Rider Haggard, the Earl of Beaconsfield and the humorist F. Anstey. Longmans also published the romances of Elizabeth M. Sewell, which could be bought in plain cloth for 1s 6d, or in extra cloth with gilt edges for 2s 6d. The titles ensured their instant appeal, which was considerable—*Laneton Parsonage*, *The Earl's Daughter*, *Home Life*, *Cleve Hall*, *After Life* and *Ursula*.

Before the passing of the International Copyright Act of 1891, American publishers could and did print and publish English or other books in the United States without making any payment of royalty to the author or copyright holders. All the most successful English books were published (or as the English said, 'pirated') in this way, and most American publishers paid little attention to the works of their own native writers, it being cheaper and easier to re-publish the most successful English novels. But from 1899 onwards there was a great awakening in American literature. Writers like William Dean Howells, Mark Twain, Bret Harte, Paul Leicester Ford and Charles Major began to cater for the taste of their readers by producing fiction about seemingly real American people, and native folklore, so that American publishers began gradually to look at the talent in their own country instead of simply reprinting the works of European writers, who were concerned mainly with their own countries.

In December 1895 the six most widely-read new books in the United States had all been British: *Days of Auld Lang Syne* by Ian Maclaren, *The Red Cockade* by Stanley J. Weyman, *The Chronicles of Count Antonio* by Anthony Hope, *The Sorrows of Satan* by Marie Corelli, *The Bonnie Brier Bush* by Ian Maclaren and *The Second Jungle Book* by Rudyard Kipling. On these books, under the 1891 copyright Act, the American publishers paid royalties to the British authors. But only four years later, in December 1899, the six most widely-read books in the United States were all by American writers: *Janice Meredith* by Paul Leicester Ford, *Richard Carvel* by the American Winston Churchill, *When Knighthood was a Flower* by Charles Major, *David Harum* by Edward Noyes Westcott, *Via Crucis* by F. Marion Crawford, and *Mr Dooley in the Hearts of His Countrymen* by Finlay Peter Dunne.

Many new American writers, who included Owen Wister, Thomas Nelson Page, Francis Hopkinson Smith, Hamlin Garland, Sarah Orne Jewett and Richard Harding Davis, were turning for their inspiration to characteristic American types, contemporary scenes and communities, local history and the growth of the nation. Their heroes and heroines replaced the dukes and foreign legionaires and European lovers who had for long been the accepted diet of the American man or woman seeking a library or bookstall volume. Thus 'Mr Dooley', a Chicago saloon-keeper created by Finlay Peter Dunne, was in his prime in the late 'nineties and early nineteen-hundreds. He and his friend 'Mr Hennissy' would discuss the contemporary American scene, politics, the activities of 'Mr Teddy Rosenfelt' and other leading personalities of the day, with touches of home-spun philosophy and wit which were hardly equalled until the arrival, much later, of the great Will Rogers.[1]

[1] Mark Sullivan, *op. cit.*

As far as advertising was concerned, it was certainly a vulgar, ostentatious age, yet much of the advertising had a freshness and flamboyance about it which are now endearing, and many of the manufacturers of household commodities—notably chocolate, cocoa and soap—employed the finest artists to illustrate their commercial appeals. Thus, some of the noted painters of the decade became associated with such products as Sunlight Soap, Lifebuoy Soap, Hudson's Dry Soap, Lux, Cadbury's Cocoa and Chocolate, and Rowntree's Cocoa and Chocolate.

In 1885, the year in which he was created a baronet, the artist John Everett Millais had arranged for his four-year-old grandson Willie (afterwards Admiral Sir William James) to sit for a painting. Millais painted the boy blowing bubbles from a clay pipe and sold the picture, which he called *Bubbles*, together with the copyright, to Sir William Ingram, owner and editor of the *Illustrated London News*, for whom he had painted several child studies. Ingram then sold the picture and the copyright to a Mr Thomas J. Barratt, a businessman concerned with the sale of soap. It was Mr Barratt who made Pears' soap a world commodity, and it was he who arranged to have a quarter of a million French centimes stamped with the words Pears' Soap' and put into circulation throughout Britain, and then charmed the Rev. Henry Ward Beecher into writing to every newspaper in the United States and Canada praising the virtues of the product.

On Barratt's advice, Pears bought *Bubbles* for £2200 and reproduced it in full colour in leading periodicals and on posters with a bar of the soap artfully introduced into the picture. At first Millais was horrified, but the colour reproductions were good and, although the advertisements created a sensation, and many people were shocked, he raised no objection. But the popular novelist Marie Corelli, among others, thought the commercial exploitation of a Millais painting was extremely vulgar. In *The Sorrows of Satan* her hero was made to say, 'I am one of those who think the fame of Millais as an artist was marred when he degraded himself to the level of painting the little green boy blowing bubbles of Pears' Soap. *That was an advertisement*, and that very incident in his career, trifling as it seems, will prevent his ever standing on the dignified height of distinction with such masters in Art as Romney, Sir Peter Lely, Gainsborough and Reynolds.'

Millais no doubt had a good legal case here, for he had not painted the picture as an advertisement, and the *Illustrated London News* was perfectly entitled to sell it. He might, also, have won a case against Pears for inserting a bar of soap into his picture. But instead he sat down and wrote to Miss Corelli, protesting that he had not painted the picture as an advertisement. 'What,' he asked, 'in the name of your Satan, do you mean by saying what is not true?'

From Folkestone, Miss Corelli wrote apologizing, saying that it was because of her admiration for the 'king among English painters' that she had become so angry at the thought of *Bubbles* being connected with soap. 'Gods of Olympus!' she wrote, she had *loved* the original painting but she hated this vulgar advertisement. Millais replied, saying that he appreciated her feelings. The two then became friends, and in subsequent editions of *The Sorrows of Satan* the hero's speech about Millais, *Bubbles*, and soap, was cut out.

Millais was by no means the only noted artist whose name appeared on, or was connected with, advertising. In the 1890s a Rowntree's cocoa poster was designed by the Beggarstaff brothers (James Pryde and William Nicholson) whose work was among the earliest fine art to be connected with advertising, and has since hardly been surpassed. Among the artists first employed by Lever Brothers were two of the outstanding humorous cartoonists of the period, Phil May (1864–1903) and Tom Browne (1870–1910), both contributors to *Punch*, *The Sketch*, *The Graphic* and other leading journals, the latter also being the creator of two classic American cartoon characters, Weary Willie and Tired Tim.

Frank Pegram, Garth Jones, Joseph Simpson, Septimus Scott, Will Owen, Bert Thomas, Harry Furniss, G. E. Robinson, Lawson Wood, Bernard Partridge and Dudley Hardy were other well-known artists who divided their time between their own cartoons and sketches and the advertisements which were commissioned by theatres, publishers, railway and steamship companies, and such enterprising firms as Lever's, Cadbury's, Pears', Hudson's, and Rowntree's. But there was nothing remarkable in using good artists; in France the artistic poster, associated with such distinguished names as Toulouse-Lautrec, had been in vogue in the 1880s.

William Lever introduced his first soap-flakes in the 1900s and called them Sunlight Flakes, but sales did not rise until the trade name was changed to Lux and the catch-phrase 'Lux won't shrink woollens' was used.

> Where have you been to, my Sunlight maid?
> To buy some Sunlight soap, she said.

A familiar sight in the streets of London in 1900 was a team of boy cyclists dashing among the horse traffic, each lad dressed in khaki uniform with a red sash bearing the words 'Bovril war cables'. The cyclists were sent out from hour to hour by the Bovril company to shops in various parts of London to announce special war news. It was claimed that by this method the news of the relief of Ladysmith was received thirty minutes in advance of any other source at shops in Norwood, Hammersmith, and other districts. Bovril also sent telegrams announcing the event to the headmasters of most of the leading schools in Britain, and several half-holidays were granted as a result.

Firms frequently used drawings of famous people, even the Queen, the Prince and Princess of Wales, and actors like Sir Henry Irving, to advertise their products. A whole-page photograph of Field-Marshal Lord Roberts in *The Sphere* (February 10, 1900) had the caption:

'Lord Roberts bears testimony to the value of Liebig Company's Extract (LEMCO) to the soldier in his *Forty-One Years in India.* The quantity of LEMCO already supplied to the British forces in South Africa amounts to the product of 4000 bullocks, or sufficient to make 5,128,192 breakfast cups.'

As we have seen, the troops in South Africa were not drinking only Lemco, but also the stagnant waters of the Modder and other foul rivers, and were dying in hundreds from disease. They were also being issued with Bovril, as Sir William MacCormack reported to *The Lancet* after the Battle of Tugela, and the Bovril advertisement later testified:

'Awaiting their turn the wounded were lying outside in rows which were being continually augmented by the civilian bearers coming in from the field. As each wounded man reached the hospital he was served with a hot cup of Bovril, large cans of which were boiling outside the tents.'

As now, actors and actresses readily gave their photographs and signatures to support advertisements. Thus Barton's Brighton Glycerine Cream (first introduced in 1849) published testimonials from 'the ever-youthful' Miss Ellen Terry ('I have used it for upwards of twenty years and still continue to do so'), Ellaline Terriss ('I shall be delighted to recommend it to my friends'), Zena Dare ('I find it excellent, especially after motoring') and Agnes Fraser ('It leaves a nice velvety tone to the skin'). Across the pages of *The Strand, The Windsor, The Sketch, The Illustrated London News, The Graphic, The Black and White Budget, Pearson's Magazine, The Wide World Magazine* and on railway hoardings and on the sides of houses there were splashed the advertisements of Lipton's Tea, Beck's Buckram Starch, Lever's Monkey Brand Soap, Dr Ridge's Food, Van Houten's Chocolate, Rowland's Macassar Oil, Holloway's Pills and Ointment, Coleman's Wincarnis 2s 9d and 4s 6d a bottle), Reckitt's Paris Blue, Vinolia Soap (whose firm sent halfpennies on three million tablets from the Vinolia War Fund to soldiers' families), Maza-wattee Tea, Rackham's Liver Pills, Glending's Beef and Malt Wine, and Page Woodcock's Wind Pills.

'The spirit abroad today is the spirit of ephemeral journalism,' said Robert Buchanan, 'and whatever accords with that spirit— its vulgarity, its flippancy, and its radical unintelligence—is certain to attain tremendous vogue.'

11

ENTERTAINMENT

Although the Victorian era as a whole was not notable for its theatrical achievements, the end of the century was dominated by a succession of famous actors whose popularity enabled them to dictate the policy of their theatres, to choose their plays, and often present them. These were the great actor-managers, most of whom had won their reputations by playing Shakespearean characters. The greatest of these, and the one most likely to be remembered today, was Sir Henry Irving (1838–1905), who had been knighted by the Queen in 1895 and was the premier actor on the English stage. The first actor to be knighted, he had made his first appearance in London in 1859 and his first real success as Digby Grant in *Two Roses*. His production of costume plays at the Lyceum Theatre from 1871 over a period of thirty years covered a brilliant series of plays, including *The Bells*, *Charles I*, *Eugene Aram*, his appearance as Shylock and Hamlet being noteworthy. At the Lyceum he was associated with Seymour Lucas (1849–1923) and Philip Burne-Jones, while his partner, the beautiful Ellen Terry (1848–1928), added lustre to a series of presentations which attracted world-wide attention.

By 1900, however, Sir Henry had a serious rival in Herbert Beerbohm Tree (1852–1917), whose lavish and spectacular productions at Her Majesty's Theatre, including most of Shakespeare's tragedies, owed much to the imagination of such eminent artists as Sir Lawrence Alma-Tadema (1836–1912) and Percy Anderson (1851–1928). But although after the death of Irving Sir Herbert Tree's revivals of Shakespeare were to place him at the head of his profession, or at least on an equal status to his contemporary Sir Johnston Forbes-Robertson, he was hardly a great Shakespearean actor. His *Hamlet* was described by W. S. Gilbert as being 'funny without being vulgar'; his *Macbeth* could never have fought a battle; his *Othello* could hardly have known jealousy and did not always know Shakespeare's lines; his Antony was anything but an orator in *Julius Caesar* and anything but a lover with Cleopatra; and although his Shylock could be as impressive as his Wolsey was dignified, neither had what critics called the authentic Shakespearean ring.[1]

However, Tree's productions were major theatrical events presented with splendour and realism, featuring living animals on the stage, streams and waterfalls, magnificent tableaux and huge crowds, processions of soldiers, priests and exotic dancers, so that audiences always had their money's worth. He told Hesketh Pearson, 'Shakespearean scholars say I'm wrong in tempting people to come to the theatre and giving them a spectacle instead of Shakespeare. But I prefer a spectacle on the stage to spectacles in the audience.'

Indeed, it was an age of stage showmanship. For his nightly production of *The Fall of Khartoum and Death of General Gordon* the circus impresario 'Lord' George Sanger employed four hundred 'supers', a hundred camels, two hundred Arab horses, the fifes and drums of the Grenadiers, and the pipers of the Scots Guards. The show ran at Astley's theatre for 280 consecutive performances; Sanger lost over £10,000, however, although the auditorium was always packed. But he did not lose money on his tremendous travelling circus, which he toured around Britain in immense horse-drawn wagons, setting up outside the big towns and delighting a vast public with a brand of vulgar, colourful, ostentatious showmanship which has never been surpassed, even by Hollywood.

At the Theatre Royal, Drury Lane, Sir Augustus Harris was producing many spectacular plays and pantomimes, but the chief dramatic event of 1900 was probably Tree's production at Her Majesty's of Stephen Phillip's poetical tragedy *Herod*, a bold

[1] Hesketh Pearson, *The Last Actor-Managers*, London, 1950.

experiment which was a marked success, being staged with great skill and acted with power. Hardly less popular was Henry Arthur Jones's drama *Mrs Dane's Defence*, acted by Charles Wyndham and his company at the new theatre which he had built in Charing Cross Road. J. M. Barrie's play *The Wedding Guest* also excited interest, but Frank Harris's comedy of manners, or 'no manners at all', as one critic said—entitled *Mr and Mrs Daventry*—was described as 'so repulsive and its treatment so crude that it had little claim to praise or success'. The star was a young lady soon to make a great reputation for herself, Mrs Patrick Campbell.

What choice would one have, if one wished to go to a London theatre in April 1900? Charles Hawtrey, one of the wittiest actors of his time, was appearing in a highly successful light comedy, *A Message from Mars*, at the Avenue; the musical comedy *San Toy* (with Huntley Wright, Fred Kaye, Hilda Moody and Hayden Coffin) was at Daly's; *Miss Hobbs* was at the Duke of York's; Edmund Payne and Katie Seymour were in *The Messenger Boy* at the Gaiety; Beerbohm Tree and Julia Nielson were in *A Midsummer Night's Dream* at Her Majesty's; George Alexander and H. B. Irving[1] were in *A Man of Forty* at the St James's; *Floradora* was at the Lyric; Mrs Patrick Campbell was in *Magda* at the Royalty; *An American Beauty* was at the Shaftesbury; Frank Benson's Shakespearean company was at the Lyceum (Henry Irving being on tour); *The Passport* was at Terry's in the Strand; and Miss Vane Featherstone and Miss Lettice Fairfax were in *Facing the Music* at the Strand.

At the London Hippodrome, not long opened, there was a variety show. Two months earlier the town had been delighted by a performance in which a horse called Good-Night had undressed itself and put itself to bed, an act which was followed by Herr Julius Seeth, standing alone in a cage containing twenty-one lions.

'The production of *Antony and Cleopatra* at the Lyceum,' said *The Sphere* (April 7, 1900), 'does not show Mr Benson at his best. Physically and temperamentally he seems to be quite incredible.

---

[1] The elder son of Sir Henry Irving.

The one moment of passion that Mr Benson shows is merely an exhibition of bad temper and jealousy on finding Cleopatra not disinclined to favour Caesar again. He entirely misses the mastering passion on which the whole tragedy is pivoted.'

Edward Rose had helped the novelist Anthony Hope to dramatize *Simon Dare*, in which Marie Tempest appeared during the year, as she did in *English Nell*. But the dramatization of Hope's *Rupert of Hentzau*, with George Alexander, failed to repeat the earlier success of *The Prisoner of Zenda*.

There were revivals by Cyril Maude at the Haymarket Theatre of *She Stoops to Conquer* and *The School for Scandal*; there was *The Casino Girl* at the Shaftesbury, and there were of course the music halls.

Although it is now customary to regard the Edwardian era as brighter and gayer than Victorian times, in fact by the latter part of Victoria's reign—the so-called 'naughty nineties'—the building of the majority of the houses of entertainment was completed. The city of Nottingham provides a good example. By 1867 it already possessed two music halls, and a third, the old Malt Cross hall, was opened in 1877. A typical Victorian music hall, this was a licensed house which also served grills; at weekends a number of popular musical attractions were presented, local and visiting artists performed, and the public ate and drank, but 'order and decorum' were rigidly enforced. The town's most successful theatre, however, was probably the Talbot Palace of Varieties, which had opened in Market Street in 1876. This had formerly been the Alexandra Skating Rink, but it continued as a music hall until 1887, when it became the Temperance Theatre of Varieties. By 1900 bolder spirits had prevailed, and the Gaiety Palace of Varieties opened its doors. In 1898 the Nottingham Empire had opened, booking the best acts available so that all the well-known stars of the halls visited the town, as they did other centres like Manchester, Leeds, Cardiff, Edinburgh, Glasgow, Birmingham, Bradford, Sheffield, and even much smaller towns.

Sometimes there were four or five music halls in the bigger places, but smaller populations had to be content with a 'number-two date' and the opportunity of seeing less successful performers, of whom there were many hundreds travelling up and down the country year in and year out, singers, dancers, red-nosed comedians, comediennes, impersonators, jugglers, conjurers, illusionists, reciters, animal trainers, some good, some bad, but most of them interesting. Indeed, provincial England was certainly not starved of entertainment.[1]

In 1900 Birmingham had 6 music halls, Liverpool 6, Manchester 4, Leeds 3, Sheffield 5, and Glasgow 6. In the provinces there were 226 Empires, Palaces of Variety, Hippodromes and other halls.

As for London, there were over fifty recognized music halls. These included: the Albert, the Alhambra, the Bedford, the Camberwell Palace, the Cambridge, the Canterbury, Collins', the Eastern Empire, the Empire in Leicester Square, the Holloway Empire, the New Cross Empire, the Brixton Empress Palace, the Euston Varieties, the Foresters', Gatti's (Charing Cross), Gatti's (Westminster Bridge Road), the Clapham Grand Hall, the Granville at Walham Green, the Hammersmith Palace, the Kilburn Varieties, the London, the London Hippodrome, the London Pavilion, the Marylebone, the Metropolitan, the Middlesex, the Oxford, the Palace, the Paragon, the Parthenon at Greenwich, the Queen's at Poplar, the Royal, Sadler's Wells, the Sebright, the South London, the Standard (later the Victoria Palace), the Star, the Stratford Empire, the Tivoli, the Varieties at Hoxton, the Victoria Coffee Palace.

With its origin in the cheap and primitive song and drinking saloons of mid-Victorian times, the music hall had developed into a semi-respectable institution. It offered a genuinely democratic form of entertainment, based on a zest for living, patriotism, sentiment, rich humour, and vulgarity. Except in the West End of London, at large theatres like the Empire, Palace, Alhambra and Tivoli, prices of admission were low. In his book *Prime Minister of Mirth* Mr A. E. Wilson has provided this budget for a night out at the old Oxford at the turn of the century:

[1] Roy A. Church, *Economic and Social Change in a Midland Town*, London, 1966.

	s.	d.
Cigarettes		3
Balcony seat	1	0
Programme		2
Two bitters during show		4
Hot supper		7
Final bitter		2
Total	2	6

A gallery seat at the Oxford cost only sixpence, and there were often as many as twenty first-class turns on the bill.

Charles Morton (1819–1904) was generally referred to as the 'father of the halls'. No one was more influential over so long a period in the development of popular entertainment. In 1849 he had taken over the Canterbury Arms as a licensed sing-song hall, with musical and comic turns, and towards the end of his life he was to run London's great Palace Theatre, a centre of variety. He rescued the early music halls from incompetent managers, a good example of his enterprise being the old Tivoli beer garden in the Strand, which was replaced in 1890 by a handsome building which was more like a club than a music hall. The variety side of this enterprise, under Edward Terry, failed because the older, rival halls were able to bar the booking of the best variety acts. When Charles Morton was called in the Tivoli was rebuilt on music hall lines, and he arranged an interchange of talent with his rivals, thus placing the theatre on a level with the Empire, Oxford, London Pavilion and others.

Later, Morton repeated this process at the Palace, when he took over the management after Sir Augustus Harris had landed the theatre in desperate difficulties by introducing what Charles B. Cochran later called 'drawing-room variety', which was eventually to kill vaudeville at the Coliseum Theatre. Morton's experiment with *tableaux vivants*—ladies in various stages of undress—was a daring innovation at the time but it had the personal support of the Prince of Wales, so there was no official objection.

The first Canterbury music hall, holding 1500 patrons, was

opened by Morton in 1852 with Sam Cavell and the Great Mackney as his comedians. There followed in the 1860s what came to be called the 'first music hall boom'. The second came in the 1880s, when Oswald Stoll and the rival firm of Moss and Thornton began building vast, palatial Empire variety theatres in the

leading provincial centres, driving many of the smaller halls out
of business. The 1860s saw the building of most of London's
famous music halls which were still busy at the end of the
century. These included Weston's, later the Royal, and finally
called the Holborn Empire (1857), the South London (1860),
the Bedford (1861 and rebuilt in 1899), Collins's (1862), the
Standard, later called the Victoria Palace (1863), the Metropolitan,
Edgware Road (1864) and Gatti's in Westminster Bridge Road
(1865). There were actually four successive music halls named
the Canterbury, all on the same site. These were the old Canterbury Arms Saloon, the Canterbury Hall (1849), the Canterbury
Music Hall (1852) and the last building (1876). One of the
theatre's greatest stars was George Leybourne, 'the idol of the
girls', who sang:

> Champagne Charlie is my name!
> Yes, Champagne Charlie is my name!
> Good for any game at night, my boys!
> Yes, good for any game at night, my boys—

Leybourne, who first appeared under the name of John
Saunders, had been a railway engine-fitter who was promoted to
the halls after singing in bars. His first London success was at the
Canterbury in 1865, where he was earning thirty pounds a week
even before *Champagne Charlie* brought him fame.

A characteristic feature of the mid-Victorian music hall had
been the introduction of international or national celebrities,
such as Charles Blondin (who had walked across Niagara Falls
on a tightrope), 'Captain' Matthew Webb (who first swam the
English Channel) and the prize fighters Sayers and Heenan. The
Prince of Wales had watched Blondin's daring achievement and
it was at his suggestion that the Frenchman came to London and
appeared at the Crystal Palace grounds, walking on a high
tightrope without a safety net.

However, it was the song-and-dance men and women,
especially the comics, whom the public preferred. Artists like
Alfred Vance (the 'Great Vance'), Charles Godfrey (the Masher
King), James Fawn (the Prince of Red-nosed Comedians), and

Arthur Lloyd (famous for his song *Not for Joseph*) were among the stars of the 1870s. Vance collapsed and died on the stage at the Sun Music Hall, Knightsbridge, on Boxing Day 1888.

It was at the London Pavilion that the 'Great Macdermott' first sang in 1877 the still famous song *By Jingo*:

> We don't want to fight, but by Jingo, if we do
> We've got the ships, we've got the men, we've got the money too;
> We've fought the bear before,
> And while Britons shall be true,
> The Russians *shall not have* Constantinople.

This was of course during the Russo-Turkish war, when Britons were split into factions who were pro- or anti-Turk, or pro- or anti-Russian. It was said that Disraeli sat in a box at the Pavilion to hear the song. G. H. Macdermott was first a labourer, then a seaman, and finally a music hall singer. Another of his popular songs was *Never Court a Girl who's a Dove, Dove, Dove!*

The third London Pavilion on the same site in Piccadilly Circus was opened in 1900 (as was the London Hippodrome) and was to remain the 'good old Pav', the home of music hall and musical shows, until 1934, when it would become a cinema. Here the comedians included Albert Chevalier, Gus Elen, Charles Coburn, and the young George Robey. Coburn's repertoire included *The Man Who Broke the Bank at Monte Carlo*, *Two Lovely Black Eyes*, and a coster song called *'E's all Right When You Know 'im, But You've Got to Know 'im Fust*. Among the other star artists who frequently appeared at the Pavilion were Harry Lauder, Dan Leno, and Little Tich, who was famous for his step-dancing in boots two feet long, and who had chosen his stage name because when he started his career the tall Tichborne claimant had gained attention in the law courts. 'Tich' had been born Harry Relph in 1868 and made his debut as a black-faced dancer in 1880, arriving on the halls four years later. He was as well-known abroad as in Britain, having taught himself German, French, Spanish and Italian. He was popular in America and in France he was idolized as 'the perfect English clown', appearing in our year of 1900 at the Exposition in Paris. He was to die in 1928, aged fifty-nine.

With the possible exception of Grimaldi, Dan Leno was the most admired and beloved comedian of the English theatre. His real name was George Wild Galvin, and he had been born in Eve Court, King's Cross, London, in 1861, a slum street now covered by St. Pancras station. Long before he considered himself a comedian he became champion clog dancer of the world, and as a boy appeared with his parents on the stage of the Argyle music hall, Birkenhead. His provincial success led to his engagement in London and he worked three halls a night, becoming a comedian at the Middlesex, where the manager suggested he should sing a comic song called *Milk for the Twins*.

Real fame came when Leno appeared in pantomime at the Theatre Royal, Drury Lane, where he was to be the leading comedian for fifteen years. It is said that as a boy he had knelt on the steps and prayed he might one day work there.

'Always he was exactly the character about whom he sang,' W. Macqueen Pope has recalled.[1] 'He could fill the stage with imaginary people and by his art you saw and heard them. He made everything real. You saw the customers when he was a shopwalker, you heard the trains when he was the guard, and when he was a huntsman there was the whole meet before you . . . but when he mentioned that he preceded the horse over the fence, you both heard and felt the impact. *The Tower of London* was a masterpiece. There he was, a guide showing the people around, but never losing sight of the refreshment room, to which he constantly drew attention. You grew thirstier and thirstier. . . . His clothes always gave him perpetual trouble, shirts and collars were always at war with him, trousers were too big and coats too long. But he always won. What he did with a harp beggars description. He would suddenly appear to be at a loss for a word, it would evade him, he would gesture, he would think and concentrate, he would have his audience on tenterhooks—they wanted to shout and tell him—and then out would come that wonderful smile of his and a word entirely different from the one

[1] W. Macqueen Pope, *Pillars of Drury Lane*, London, 1954.

19. G. A. Smith's film studio at Hove in 1900, showing stage set for filming
Mary Jane's Mishap

20. The Paris Exposition, 1900

21, 22, 23, 24. England's four greatest music-hall stars: Little Tich, Dan Leno, Marie Lloyd and Albert Chevalier

they expected would knock them out of their seats with laughter.'

Dan Leno was to die tragically and suddenly in 1904, aged forty-three, after his release from an asylum. Crowds three deep were to line the funeral route of over three miles. It is typical of the time that he was not listed in *Who's Who*.

Albert Chevalier (1861–1923) was a coster comedian who made his debut at the Pavilion, being paid £12 a week in 1891 for three performances a night. But even before 1914 he was to earn several hundreds a week singing *My Old Dutch, Knocked 'em in the Old Kent Road*, and other favourites.

Other darlings of the halls at the turn of the century included Harry Champion (1866–1942), whose *Any Old Iron* is still sung, G. H. Chirgwin (the White-Eyed Kaffir), the coster comics Alec Hurley, Gus Elen, Joe Elvin, the Dickens impersonator Bransby Williams, and the comediennes Florrie Forde, Vesta Victoria, Vesta Tilley, and Marie Lloyd (Mrs Alec Hurley). Born in Leeds, Vesta Victoria (1874–1951) was the daughter of a music hall artist named Joe Lawrence and she made her debut when only four, her later success including *Our Lodger's such a Nice Young Man, Daddy Wouldn't Buy Me a Bow-Wow* and *Waiting at the Church*. She was to retire in 1920 but would return for a few years in 1926.

Marie Lloyd, born Matilda Wood at Hoxton in 1870, the daughter of a waiter at the Grecian Saloon, was probably the most popular of all the women artists of the halls. She made her debut as Bella Delmere in 1885, singing *The Boy I Love is up in the Gallery*. Her extensive repertoire included *Then You Wink the Other Eye* (1890), *Oh, Mr Porter* (1893), *A Little of What You Fancy Does You Good*, and *Twiggy-Voo*. She sang in a rich, fruity cockney voice and her songs were often saucy. Of her legendary gifts, Charles B. Cochran was later to say, 'She had, beyond any artist that I have ever seen, the supreme gift of timing. The delicacy of her indelicacies was delicious. I unhesitatingly place her among the very great artists I have seen in my life.' During her thirty-five years at the top of her profession she probably earned about £250,000, at a time when income tax was very low, but when she died in 1922 she left nothing but the previous week's salary, having given away or spent all her money, mostly for the benefit of other people.

George Robey, later to be called 'the Prime Minister of Mirth', had made his debut in 1891, his first hit being *The Simple Pimple*, written by E. W. Rogers. With his large eyebrows, a clerical coat, and a flat bowler hat, he at once claimed distinction, both for his ability as a performer and for the audacity of some of his material. After telling a particularly risqué joke he would look surprised, raise his eyebrows, adopt a scandalized air, and advise the audience: 'Please! I meantersay! Kindly temper your hilarity with a modicum of reserve!' Thus the vulgar, rich way in which he put over songs like *Bang Went the Chance of a Lifetime*, *Archibald, Certainly Not!* and *Oh, How Rude!* led the audience to see more in the words than was at first obvious. He even appeared, in his younger days, dressed as the Queen, the widow of Windsor. He was to be knighted in 1954, in the last year of his life.

It was in 1900, at Gatti's, that Harry Lauder made his first London appearance after working for ten years in a Scottish coal mine and performing in working men's clubs as an amateur. He introduced his particular style of homely Scots songs to English audiences, including *The Safest of the Family*, *I Love a Lassie*, *Just a Wee Deoch-an-Doris* and *Roamin' in the Gloamin'*, and he was one of the first music hall artists to record for the phonograph. He was to be knighted for his war service in 1919, and would die in 1950 at the age of seventy-nine.

Vesta Tilley, described as 'the London Idol', had first appeared in 1869 at the St George's Hall, Nottingham, where her father was the chairman and master of ceremonies. A year later she donned a boy's suit and became a male impersonator, arriving in 1878 at the Royal Holborn. Her popular character studies of smart men-about-town, 'mashers', soldiers and sailors, set the pattern for her many imitators and rivals. Her successes included *Following in Father's Footsteps*, *Jolly Good Luck to the Girl who loves a Soldier* and *The Army of Today's All Right*. She married Walter de Frece, a music hall proprietor and MP, and later became Lady de Frece, living to the age of eighty-eight.

There were of course many others, too numerous to mention in detail—the great male impersonators, Fanny Robina, Millie Hilton and Ella Shields; Tom Leamore singing *Percy from Pimlico*; the eccentric Nellie Wallace with her moth-eaten fur tippet; George Beauchamp singing *Get Your Hair Cut* and thus adding an expression to the English language which has certainly not died; the Canadian R. G. Knowles; the eccentric comedian T. E. Dunville; the ventriloquist Fred Russell; Marie Kendall; Wilkie Bard; and Arthur Roberts (1852–1933) whom James Agate thought 'one of the greatest artists the English music hall has ever known. . . . His ten minutes were the most delirious known to the evening-dress habitués of the halls.'

The many black-faced coon singers were headed by Eugene Stratton, G. H. Chirgwin (the White-Eyed Kaffir) and later G. H. Elliott. Stratton had been born in America and arrived in England in 1881 with a minstrel show, going on the halls with his act in 1892. Many of his songs were written by Leslie Stuart, the most popular being *The Lily of Laguna* and *Little Dolly Daydreams*. G. H. Chirgwin first appeared at the Oxford in 1878, and later adopted a diamond-shaped white patch around his right eye. G. H. Elliott was not to appear in London until 1902, singing coon songs and dancing in the same tradition.

Ada Reeve was born in Whitechapel in 1874, first appearing as a child singer and making her music hall debut at Sebright's, Holloway, in 1886. Two years later she was singing at Gatti's, Charing Cross, and in 1893 she toured America. In 1894 George Edwards engaged her for musical comedy at the Gaiety, and she continued to appear before the public, singing on her ninetieth birthday in 1964 in the theatre under the arches in Villiers Street, London, where she had first appeared in 1888.[1]

Bridging the gap between the music halls and the legitimate stage were the popular musical players, of whom Sir Henry Lytton (1865–1936) was the undisputed king, a Savoyard who appeared in Gilbert and Sullivan's satirical comic operas and later in musical comedy.

Gilbert and Sullivan drew on public figures and national events

[1] Raymond Mander and Joe Mitchenson, *British Music Hall*, London, 1965.

179

and failings for their satire and everyone knew at whom and at what the arrows were aimed. The music halls were more blatantly patriotic and jingoistic. With full sincerity a vocalist would sing of *The Union Jack of Dear Old England* and the audience would join in the rousing chorus. 'In time of war and political stress,' wrote J. B. Booth, 'the music hall bards reflected the national feeling, for in the old days some of us remember we were a singing nation in moments of strain.' Thus Charles Godfrey sang *On Guard*, while *Her Lad in the Scotch Brigade* was a Sudan war song which was still topical when the Boer War started. George Lashwood sang *The Death or Glory Boys* and *The Gallant Twenty-First*, and *Tommy, Tommy Atkins* lived on for long after Hayden Coffin introduced it in 1893 in *A Gaiety Girl*. Leslie Stuart's stirring *Soldiers of the Queen* (1881) had not died by the end of the reign, while *Goodbye, Dolly Gray*, sung by the Australian baritone Hamilton Hill in 1900, still conjures up a picture of a soldier in khaki leaving on a troop train or liner for South Africa, perhaps never to return:

> Goodbye, Dolly, I must leave you,
> Though it breaks my heart to go.
> Something tells me I am needed
> At the front to fight the foe.
> Look! the soldier boys are marching,
> And I can no longer stay.
> Hark! I hear the bugle calling;
> Goodbye, Dolly Gray.

Farewell, My Bluebell was another Boer War song (with its soldiers' parody *I Shall Be Boozing at the Old Blue Bell*), as were *Goodbye, Little Girl, Goodbye, You Can't Call Them Traitors Now* (in praise of the Irish troops in the war), and Leo Dryden's *Bravo, Dublin Fusiliers!*

Many of the songs sung in the halls and played on street barrel-organs in the 'nineties had been written in the 'eighties, or earlier. The vogue of the bicycle was reflected in one of the most popular verses, still with us today, known as *Daisy Bell* and first sung in 1892 by Katie Lawrence wearing bloomers and woollen stockings:

Daisy, Daisy, give me your answer true.
I'm half crazy, all for the love of you!
It won't be a stylish marriage,
I can't afford a carriage,
But you'll look sweet
Upon the seat
Of a bicycle built for two!

Four years later had come *There'll Be a Hot Time in the Old Town Tonight*, an American favourite which enjoyed a moderate success in Europe. Other popular songs of the period included *After the Ball* (1892), *Where Did You Get That Hat?* (1888), *Little Annie Rooney* (1890), *Only a Bird in a Gilded Cage* (1899), *Ta-ra-ra Boom de-Ay* (1892), *Two Little Girls in Blue* (1893), *The Rosary* (1898), and *And Her Golden Hair Was Hanging Down Her Back* (1894). From about 1870 onwards sentimental, humorous or patriotic songs had helped to lift the working classes a little way out of their drab lives. The most successful had simple refrains, like *Comrades, Let 'Em All Come* (sung by Harry Randall), *A Boy's Best Friend is His Mother, Ask a Policeman, The Miner's Dream of Home, Molly and I and the Baby, Down the Road*, and the evergreen *At Trinity Church*, sung by Tom Costello.

Most of these songs originated in the period 1890–1895, and were to continue into the Edwardian period and beyond. Gus Elen's memorable *If It Wasn't for the Houses in Between* was as much a social commentary as *Glorious Beer*, the comical *At the Football Match Last Saturday*, the sentimental *Shall I Be An Angel, Daddy?* and *Three Little Words* (*I Love You*). The song *Let 'Em All Come* spilled on into the 1914 war, but few today recall the words of *Blind Little Irish Girl* or *Creep Mouse*.

Writers and singers were nothing if not topical. Winston Spencer Churchill's adventures in South Africa led the comedian T. E. Dunville to appear in 1900 as 'Brimstone Chapel', dressed in khaki and hung with countless water bottles, field glasses and military accoutrements, to sing *The War Correspondent on the Front*. And there was also Florrie Forde, who had arrived in

England from Australia in 1897 and was already buxom, singing *Has Anybody Here Seen a German Band?*, *Flanagan*, *Down at the Old Bull and Bush* and *Has Anybody Here seen Kelly?*.

Raymond Mander and Joe Mitchenson have pointed out that, although the music hall had now moved away from the public house and was filled by middle-class patrons as well as the working classes, a visit to a hall was still taboo to many people unless they wished to be considered 'bohemian' or 'fast'. Respectable middle-class families could see the music hall stars only at Christmas in the pantomimes. It was Sir Augustus Harris who, in 1880, banished from Drury Lane the old-fashioned traditional pantomimes and imported comics and singers from the halls, introducing feminine principal boys for the first time, with eccentric dames played by Dan Leno.

Indeed there were two kinds of music hall, and something for everyone. Some were classed as 'low'; others were 'high' or 'family'. In 1900 The Palace in Cambridge Circus was 'refined', and it suffered from this defect, while the Empire in Leicester Square was described as 'one of the most gorgeously appointed and most fashionable variety theatres in Europe, and one in which evening dress is very much in evidence. ... No one can deny the dazzling brilliance of the scene at, say, 10.30 p.m.; no wonder that the Empire lounge should be the favourite resort of the Oriental potentate in London.'

Far from the gaslight and evening entertainments of the cities there were more humble amusements, which have vanished as surely as the real music hall has disappeared. People sang or played the piano or entertained at home, and most seaside towns of any size had their pierrots or minstrel shows or children's entertainers, often appearing on the end of the pier or on stages erected on the sands. Thus the Thespian Concert Party at Bognor in 1900 was headed by 'Uncle George' (George Edgar) and the troupe included Gus Davis from the Moore and Burgess Minstrels, Charles Crannis (ventriloquist), Fred Warwick (versatile comedian) and Harry Everett (pianist). Their humour was topical; their songs were catchy; the audience joined in. Maybe they were not great stars, but in their time they were good family entertainers.

The troupe had been in Bognor since 1897 and performed twice daily during the summer on the sands and West Parade, and also at the Pier Hotel in the evening after 9 p.m. A children's singing competition was held, a fresh song being taught each week.

Their rivals at Blackpool, Scarborough, Ilfracombe, Margate, Hastings, Ramsgate, Newquay, Ryde, Paignton, Torquay, Weymouth, and in dozens of other resorts around the coast of Britain, were at this time energetically singing and dancing or playing harmoniums or pianos to delight visitors. A week or a fortnight's holiday was as much as most families could afford and a great deal more than was possible for many people:

> Oh, I do like to be beside the seaside,
> Oh, I do like to be beside the sea...

In America at this time the songs of the 'nineties were still very much in vogue and were being imported to Britain, English comedians singing the ever-popular:

> Where did you get that hat,
> Where did you get that tile?
> Isn't it a nobby one
> And just the proper style?
> I should like to have one
> Just the same as that!
> Where'er I go they'd shout 'Hello!'
> Where did you get that hat?

Other American songs of the period still popular in 1900 included *Sunshine of Paradise Alley* (1895), *The Picture That is Turned to the Wall* (1891), *Sucking Cider Through a Straw* (1891), *The Moth and the Flame* (1898), *She Was Bred in Old Kentucky* (1898), *The Cat Came Back* (1892), *And Her Golden Hair Was Hanging Down Her Back* (1894), *Rastus on Parade* (1896), *Two Little Girls in Blue* (1893) and *My Sweetheart's the Man in the Moon* (1892). *The Rosary* was sung for the first time in Boston by Francis Rogers in February 1896. As in Britain, the interest in music and the sale of sheet music were greatly stimulated by the increase of wealth in the middle classes that enabled larger numbers of people to play musical instruments at home, the old upright piano being especially popular and convenient in front parlours, where it was almost a status symbol.[1]

Some of the world's best-known military marches were being composed by John Philip Sousa, for twelve years leader of the United States Marine Band. His marches not only inspired the nation but were taken up wherever there were military bands, often served as dance music, and directly inspired the two-step. He received only ninety dollars for writing *Stars and Stripes Forever* and had sold his first song to a publisher by trading it for a cheap dictionary. Among Sousa's other rousing marches are *The Washington Post, Liberty Hall, High School Cadets, King Cotton* and *El Capitan*. In many ways he represented the new, vigorous, national feeling which was emerging in his country.

Although in retrospect the Victorian music hall appears to have been a most attractive institution, one to which most of us would like to be whisked back through the years, even if only for a night, yet there was clearly a similarity, a constant repetition, in most of the programmes. The same songs continued to be sung year after year, artists copied one another, there were hundreds of almost identical comedians, and many not only looked alike but stole one another's gags, eccentricities, and techniques.

A Tivoli programme chosen at random during the winter of 1893 shows how, by later standards, the choice of artists was curiously unimaginative and the turns lacking in contrast. The first four turns were comedians—Arthur Rigby, George Robey, Harry Freeman, and Edwin Boyle. Then came a singer and a black-faced stump-orator, and three more comedians—Dan Leno, Kate James and Albert Chevalier. A serio-comic, a dancer, and Eugene Stratton, and then the balance of the programme was devoted to more comedians, including Little Tich and Harry Randall. Altogether there were thirteen comedians in a programme of twenty-seven items, and throughout the whole evening there was never more than one person on the stage at a time. To be able to live together on the same bill each of the thirteen had to develop a distinct brand of humour, a charac-

---

[1] Mark Sullivan, *op. cit.*

teristic and unmistakable make-up and line of business. But what a bill!

The artists, their turn at one theatre finished, went on to the next. Still in make-up, they got into the cab waiting for them at the Tivoli stage-door and went to the Oxford; from there to the Pavilion; and then probably to an outlying hall. Three or four appearances in an evening in different places was just part of their routine.[1] Thus the male impersonator Millie Hilton had made her début at the Cambridge, the Canterbury and the Metropolitan on the same night in 1888, and the success of Lottie Collins singing *Ta-ra-ra-Boom de-Ay!* at the Grand, Islington, led to her introduction, with the same song, into the Gaiety theatre at the same time as she was playing at Islington.

Few of us would not grasp the opportunity to return for a short time to the so-called 'good old days' and judge for ourselves what these singers and comedians were really like. But were they so talented? Two long-playing gramophone records give us some idea, although the recordings, made long before the introduction of the electrical process, are primitive. The first, entitled *The Golden Age of the Music Hall* (Delta records, No. TQD 3030), gives us songs by Gus Elen, Vesta Victoria, Albert Chevalier, Marie Lloyd, Dan Leno (reciting *The Robin* and *The Tower of London*), Louis Bradfield, George Robey, Arthur Roberts, Henry Lytton, Little Tich and Florrie Forde. The second, *Golden Voices of the Music Hall* (Decca, Ace of Clubs series: ACL 1077), presents Ella Shields, Tom Leamore, Nellie Wallace, Gus Elen, Hetty King, Albert Whelan and Gertie Gitana. Spanning the years, they tell us something of what these artists were really like. Although the recordings are antique by modern standards, and are sometimes faint and scratchy, the artistry is distinctly apparent, enabling us to hear the voices of entertainers of a bygone age, and the songs with which they delighted their public.

[1] Felix Barker, *The House that Stoll Built*, London, 1957.

12

ANIMATED PICTURES

The Victorians liked optical illusions and made toys in which men or animals appeared to run or move in rotating cylinders. Magic lanterns had been in vogue since the sixteenth century and were immensely popular in Victorian households, schools, village institutes, working men's clubs and town halls, where visiting lecturers used them to illustrate wordy talks about darkest Africa, the wonders of South America, unknown China, and so on. It was not until the late 1880s that the American George Eastman, founder of the Kodak company, successfully substituted sensitized celluloid film for the glass plates and papers which had hitherto been used for negatives. Thus the cheap Kodak 'Brownie' camera prepared the way for the perfection of cinematography.

On June 21, 1889 a British photographer named William Friese-Greene took out a patent in London covering many of the principles of modern cinematography. His experiments had proved that a length of film could pass through a projector with an intermittent movement, each frame being momentarily held in front of the lamp, a shutter masking the change from frame to frame.

The discovery of motion pictures has been attributed to several people, pioneers in America, France, Britain and Germany, and is still disputed. William Friese-Greene's claim is probably the best, but there were many other contributors to the final solution and the development of the invention: Thomas Armat, Birt Acres, Max Skladanowsky, Louis le Prince, the Lumière brothers, Thomas A. Edison and his English assistant Kennedy Dickson,

Robert W. Paul and others, have all been held to have invented cinematography.

On 20 February, 1896 a programme of short films was first publicly projected to an audience in Britain, having already been seen in France. The occasion was the presentation by the brothers Louis and August Lumière of a performance of what they called their Cinematographe at the Marlborough Hall in Regent Street, London, on the site of the modern Polytechnic. In the first programme there was sandwiched between a short film taken at the Lumière photographic factory at Lyons and a picture showing the arrival of the mail boat at Folkestone a brief comic interlude entitled *Teasing the Gardener*. In this a child was seen stepping on a hose. The gardener, looking into the hose, suddenly got wet.

While Felicien Trewey, on behalf of the Lumière brothers, was introducing the programme at the Marlborough Hall, a London instrument-maker named Robert W. Paul was demonstrating his Theatrograph projector privately. A few months later he showed his first coloured moving pictures, hand-tinted by a lantern slide colourist.

To feed the Cinematographe, the Theatrograph, and the many rival machines which soon appeared, large numbers of new films were required. At first familiar scenes and brief incidents were captured by the cameras; the novelty of what were called 'animated pictures' was so great that almost anything, from a coastal gale to a lion in the London Zoo, was considered entertaining. The first story films were simply little incidents, often comic, enacted either by hired players or friends of the 'film manufacturer'. From the earliest days of the film up to 1910 the average moving picture only took from one to fifteen minutes to show. The first films were merely brief glimpses of everyday scenes, but people flocked to see them in local halls, converted shops, circus side-shows, and the music halls, where they were presented as an act.

In America the inventor Thomas Edison was making films for his Kinetoscope peep-show cabinet. Although other pioneers were projecting pictures on to screens he saw no future in this and preferred the 'coin in the slot' principle, which had the disadvantage of allowing only one person at a time to view the pictures. Looking through a narrow slit in a rotating shutter at a continuously running strip of film moving in front of an electric light bulb, the spectator watched a short comedy sequence or a street scene, or a series of pictures filmed on Long Island, produced by the Edison Company.

Kennedy Dickson presented to Edison what was probably the world's first 'talking film'. Dickson himself was seen in the Kinetophone peep-show cabinet, walking across a room and raising his hat, while his voice was heard to say, 'Good morning, Mr Edison. Glad to see you back. Hope you will like the Kinetophone. To show the synchronization I will lift my hat and count up to ten.'

Four years later Dickson built what was called the 'Black Maria' studio at West Orange, New Jersey, a dark shed mounted on a revolving platform to catch the sun. And it was here, in 1894, that an employee named Fred Ott was filmed sneezing, a comic picture which was seen but not heard in hundreds of peep-show machines all over the world.

In June 1895, five months after the first Lumière show in France, Thomas Armat of Washington discovered the principle of modern film projection, and in September successfully demonstrated a greatly improved machine at the Cotton States Exhibition in Atlanta, Georgia. The films he showed were those issued by Edison for his peep-show, and his projector was called the Vitascope. Soon afterwards Armat showed his pictures to Koster and Bial's music hall in Herald Square, New York, including in his programme two Lumière films, *Mammy Washing Her Child* and *Teasing the Gardener*. In the same year Max Skladanowsky exhibited a programme of films at the Winter Gardens, Berlin.

In 1896 Bert Bernard took the first film of the Lord Mayor's show in London, and a year later he filmed about 1200 feet of stock during the passing of Queen Victoria's Diamond Jubilee procession.

'Very tiring to the eyes,' said the Queen, 'but worth a headache to have seen such a marvel.' Although she had accepted spectacles in 1877 because of her failing eyesight, it was not until 1899 that she wore them in public.

In 1896 Robert W. Paul, who had adapted an Edison peep-show machine as a projector, decided to film the Derby. Hiring a wagonette, he drove to Epsom and set up his camera near the racecourse rails. A showman, seeing the camera and its handle, thought he was setting up a rival peep-show and tried to turn Paul's wagonette over. The police were summoned.

'We were given a pretty rough handling,' Paul recalled later.[1] 'At first the policemen thought it was a fracas between a couple of rival Punch and Judy men, but when I explained matters they were very interested. Sending the gypsy about his own business, they helped me tie my vehicle to the rails so that no one could shift it.'

The pictures were good, the race being won by the Prince of Wales's horse Persimmon, a popular victory. Hitherto Paul had been showing Bert Bernard's films at the Alhambra Theatre, Leicester Square, as part of the variety show. Now he quickly developed his Derby film and showed it that same night to an enthusiastic theatre audience at the Alhambra.

'They went crazy,' he recalled. 'The win was a popular one with the crowds and when I ran the film the following night they would not let me go. I had to re-wind the film and show it over and over again. They stood on the seats and cheered it every time. Then they sang *God Bless the Prince of Wales*. I remember that some of the artistes on the bill were a little jealous; I felt a little guilty about it myself for I suddenly realized while I was rewinding between one of the many repetitions of the film that, apart from the hire of the wagonette, the picture had only cost me fifteen shillings to make. People came to see it night after night and I showed it at other halls, and I was receiving a pound a minute for showing it every time it went on the screen.'

From 1896 onwards Robert Paul's motion-picture business in Hatton Garden boomed and he was besieged by customers demanding to buy projectors. The Alhambra contract had originally been for a fortnight, but Paul stayed on for four years

[1] Leslie Wood, *The Miracle of the Movies*, London, 1947.

and with the help of Sir Augustus Harris of Drury Lane gave film shows at Olympia and in many theatres and music halls. Short comic incidents were filmed on the roof of the Alhambra, and an outdoor 'stage' was later built in a field at New Southwick, where little comedies, tragedies, melodramas and many 'trick' and 'magic' subjects were produced. As early as 1899 this pioneer studio was equipped with a camera trolley, a moving stand fitted with wheels, on which the camera could achieve tracking and zooming shots while the players walked or stood still, thus adding an extra dimension to the moving pictures, although for some fourteen years the static camera was still generally used in both Europe and America.

Another pioneer at work during the period was Cecil M. Hepworth, regarded by many as the 'father of British films'. An expert with magic lanterns and optical lenses, he first became interested in the new phenomenon in 1893 when Birt Acres told him he had been invited to show some of his films at Marlborough House on the occasion of the wedding of the Duke of York to Princess Mary (May) of Teck.

'At that time I had never heard of films,' said Hepworth later. 'I could only guess what he was talking about, but I must have surmised that some kind of lantern was involved and that would have been enough for me. . . . We duly arrived at Marlborough House with the gear, projector, lamp, resistance and wire and all the rest of it. The whole place was gaily decorated and there was a considerable air of fuss and tension. Birt Acres was a man who perspired easily. He fully lived up to his reputation in this respect. We set the apparatus up in a sort of tent which was an annexe to the room where the guests were to assemble for the show. I remember being mildly surprised when the Prince of Wales came over and talked to us when we were getting the show ready in this kind of small ante-room. He seemed to speak with a fairly strong German accent. But I do not remember being greatly impressed with the pictures. . . . One of them did startle me, though; it was a picture of a great wave rushing into the mouth of a cave and bursting into clouds of spray.'

Hepworth's first motion picture camera was made at Prest-

191

wich and was owned by Thomas R. Dallmeyer, who asked Hepworth to accompany him to film the Diamond Jubilee of 1897, but the camera unaccountably jammed at the critical moment and no pictures were taken. Bert Bernard, with his camera at a different vantage point, outside St Paul's Cathedral, was more fortunate.

For the Warwick Trading Company, a firm founded by the pioneer Charles Urban, young Hepworth filmed the Oxford and Cambridge boat race of March 1898, and then went on to make his own films of many topical events, using a villa at Walton-on-Thames, Surrey, as his laboratory, workshop, and headquarters. The Warwick Company, like its many rivals in 'Flicker Alley' (Cecil Court, St Martin's Lane, London), was a firm which made, bought and sold motion pictures by the foot. Hepworth had a small bank balance, due largely to his having invented an arc lamp and a developing machine for film stock. From his little house in Walton, The Rosary in Hurst Grove, he decided to supply Flicker Alley with the films they needed. The rent was £36 a year, and here, within the narrow confines of his back garden, front sitting-room, kitchen, bathroom and scullery, he wrote, produced, developed and printed for distribution a regular supply of short films. At first he made pictures for a small market; later he produced them for the world. The scullery housed a second-hand gas engine which provided the power; the two bedrooms were fitted out as film processing and drying rooms, and the front room became an office. The first 'studio' was the back garden, where after a few months an eight-by-fifteen-foot wooden platform was erected, with upright posts to support the modest scenery, which Hepworth helped to paint. History was made and recorded at Walton, and by 1903 a real 'studio' was erected in the garden, a building with a glass roof to keep out the rain and catch the sun. There were ten Westminster incandescent arc lamps to supplement the natural light.

Hepworth's 'actualities' or 'topicals', as they were called, were popular. 'I found that the Henley Regatta of 1900 attracted our roving attention for seven scenes, and that perhaps suggested the possibility of taking two or three 'scenics' on the upper

25. Worcester horse tram, 1890

26. Piccadilly Circus in 1899

27. L. & N.W.R. four-cylinder compound engine *La France*, built in March, 1900 and sent to the Paris Exhibition where it won the gold medal for excellence of workmanship

Thames, punctuated with a river panorama of a Cornish village. Then we became patriotic and immortalized some modern war-ships, contrasting them with the old sailing frigates used as training ships for the Navy.'[1]

The topical appeal of news in films was apparent. The departure of the City Imperial Volunteers for South Africa was filmed in January 1900, Hepworth standing on the gangway of the *Garth Castle* to photograph the troops, with his camera cranking as they came up on the ship. The record of Queen Victoria's visit to Dublin ran to three little films totalling 250 feet. The arrival of HMS *Powerful*, with the returning heroes of Ladysmith on board, was another scoop, as was Hepworth's filming of the solar eclipse of May 1900, for which he took his camera and equipment to Algiers. No less enterprising was the American Biograph Company, which despatched an English cameraman, Mr J. Rosenthal, to South Africa on the outbreak of war, thus securing the first motion pictures of an army in action.

A notable French invention of the time was the Cinéorama, developed and patented in 1897, when practical projectors were in their infancy. To view this entertainment 200 people stood or sat in the basket of a balloon while above their heads hung the lower part of a huge gas bag and around them were all the proper rigging and ballast. The great craft was still at anchor. Then, suddenly, the captain of the balloon announced, 'Ladies and gentlemen, we are about to leave the garden of the Tuileries. Cast off!' The balloon seemed to ascend, as hand-coloured films in ten motion-picture projectors beneath the basket threw on to a circular wall some 300 feet in circumference a vista of Paris of 1900 falling away below the spectators. Then came 'a minute of obscurity', or 'fade', while the officer announced, 'We are about to land in the great square of Brussells'. After that the balloon took its passengers to England, the Riviera, Spain, Tunis, the Sahara, and back to Paris for the final descent. On the trip the balloonists saw such spectacles as a bullfight, a carnival, cavalry charges, a storm at sea, and a desert caravan of camels.

The Cinéorama was one of the features of the great Paris

[1] Cecil M. Hepworth, *Came the Dawn*, London, 1951.

exhibition of 1900—well named 'L'Exposition Universelle'—
and here there was not only a round cinema screen but also other
film shows which broke experimental ground. Visitors heard via
the phonograph, as well as saw, three exhibits of 'talkies', one of
them graced by the French stage stars Sarah Bernhardt and
Benoit Coquelin. *Maréorama* set its audiences on the bridge of a
steamship, and took them out of the harbour of Marseilles into a
storm at sea, and on to Algiers. This anticipated by four years
the American *Hale's Tours* that seated the spectators in a railroad
car. In England Cecil Hepworth had already mounted his camera
on to the front of moving locomotives for his *Phantom Rides*.
Finally, Paris saw pictures on a screen 70 feet wide by 53 feet
high.

When the Lumière brothers were asked to create an *écran géant*
for the exhibition's Galerie des Machines, they began by installing
a screen 100 by 80 feet, as high as a six-storey house. Alterations
in the building before the fair opened forced them to reduce the
screen to 70 by 53 feet, still twice the height of a cinema screen
today. By immersing the giant cloth in a tank of water they were
able to make it translucent and managed to show their films to a
gigantic audience of 25,000 at a time, half on each side of the
screen. It would not be until 1919, at a summer conference of the
Methodist Church at Columbus, Ohio, that Lorenzo Del Riccio
was to set up the world's largest screen, 165 by 135 feet. [1]

By 1900 there were several small film-production centres in
England turning out short subjects and little features or 'picture
plays' every week. Some were converted greenhouses; some
were open-air 'stages' in back gardens; others were old factory
buildings. One was at Loughborough Junction, where on a
rented plot of land a wooden platform served as a stage for the
Drury Lane impresario Arthur Collins, who 'stage managed' (or
directed) animated pictures for the English branch of the famous
French firm, the Gaumont Company. The scenery and wings in
these open-air 'studios' resembled theatrical scenery, sometimes
had footlights, and were often borrowed from theatres.

G. A. Smith's little 'studio' at Hove, Sussex, was in full

[1] Kenneth Macgowan, *Behind the Screen*, London, 1966.

production in 1900, a weekly quota of short dramas and comedies and local actualities being made. Another Hove pioneer was J. A. Williamson whom Smith introduced to films. He was probably the first man to cut his scenes from medium shot to close-up, while, like Hepworth at Walton-on-Thames and Robert Paul, he employed a camera mounted on wheels. The curious may still see the name 'Kinemacolor' painted faintly on the wall of his studio close to Hove station, on the south side of the Hove-Brighton railway line.

Meanwhile in Paris the pioneer of trick and table-top photography, Georges Méliès, who had started as a conjurer, was turning out hundreds of 'magic' films. He had owned the Théâtre Robert-Houdin, a house devoted to mystery, and he discovered in the motion picture a new way of producing magic. He offered the Lumière brothers 10,000 francs for one of their cameras, and when they refused he made one from parts supplied from England by Robert Paul. In April 1896, when the American Vitascope first reached New York, Méliès was already showing trick motion pictures at the Théâtre Robert-Houdin, and in this year he made more than seventy-five little films of about sixty-five feet. He learned how to produce ghosts by double exposure; he developed the 'fade', slow motion and fast motion, and in the spring of 1897 he built his first studio, glassed-in at a time when most other pioneers were filming in the open. His *Dreyfus Affair* (1899) was the first of his long films, running to about 715 feet and, for probably the first time in motion-picture history, there were as many as twelve long scenes. By 1902 he was to employ thirty scenes in his famous *A Trip to the Moon*, and forty-three in *An Impossible Voyage* (1904). *Joan of Arc*, made in 1900, was described in his catalogue as 'a grand spectacular production in twelve scenes. About five hundred persons enacting the scenes, all superbly costumed. Running time about fifteen minutes.' Between 1896 and his retirement in 1913, Méliès made some five hundred films.

The Electric Palace, Gems, and Coronation Theatres were yet to come, but they were not far off. Meanwhile, in 1900, British showmen were inviting patrons into tents and halls and converted shops to watch the first boxing film made under artificial light, the Jeffries-Sharkey championship fight which had been filmed by William A. Brady on behalf of the American Mutoscope Company. The heat from about four hundred arc lamps suspended above the ring had almost cooked the boxers. The novelty attracted thousands of patrons into the picture houses, or cinemas as they were now sometimes called. But 'going to the pictures' regularly was still generally regarded in Britain as an occupation for housemaids and children rather than for gentlefolk. Furthermore, there was always a serious risk of fire because at this early date there were few regulations for the showing of films, and the highly inflammable film often dropped down from the projector into an open basket among the audience, with their cigarettes and pipes.

Another immensely popular subject at this time was *Our Navy*, followed later by *Our Army*. One critic wrote, 'It is quite sensational to see the *Turbinia* come tearing full on the audience, hurling aside the foaming water as she whizzes in and out of sight.' As with many early film shows, an explanation of each picture was given by 'a gentleman who is an adept at this sort of thing and who loses none of his opportunities to fan the patriotism of his audience into enthusiasm'.

'It is astonishing how soon one grows accustomed to new wonders,' said the *Brighton Herald* on December 8, 1900. 'Otherwise the exhibition of animated photographs now on view at the West Street concert hall would be nothing short of sensational. As it is we have been trained within a very brief space of time to accept photographic records of events, showing all the life and movement and excitement of a scene, almost as much a matter of course as a newspaper record. The Biograph has speedily taken a place in our life as a supplemental chronicler of the more notable events of the day in all quarters of the world, and a highly interesting chronicler it is, enabling us to realize the spirit of scenes with an actuality and vividness hitherto unattainable. This week, at the West Pier concert hall, scenes of this kind of the highest interest are brought before the eyes of the spectators with impressive interest, the medium being the

American Biograph, identical with that shown at the Palace Theatre, London.'

On this occasion the films were accompanied by a piano, and at intervals solos, duets and trios were contributed by a concert party—to give the projectionist time to change the film. The war in South Africa was prominently featured, the camera-operator Mr J. Rosenthal having secured pictures of Lord Roberts meeting Baden-Powell in Pretoria, while another operator took pictures at Aldershot of the returning General Sir Redvers Buller being triumphantly drawn along in his carriage by firemen. The Queen and the Prince of Wales were also seen reviewing troops. The *Brighton Herald* remarked:

'The keen interest of Her Majesty is obvious. As she sits in her carriage right in the forefront of the great picture one notices that she several times raises her field glasses to her eyes. Other interesting royal pictures present the children of the Duke and Duchess of York playing at soldiers, and the Queen nursing the new baby whilst the other children are ranged around her.'

The programme also included scenes of the aged Pope Leo XIII, giving his benediction, the launching of the liner *Oceanic*, cavalry jumping hurdles at Aldershot, a man being rescued from the sea and being taken aboard HMS *Repulse*, a torpedo-boat destroyer ploughing through the water at full speed, and a visit to the Paris Exhibition.

Could anyone ask for more, for threepence?

13

THE KHAKI ELECTION

The Marquis of Salisbury (1830–1903), Disraeli's successor as leader of the Conservative party, was more attuned to the early nineteenth century than to later Conservative democracy. Lord Robert Cecil, as his courtesy title had been, was the second son of the second Marquis of Salisbury, the representative of a noble family which had produced important statesmen in the time of Queen Elizabeth I. He had been elected to the House of Commons in 1853 and continued to represent Stamford until he became a peer in 1868.

Salisbury's maiden speech in the Lords had been in opposition to Lord John Russell's proposed university reforms. He distrusted Disraeli and disagreed with him on the question of admitting Jews to parliament, as well as on parliamentary reform. He was the constant defender of tradition, and the maintenance of the Empire was his principal theme. Supported by the Liberal Unionists he had strongly opposed Gladstone's plan to grant Ireland home rule.

Of the years in which Salisbury was Prime Minister, 1885–86, 1886–92 and 1895–1902, the middle period marked his greatest achievements. He managed to keep out of war with France, and in 1889 he provided, by the Naval Defence Act, for the construction of ten new battleships and sixty cruisers within four and a half years. He administered both the Golden Jubilee of 1887 and the first imperial conference. He was an empire-builder whose territorial acquisitions, according to his opponent Lord Rosebery, added an extra two and a half million square miles to the Queen's dominions within twelve years. But his lack of vigour in the conduct of the Boer War, due partly to the fact that he was over seventy and had just lost his wife, who had been his staunch companion throughout his career, was not in his favour.

The Liberal Imperialists were led by Lord Rosebery, the last Liberal Prime Minister before 1900 (1894). The Liberal Unionists were led by the Duke of Devonshire, and there was also the old guard of Liberals who looked with suspicion on imperialism and retained the non-acquisitive political theories of Gladstone.

'Lord Salisbury has returned to work, finding in its abstraction some surcease from abiding sorrow,' Sir Henry Lucas recorded in his diary on December 10, 1899. 'He has been deeply touched by the manifestations of national sympathy in his bereavement, a demonstration made without reference to political or social distinction. He is agreeably surprised to find how wide and deep is his personal popularity. The guerdon is the more pleasing since it was never so sought. Beyond all public men, not excluding the Duke of Devonshire, whom in this respect he resembles, Lord Salisbury has never courted the favour of the masses. On the contrary, he has, upon occasion, sometimes perhaps without occasion, gone out of his way to flout them. It is impossible that a statesman of his clear judgment and long experience should really regard the House of Commons as an inconsiderable body compared with the House of Lords. Nevertheless, he with great success systematically affects that conviction.... He never condescends to visit the House of Commons. Herein he differs from the Duke of Devonshire, who is generally seen yawning in the front row of the Peers' gallery on nights when it is crowded in anticipation of a big debate. I cannot call to mind any occasion when Lord Salisbury has been seen looking down on the assembly in which, first as Lord Robert Cecil, then as Lord Cranborne, he earned his spurs in the political lists. Behind this aloofness and scornful mien he only partially conceals a kind heart and a highly sensitive nature.'

Soon after the close of the parliamentary session of 1900 the country began to consider the possibility of an early dissolution. The Conservative government in power under the leadership of

Lord Salisbury, who was also Foreign Secretary, might still have had a further year or more of life, but the government decided to go to the country and face its opposition. The Boer War had not proved to be the quick, easy campaign which had been anticipated. Meanwhile there were some doubts, even among the Liberals, whether Lord Rosebery was capable of fulfilling, or really wished to accept, the full policies of Liberalism as Gladstone had practised them.

Generally speaking, the Conservatives were imperialist and pro-war, while the Liberals were inclined to be against the conflict, and in many cases were actively pro-Boer.

Parliament was dissolved on September 25th. The same issue of the *London Gazette* which announced the dissolution contained the royal proclamation of the formation of the Commonwealth of Australia, whose parliament was to be opened by the Duke and Duchess of York, later to be King George V and Queen Mary. It was therefore no coincidence that one of the important issues in the selection was whether or not the South African Republic should also be granted self-government.

From Lord Salisbury's point of view an early election was preferable because the military position in South Africa, although not resolved, was at last apparently favourable to the British. Never again might the Conservatives be so popular and the opposition so split. Because the war was the main bone of contention, the election came later to be called the 'khaki election'.

The electioneering was noisy and exciting. In his speeches up and down the country Joseph Chamberlain frequently referred to the telegram sent to him by the Mayor of Mafeking which had contained the words: 'A seat to the Liberals is a seat given to the Boers.[1] Addressing a crowded meeting at East Manchester, the Conservative candidate Mr A. J. Balfour told the electors that 'the lesson which has been indelibly pressed on the South African mind by the portion of our dealings with the Transvaal which so ingloriously ended at Majuba is that, from a radical administration, neither firmness of purpose nor consistency of policy need be

[1] D. H. Elletson, *The Chamberlains*, London, 1966.

anticipated in the face of Boer persistence'. This reference to the defeat on Majuba Hill back in 1881, and to the immediate peace terms then made with the Transvaal by Gladstone's government, was a reminder that the Liberals had at that time quickly come to terms with the enemy, and might do so again if returned to power. Mr Balfour ended his speech with an appeal to 'every citizen, therefore, who desires that the blood which men of our race from every quarter of the world have so freely shed in defence of the Empire, shall not have been shed in vain'. It had been said before, and would be said again.

The Liberals had little doubt that they faced defeat at the polls. At Leeds, on September 18th, Mr Herbert Gladstone, the opposition's chief whip, did not conceal his fears, but stated that his party was not in a position to form a government capable of retaining power. He argued that unless the Liberals could win 160 seats from the Conservatives no responsible statesman would undertake to form a government.

Lord Salisbury countered by publishing a letter urging all Conservatives to vote and thus to settle not only the South African problem but also the reform of the country's military organization and the nation's policy on China. He went before the electors as representing a united party promising the success of British arms against the Boers.

The Liberals were not completely united in their opposition to the war, and their position was made even less secure by division on other problems, such as Irish Home Rule and legislation for temperance safeguards. As the election campaigns proceeded, it became clear that they were placed at a serious disadvantage by the issue of the war and the divided loyalties within their ranks. Finally, because there was little expectation that they could win, the country began to lose interest in the election. Sir Henry Campbell-Bannerman was now leading the Liberals in place of Lord Rosebery, but he was faced with the fact that Lord Roberts was turning the tide against the Boers and that Lord Salisbury's choice of an early date for an election was a wise one from a Conservative point of view.

The result at the polls was a considerable victory for the

Conservatives and Unionists, who altogether returned 402 members, the Liberal and Labour members together numbering only 186. The Conservatives thus gained their vote of confidence from the country. Lord Salisbury returned to power as Prime Minister and Lord Privy Seal, but decided to relinquish the position of Foreign Secretary to the Marquis of Lansdowne. Little new blood was injected into the government's front bench as a result of the re-shuffle, critics of the new Cabinet pointing out that it consisted of several members of the same family and that with twenty members it was unusually large. The new session began on December 3, 1900.

The Queen described the result as being 'wonderfully good' and was grateful that Mr Gladstone's influence had not been revived while her 'poor soldiers' were fighting for their country overseas.

This parliament was notable for several new members. Andrew Bonar Law, quiet, unassuming and methodical, was returned for the City of London, and Winston Spencer Churchill, fresh from his exciting adventures as a war correspondent at the front, won his seat for the constituency of Oldham, but only by a narrow margin and after a recount. Both were later to become Prime Ministers.

Churchill had failed to gain the seat in July of the previous year, before going out to South Africa, but he had returned as a hero and there was no doubt about his ability as a speaker. Joseph Chamberlain appeared for him on the platform, and the result was a victory both for Churchill and for one of the Liberal candidates, Oldham in those days being a constituency with two members:

Sir Alfred Emmott (Liberal)	12,976
W. S. Churchill (Conservative)	12,931
Walter Runciman (Liberal)	12,709
C. B. Crisp (Conservative)	12,522

In those days polling was spread over a period of three weeks, so that the early results could have a considerable influence on the later votes in the rest of the country. The young Churchill's gain naturally put the Conservatives in good heart, and a telegram of congratulations reached him from Lord Salisbury. Next day Arthur Balfour, who had found it impossible to assist him at Oldham, asked Churchill not to return to London but instead to speak on his behalf at Manchester. For the next three weeks Churchill was the star speaker in tours of marginal constituencies. First he spent two days at Joseph Chamberlain's home, Highbury, Birmingham, from where he was carried from one Midlands meeting to another by special train. Then he travelled more widely afield, to wherever the party managers thought he would be most helpful in swaying votes. Thus, many thousands of the people of England saw and heard for the first time the man who was to become one of the greatest wartime statesmen in the nation's long history. 'Quite a few victories followed in my wake,' he was later to recall. It seemed to him like a triumphal progress.[1]

Joseph Chamberlain wrote to his wife that the campaign as a whole had been 'fought with the greatest malignity by the baser sort on the other side'. No doubt in this attack he included the brilliant young ex-solicitor David Lloyd George, who had been Liberal member for Caernarvon since 1890 and was regarded as one of his party's most promising supporters. Throughout the electioneering Lloyd George frequently stated that the South African war was the work of one man, Joseph Chamberlain, who had willed it, planned it, brought it about, profited by it, and was now unnecessarily prolonging it. At Llanelly, Wales, in October, he described the progress of what he called 'Chamberlain's war'. Last year, he said, the public had been relieved to hear that the war was over. 'How handy, just in time for the General Election in October!' Then, 'Hallo, what's this? Still on in November— and another little bill for a few million pounds. That was *last* November. Now, after twelve months more fighting, how did we stand? We had a government which would not make peace and even yet did not know how to make war.[2]

Later, in December 1901, the fiery Welshman was to carry his attack right into Joseph Chamberlain's camp, invading his

[1] Randolph S. Churchill, *Winston S. Churchill*, Vol. 1, London, 1966.
[2] Frank Owen, *Tempestuous Journey*, London, 1954.

stronghold of Birmingham, where the listeners, accustomed to the incisive imperialism of Chamberlain, who had done much for their city and its prosperity, were to rise in protest against the intruder, smashing windows in the Town Hall, breaking open doors, ransacking the place, and forcing the future Prime Minister of Britain to escape from their wrath by disguising himself as a policeman.

At this time the Labour movement was still in its infancy, but it was growing fast. Throughout the 1890s, James Keir Hardie had fought strenuously to convert the labour unions to a policy of independent representation in parliament. Within the Trades Union Congress he encountered stiff opposition from the Liberal–Labour members, but in 1900 he was able by means of an innocuously worded resolution to secure the establishment of a Labour Representation Committee, whose purpose was to return Labour members to Westminster.

A Scot, Keir Hardie had started work in the coal mines when he was ten and when in 1892 he made his first appearance in the House of Commons—heralded by a brass band—he wore his miner's cap and a rough tweed suit, in marked contrast to the smart top hats and frock coats around him. He had refused the offer of a safe Liberal seat with £300 a year, preferring to organize the Scottish Labour Party and so enter parliament as a Socialist. It was in the 1900 election that two candidates of the Labour Representation Committee were elected to parliament, Hardie being one. By 1906 the Committee was to be known as the Labour party, when twenty-nine of its members would be elected, including James Ramsay Macdonald and Philip Snowden. But this milestone in the emancipation of Britain's working-classes was, in 1900, still a long way off.

In late Victorian England there were two kinds of socialism. One, headed by the writer and artist William Morris (1834–96), was generally known as Guild Socialism, its inspiration being derived from the craftsmanship of the medieval workman. John Ruskin had been among the first to insist on the importance of enabling a man to express himself in his work, and he maintained that the routine labour of the factory hand was morally and physically degrading. The dignity of work was the first concern of the Guild Socialists.

The other group was the Fabians, a society founded in 1883, taking its name from the Roman general Quintus Fabius Maximus, who had triumphed over Hannibal without giving direct battle. They largely accepted the Marxian analysis of society, but believed in a step-by-step advance towards socialism instead of a violent revolution. In its early days the two most notable members of the society were Sidney Webb (1859–1947) and George Bernard Shaw (1856–1950). In his *Tract No. 70: Report on Fabian Policy* (1896), Shaw stated: 'The object of the Fabian Society is to persuade the English people to make their political constitution thoroughly democratic and so to socialize their industries as to make the livelihood of the people entirely independent of private Capitalism'.

14

THE HORSELESS CARRIAGE

The turn of the century saw the development of the internal combustion engine and the 'horseless carriage' or 'automobile' or 'motor-car', as the new wonder came to be called. It was an invention which was to revolutionize transport and the way of life of millions of people all over the world. Yet Queen Victoria never entered a motor-car and she never saw an aeroplane.

Although at the end of the century the railway and the horse were still the principal means of conveyance and would remain so for several years, the motor-car, at first regarded with fear and dislike, was eventually to force the horse off the highway and close many railway lines.

While the motor vehicle originated in Europe the industry was to be developed mainly in the United States, where the economic climate of the coming twentieth century was to be favourable to mass-production. The majority of the early European vehicle builders were obsessed with the idea of a 'horseless carriage', a mechanically propelled coach or cab, and one of the first British companies to make motor vehicles was called the Great Horseless Carriage Company. The engine in the early, pre-1900 vehicles was usually hidden under the floor or behind the rear seats and the bodywork of the cars was coach-built and heavy.

The formation in 1895 of the British Motor Syndicate, and then the Great Horseless Carriage Company, was an attempt by a financier named Harry John Lawson, who believed passionately in the future of the petrol-driven motor-car, to corner the entire

British industry. Incompetent management and financial fraud led ultimately to the collapse of the companies.

No single invention was to contribute more to the motor-car's gradual conquest of the public highway than the development of the pneumatic tyre, patented in 1888 by a Scots veterinary surgeon named John Boyd Dunlop, who had devised an inflated tyre for his son's bicycle and had at first no intention of marketing

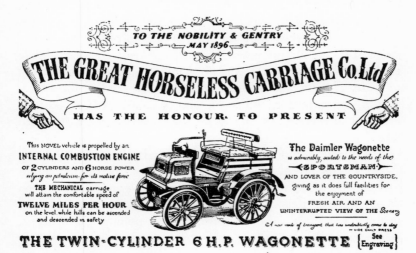

TO THE NOBILITY & GENTRY
MAY 1896

THE GREAT HORSELESS CARRIAGE Co.Ltd

HAS THE HONOUR TO PRESENT

This NOVEL vehicle is propelled by an INTERNAL COMBUSTION ENGINE OF 2 CYLINDERS AND 6 HORSE POWER relying on petroleum for its motive force THE MECHANICAL carriage will attain the comfortable speed of TWELVE MILES PER HOUR on the level while hills can be ascended and descended in safety

The Daimler Wagonette is admirably suited to the needs of the SPORTSMAN AND LOVER OF THE COUNTRYSIDE, giving as it does full facilities for the enjoyment of FRESH AIR AND AN UNINTERRUPTED VIEW OF THE Scenery A new mode of transport that has undoubtedly come to stay — VIDE DAILY PRESS

THE TWIN-CYLINDER 6 H.P. WAGONETTE [See Engraving]

his invention. The first pneumatic tyre for cars was made in 1895 by the Michelin brothers, but until then only solid tyres were available, and these seriously limited the vehicle's speed and performance.

The coming of the motor-car was soon to disrupt town and country life. While the streets in the cities and towns were heavily congested with horsedrawn traffic—omnibuses, trams, dray wagons, carts, vans, cabs and private carriages—the villages and country lanes were relatively free of traffic, and the roads were usually in poor condition. Horses and bicycles were used for getting from one village to another, unless there was a railway nearby. The clergy, doctors, lawyers, farmers, local landowners and retired gentlefolk owned their horses, carriages, or ponies and traps; the tradesmen and commercial folk had vans and carts.

Blacksmiths' shops, due almost to vanish from the scene after the 1914–18 war, were busy, as were the knackers' yards and the sea traffic in live, old, worn-out or unwanted horses which the hungry European continent devoured as meat.

'English villages at the turn of the century would seem quiet to village people today, for there was little traffic,' recalls a country doctor.[1] 'The carrier would go to the nearest town, maybe once a week, and would shop for the whole village. Sometimes one of the villagers would travel with him, but it was a big occasion when they did, and it was talked of for weeks afterwards. . . . When people were dependent on horses they could not get far and made do with what the village could provide. There would be the village shop, the saddler, the wheelwright, the carpenter, and so on, and of course pedlars. No one dreamed of travelling to a nearby town every week as they do now.'

The first automobiles or horseless carriages were driven by steam, and then by electricity, not petrol. Nicholas Joseph Cugnot of Lorraine made a large, heavy, steam-driven tricycle in 1769 which ran for twenty minutes at $2\frac{1}{2}$ m.p.h. and carried four people. Cugnot's steam vehicles were popular in Europe, especially in Britain. Steam 'buses were running to Paris as early as 1800, Oliver Evans ran an amphibious steam dredge in Philadelphia in 1804, and in the 1830s several steam-driven stage coaches were in regular service in England. Later came the electric automobile, which achieved such popularity that at the first American motor show held in New York in 1900 more than one-third of the exhibiting space was taken up with displays of electric cars and nearly all the rest of the space was devoted to steam cars. Only a small fraction of the hall went to petrol-driven cars. But soon the electric car was to lose the race, mainly because its power could be renewed only at electric charging stations in the cities, while the steam car fell behind because it was generally considered dangerous and difficult to work, although it was in fact more comfortable, less noisy, not so smelly, and easier to control than its first petrol-driven rivals.

[1] Noel Streatfeild (ed.), *The Day Before Yesterday*, London, 1956.

Jean-Joseph-Etienne Lenoir of Paris (who died almost un-known in 1900) was one of the important inventors of the modern motor-car. He devised a vehicle which used air instead of water as complementary fuel and eventually enabled a small car to travel for a thousand miles without re-provisioning. Lenoir's car of 1862, foreshadowed by a specification on view at the Great Exhibition of 1851, used some kind of petroleum spirit vapour; it worked satisfactorily, and it actually had electric ignition. Although the claim to have produced the world's first car has been disputed, Lenoir's right is supported by the grant of a master patent, No. 43,624 dated 1860.[1]

Austrian authorities, however, maintain that the earliest genuine modern car came from Siegfried Markus of Vienna in 1875.[2] But there is no doubt that two of the most important contributors to the development of the petrol-engined auto-mobile were the German pioneers Karl Benz (1844–1929) and Gottlieb Daimler (1834–1900). Benz ran his first car in 1885 and Daimler perfected his first a year later. The firm of Daimler-Benz was founded in 1895, but there is no record that Benz and Daimler ever met.

Karl Benz was dedicated to the belief that the internal com-bustion engine would revolutionize transportation. His 1885 car circled a cinder track beside his small factory while his workmen and his wife ran along beside the little vehicle clapping their hands. The car made four circuits before breaking a chain. In the autumn of 1885, when Benz demonstrated his invention publicly, he forgot to steer and smashed the car into a brick wall. His first automobile sale was made in 1887 to a Parisian named Emile Rogers. A year later he was employing fifty workmen to build his tricycle car and in 1890 he began work on a four-wheeler.

Daimler's 1889 model had a framework of light tubing and a rear engine. It was driven by a belt, was steered by a tiller, and had four different speeds.

The Daimler-Benz claim to have invented the automobile was

[1] G. R. Doyle and G. N. Georgano, *The World's Automobiles*, London, 1963.
[2] The Markus celebrated its seventy-fifth birthday in the streets of Vienna in 1950 by travelling at 3 m.p.h. The name is sometimes spelled Marcus.

attacked in 1895 when US patent No. 549,160 was granted to George B. Selden as the inventor. Selden had filed a claim on May 8, 1879, although he had not at that time built a vehicle. He succeeded in keeping the patent pending for sixteen years.

Other pioneers were Emile Levassor, the Marquis de Dion, and M. Bouton. They produced great advances in the construction of the explosive cylinder, with proper timing and valve work. Emil Jellinek, an associate of Daimler, had a daughter named Maja, which name he used for the Austrian version of the Daimler. To the super-car made at Canstatt the firm allotted the name of Emil's other daughter, Mercedes.

In 1887, Emile Levassor, of the French firm of Panhard and Levassor, makers of wood-working machinery, secured the French patent rights in Daimler's motor-car and produced a vehicle whose general mechanical lay-out was to remain standard for the next eighty years and more, except for the substitution of a live axle for a chain drive. Even then, the live axle, to be produced later by Renault Frères, would not quickly replace Lavassor's chain drive. By 1891 the Panhard-Levassor was in regular production and most of the early motor-cars which found their way to other European countries were either French of German.

Development in Britain went ahead when Evelyn Ellis imported a four horse-power Panhard-Levassor from France in 1895. At that time every mechanically propelled vehicle on Britain's roads was restricted to a speed limit of 4 m.p.h., and one member of the minimum crew of three was required to walk at least twenty yards in front to warn others of the monster's approach. It was not until 1896 that the Locomotives on Highways Act raised the speed limit to 14 m.p.h. and a man on foot was no longer needed. To celebrate this freedom the Motor Car Club organized a great emancipation run from the Hotel Metropole in London to the Hotel Metropole in Brighton, on November 14, 1896. It is recorded that a red flag—the symbol of oppression which an earlier law had said must be carried in front of a mechanical vehicle on the roads—was ceremoniously destroyed before the run began. Many cars broke down on the journey and

Punch humorously reported that 'many of the guests of the Motor Club went to Brighton on Saturday last by a horseless carriage—supplied by the London, Brighton and South Coast Railway'.

In France, Miss Vera Hedges Butler, the daughter of the balloonist Frank Hedges Butler, was the first woman to gain a driving certificate. She drove from Paris across the Alps to Nice, and was in the Paris-Marseilles race of 1896 when pneumatic tyres were first used, and in the 1000 Miles Rally of 1900. *Teuf-teuf* was the onomatopoeic name given by the French to their early cars, this aptly describing the noise of the engines, and the equivalent in France of the Veteran Car Club of Great Britain was later named *Les Teuf-teuf.* In April 1899 *Punch* reported that the latest Parisian fashion colour was *'rouge automobile'*, which the *boulevardiers* described as *très* smart or *teuf-teuf,* 'a word derived from the sound of the *petrolette'*.

At first, because of her laws, Britain lagged far behind in the motor-car race. But there were signs that the days of the horse-drawn vehicle were numbered. In October 1896 there was a cab strike in London and *Punch* warned the cabbies:

> Hansoms and growlers together,
> Fares don't care for your love or your war!
> In this coming November
> Just please to remember
> You've a rival—the new motor car!

This was followed in November by Phil May's conception in *Punch* of the motor 'bus whose cabby driver 'can't stop the bloomin' thing'. The *Punch* volume for 1898 ended with a drawing of Santa Claus driving from the North Pole in a horseless carriage stacked with toys.

In 1900 *Punch* depicted Mr Jenkins driving his wife in his new motor-car to Epsom, but 'to make sure of arriving there, he thought it only wise to bring his horses as well, in case anything went "wrong with the works" '. A coachman sits at the back of the car, leading the horses on a rein, and a Fortnum and Mason picnic basket is strapped to the front of the car.

René Panhard's business association with the French bicycle-maker Armand Peugeot put Peugeot among the few early motor-car manufacturers, and in 1890 Peugeot introduced his first petrol-driven quadricycle.

The first firm to manufacture gasoline automobiles on a large scale in the United States was probably the Duryea company, formed in 1895 by Charles E. Duryea. This was so successful that Duryea was able to open subsidiary factories in Liège in Belgium, and Coventry in England. In the same year America's first automobile journal appeared, *The Horseless Age*, started by E. P. Ingersoll. *It's All U.P. With the Poor Gee-Gee* went a popular song a year later, but horses stayed on the roads for many years.

In 1900 there were still only twelve firms making motors in the USA and they produced some 4190 vehicles; by 1910 there were to be sixty companies with an annual production of 187,000. Most of the firms started with little capital, the Ford Motor Car Co. (1903) with 28,000 dollars, the Hudson company with less. Motoring was still only for a minority. Public garages could be found only in the largest cities, and then infrequently, cars usually being kept and maintained in stables, where servants more accustomed to caring for horses often felt no interest. There was little encouragement for the early motorist, either in America or Europe. The roads were usually narrow and muddy, the vehicles were often awkward and complicated and frequently broke down, and large sections of the public considered the invention an unmitigated nuisance and called it a 'devil wagon'.

In 1899 a law was passed which made it illegal to take a horseless carriage into Central Park, New York. Under such restrictions and with the newspapers constantly making fun of the new wonder of the roads, the early manufacturers in Europe and America concentrated on turning out vehicles for the wealthy, the eccentric, and 'to order'. But in 1900 some American industrialists began to make cars for the average man at reason-able prices, and the fine craftsmanship and quality coachwork which had distinguished the early European models was gradually to be replaced over the years by quality mass-production which was to make the automobile available not to hundreds but to millions, and eventually hundreds of millions of people, many of whose parents had not even owned a horse and cart.

Among the American pioneers, Ransom Eli Olds has a prominent place. The Olds Motor Vehicle Co. Inc. was founded in 1897 to make and sell cars, and it was followed in 1899 by the Olds Motor works which took over the earlier company. In 1900 the 3 h.p. Oldsmobile was the first commercially successful American automobile. Four hundred and twenty-five models were to be sold in 1901, over 2000 in 1902, about 4000 in 1903, and about 5000 in 1904. The big boom was not to start in America until 1904–08, when some 241 rival manufacturing or assembling companies would be in business.

The Olds works in Detroit was in 1900 the world's largest motor-car factory. Parts were ordered in lots of a thousand; 2000 sets of transmission gears from Dodge Brothers; 2000 motors from Leland and Faulkner. They sold the first car for 600 dollars, the next for 650. The firm was started with only 200,000 dollars but during its first two years it paid out 105 per cent in cash dividends. Soon America was to steal the automobile markets of the world from Germany, France, Britain, Italy and Belgium, where cars were until the 1920s still to be made with all the slow perfection and ponderous craftsmanship of the old carriage and coachwork trades.[1] The elegant, long Rolls-Royce Silver Ghost, later to be christened by Lord Northcliffe 'the best car in the world', would not become the pride of the Motor Show until 1909.

Henry Hewetson, a tea merchant of Mark Lane, London, was one of the first men to use a petrol-driven car in Britain. In *A History of Ten Years of Automobilism* the late Lord Montagu of Beaulieu tells how in 1894 Hewetson happened to be in Mannheim, where a friend showed him his Benz car. He immediately went to the Benz company and ordered a two-seater 3 h.p. model for about £80, with the object of shipping it to England, but they explained to him that although motor-cars were allowed on the Continent they could not be driven freely in England until

[1] Mark Sullivan, *op. cit.*

a special law was passed. This was true, but it seemed so ridiculous to Mr Hewetson that he decided to take the risk, and the car was delivered to him at Catford at the end of 1894.[1]

Some of the manufacturers were to last for only a few years; others were to span over half a century. In Jackson, Michigan, the Clark-Carter company lasted only from 1900 to 1908. The Century Motor Vehicle Company of Syracuse, founded in 1899, was to cease production in 1903, like the Graves-Condon company in Amesbury, Massachusetts. Others did better. The Star Engineering Company of Frederick Street, Wolverhampton, made cars from 1899 to 1935, and the Albion Motor Car Company of Scotstoun, Glasgow, made them from 1900 to 1913 and then produced commercial vehicles.

The little Swift, first made in Coventry in 1899, was to continue production until 1931, while the Studebaker company of South Bend, Indiana, with a historic record of carriage-building since 1852, was to introduce its first electric car in 1902 and then to provide the world with millions of high-quality gasoline automobiles.

One of the important developments, from a commercial point of view, was the motor-car race. The world's first real car race was probably the contest held on June 11–13, 1895 from Paris to Bordeaux and back, which was won by a Panhard-Levassor at an average speed of $15\frac{1}{2}$ m.p.h. over the 740-mile course. Four years later the Paris-Ostend race was won by the Honorable C. S. Rolls driving another Panhard, the second place being taken by an English Daimler driven by Lord Montagu of Beaulieu. In 1907 the Napier was to establish the twenty-four hours world speed record, which would remain unbeaten for seventeen years.

Although from November 1, 1896 a motor car could be driven along a public highway in Britain without breaking the law, the English manufacturers still lagged far behind their European competitors at the turn of the century. Nearly every car that took part in the first great London to Brighton emancipation run was foreign-made. Three years after the change in the law a motor-

[1] W. J. Bentley, *Motoring Cavalcade*, London, 1953.

car was still 'something of a surprise packet even in the streets of London, and almost a nine days' wonder in the country districts'.[1]

The first licence granted to a public motor cab in London was issued in 1897, the vehicle being electrically-driven and termed by the Scotland Yard authorities a 'mechanical Clarence'.

By 1900 there were about a hundred car factories in Europe, mostly small, and a year later the total number of automobile-makers throughout the world was estimated to be 300. By this time there were believed to be some 10,000 cars in Britain, a figure which was to rise in fifty years' time to 2,350,000 cars and 910,000 lorries. In the boom period cars were made not only in America, Britain, Sweden, Belgium, France, Italy, Germany and Holland but also in Hungary, Russia, Sicily, Canada and Tasmania. By 1906 there would be 810 car-making firms in existence, a figure never exceeded before or since. In 1903 the Ford Motor company was to start production, selling its first car a month after the opening of the factory and producing 1700 vehicles in its first year. By 1908 Henry Ford would be selling 8000 vehicles a year, his policy being to make vehicles strong enough to run for five years but at such a low price that their owners could afford to replace them. Although not the originator of mass-production, he was the first person to produce vast numbers of cars.

The English-built Napier was the world's first six-cylinder car, its four-cylinder cousin winning the 1902 Gordon Bennett race for England against all Continental drivers, an achievement of major importance. When for the first time the long stretch of Porlock Hill was conquered by a 16 h.p. Napier, in August 1900, the time of the run was seventeen minutes, thirty-five seconds—about 10 m.p.h.

In Britain the Daimler Motor Syndicate was founded in 1893 to acquire the British rights in Gottlieb Daimler's German engine patents, held by an English manufacturer named Frederick R. Simms. With Simms on the board the company changed its name in 1896 to the Daimler Motor Co. Ltd. and was for a time

[1] *The Harmsworth Magazine*, April 1900.

involved in the grandiose schemes of H. J. Lawson's Great Horseless Carriage Company. When Lawson failed the company was reformed, and in 1910 it was to become part of the Birmingham Small Arms group. The first English Daimler was on the road in 1897, and the success of its later models owed a great deal to royal patronage.

In May 1896 the Prince of Wales had opened an exhibition of cars and motor-cycles at the Imperial Institute, London, and had ridden in two Daimler cars, one driven by Mr E. M. C. Instone, the new secretary of the Daimler company. In 1898 the company was asked to show the Prince its cars while he stayed at Warwick Castle. Five models were sent over from Coventry with a Mr Critchley, who drove the Prince, with the Countess of Warwick and Lady Randolph Churchill, to Compton Verney and Wellesbourne, where they had lunch. However, the first royal outing was hardly a success because they were hit by a storm and the Prince had to abandon the car and return to Warwick in a closed carriage.

The first of many royal Daimlers was ordered in May 1900, following a visit by Lord Montagu of Beaulieu to Highcliffe Castle, near Christchurch, Hampshire, the home of Colonel Montagu-Stuart-Wortley, which had been rented to the Prince's friends Mr and Mrs George Cavendish-Bentinck, with whom the Prince was staying.

On this occasion, the present Lord Montagu of Beaulieu has recalled,[1] his father 'had been specially invited to lunch in order to give the royal party a drive in the afternoon. This went off extremely well and after the trip the Prince closely questioned my father on the car and asked his advice as to what sort of vehicle would be most suitable to him. A few weeks later my father was summoned to Marlborough House and asked to bring the Daimler with him. It was examined by members of the household—no doubt including the Master of the Horse—and shortly after this an order was placed with the Daimler Car Company for a car similar to my father's. This started a long association between the Daimler company and the royal family.'

[1] *Daily Telegraph*, May 27, 1966.

Later, as King, the first royal patron of the automobile owned two Mercedes, a Daimler, a small Renault and a 'landaulette', while Queen Alexandra had a Wolseley. The royal cars had no number plates and always attracted attention. Once when the King left his car to walk along the sea-front at Hove the towns-people, seeing it parked, began to look for him. As he strolled along with his equerry a boy went up to him and asked: 'Please mister, can you tell me the time?' 'Yes,' replied the King, 'it is a quarter to one.' The boy complained that he had been 'waiting for two hours to see the blooming King, and I'm not going to wait any longer!' 'Neither am I,' answered the King, much amused.[1]

Lord Montagu recalls that shortly after the delivery of the first royal car, the linkage in the steering in his father's car failed on one of the country roads near Beaulieu. Knowing that a similar weakness might endanger the Prince's life, his father immediately sent a telegram to Marlborough House, and the necessary modification was made. The Prince's first car was a phaeton type fitted with a 6 h.p. Daimler motor, to carry four people. The Daimler company undertook that His Royal Highness would be 'personally instructed in its management'.

Although by 1900 the motor-car had scarcely begun to affect British public life, the Automobile Club of Great Britain and Ireland ('with which is incorporated the Self-Propelled Traffic Association'), later to become the Royal Automobile Club, decided in the spring to entertain the chief constables of several counties to luncheon at Sheen House Club, Richmond, where motors would be displayed and demonstrated. They considered that it was time that the automobile became respectable, for there had been many examples, especially in the Home Counties, of discrimination against motorists in police cases. The guests were driven around Richmond Park and were later asked to express their views on the importance of the motor-car in transport.

The success of this meeting prompted Claude Johnson, the first secretary of the club, to organize a 1000-mile trial run, the first of its kind in the world, to Edinburgh and back. Starting on

[1] Alison Gernsheim, *Edward VII and Queen Alexandra*, London, 1962.

April 23, 1900, it was timed to finish in the second week of May. Sixty-five out of eighty-five entries completed the run, and of these only eleven did not break down at some time. The run had its base line between London and Bristol and its apex at Edinburgh. Describing the event as 'a really great and picturesque idea', *The Autocar* stated that 'no better plan for familiarizing the public with cars and their capabilities could possibly have been devised'.

Anxious to gain publicity for his rally, Mr Johnson approached Alfred Harmsworth,[1] the proprietor of the *Daily Mail*, who at once supported it in his newspapers, at a time when many other journals were deriding the automobile as being 'a disagreeable and unnecessary plaything of a few cranks'.

Harmsworth himself had written in the *Daily Mail* on May 4, 1896: 'It only needs the support of influential people to make the application of automobilism to road travel widely popular.' He took part in the run as far as Manchester, driving his 6 h.p. Panhard-Levassor, with a passenger. The car was considered 'the last word' and was admired as much by the experts as by the many gaping sightseers along the route. He had bought it for £800 in the spring of 1899, although he had motored in France before then. One of his first passengers was his mother, and another was the poet W. E. Henley. The little yellow, high-seated car was the first seen in many towns and villages of south-east England.

Another distinguished motor in the historic run was the Wolseley Voiturette, the first car designed and built by Herbert Austin, which had been shown at the Crystal Palace Exhibition of 1896. In June 1898 Austin had driven it from London to Rhyl and back at an average speed of eight miles an hour, without a breakdown. At the time of the great rally it was the standard Wolseley, available to the public at £225, and at the end of the run it was awarded the £10 first prize in its class by the *Daily Mail* and a silver medal by the Automobile Club de France.[2]

[1] Later Lord Northcliffe.

[2] The Automobile Club de France had been founded in 1895 by Baron von Zuylen, Count de Dion, and the Paris editor Paul Meyan.

Soon the names of Austin and Wolseley were to mean motoring for the thousands, and ultimately for the millions.

Breakdowns and accidents were frequent during these early years. Setting out on August 8, 1899 to visit Rudyard Kipling at Rottingdean, Sussex, Alfred Harmsworth had got no farther than Wimbledon, on the outskirts of London, when the car broke down. On another occasion, when driving to Broadstairs in Kent, his French chauffeur panicked at the sight of a horse crossing the road and ran the vehicle up on to a bank, where it overturned and pinned its distinguished owner underneath. He was pulled out, badly shaken, his arm temporarily paralysed, the victim of one of the first recorded motor-car accidents.[1]

What was described as a 'distressing fatality', in which the part played by a motor-car was not very clearly defined, occurred at Hove, Sussex, in April 1900. The victim was a young carter who was leading his horse along a main road when the animal was frightened by a passing car. The boy was run over and killed by his own cart. Motors came along the Lower Shoreham Road too frequently, said a witness. The car driver said he was travelling with eight passengers in his vehicle, which was licensed, and was 'the quietest thing in Brighton'. He was going along at about 6 m.p.h. The jury expressed the opinion that 'all motor-cars should be driven with the greatest care from Hove Street to King's Gardens'.

When a summons for riding a motor-cycle to the public danger was brought against a Brighton publican, the police gave evidence that he had 'come down the Queen's Road on a motor-quadricycle at the rate of fourteen or fifteen miles an hour'. The pace was so alarming that a policeman had called out to people to beware, because a runaway was coming. As the driver passed him the policeman held up his hand for the machine to stop but the quadricycle not surprisingly 'continued at the same furious pace'. Fortunately the only traffic in the road was a horse omnibus and a cab, which the defendant passed 'by a miracle'. People came running up to see what had happened. 'I think,' said Mr Bunbury, the magistrate, 'that bicycles and motor-cars ought to proceed

[1] Reginald Pound and Geoffrey Harmsworth, *Northcliffe*, London, 1959.

in main streets even slower than the horse traffic. A horse does give ample warning of its approach, which these vehicles often do not. One pound fine, and costs.'

At Cardiff a driver was summoned by the police for driving a car 'at a greater speed than reasonable'. The stipendiary magistrate, accepting the evidence of a police constable that the car was propelled at a rate of ten miles an hour, which he held 'with great confidence to be an unreasonable and dangerous speed', imposed a fine of £5. But police evidence was often misleading, for there was no way of proving or checking speeds. Thus a driver summoned for 'furiously driving a motor car in Brighton Road, South Croydon', was described by the police and various witnesses as having driven at speeds ranging from 16 to 150 miles an hour.

Motors were at first debarred from many public places, such as Windsor Park, the Barge Walk at Kingston-upon-Thames, several parts of Scotland, Central Park, New York, parts of Pennsylvania, and many private roads and parks. In 1899 Lord Montagu of Beaulieu was prevented by the police from entering the sacred precincts of parliament in a car. In some towns in the United States motorists were compelled to alight from their vehicles before entering a populated area at night in order to fire signal flares as a warning to the inhabitants. It was not unusual, in rural areas in Europe, for these extraordinary monsters to be stoned by rustics. Petrol could be obtained in only a few towns, and was often dispensed by chemists. The *Motor Car Journal* for March 1901 stated that 'motorists touring towards Land's End, Cornwall, will be glad to know that motor spirit can always be obtained from Mr Wm. Prockter of Launceston'.

In Italy the industry had developed mainly in Turin and Milan, the famous FIAT company (Fabbrica Italiana Automobili Torino) being formed in 1898, but the comparative poverty of the country in the early stages of the development of the industry was a serious handicap to the achievements of her engineers and designers.

In Denmark, the Hammel (traditionally dated 1886–7 but possibly older) was the oldest car. It was built by H. F. Hammel and H. U. Johansen; it was water-cooled, and had a reverse gear.[1]

In parts of the Empire where the importing of vehicles from Europe and America was at first expensive and difficult, enthusiasts attempted to build, or assemble their own cars. One of the pioneers in Australia was Herbert Thompson of Armdale, Victoria, who in 1896 constructed a steam-powered 'motor phaeton'. There is also evidence that Charles Highland of Sydney built a three-wheeled car in 1894 and fitted it with a Daimler petrol engine. This was probably Australia's first petrol motor-car but it was reported to have burst into flames and never to have progressed farther than the length of a street. Two years later Mr Highland built a new car with a de Dion engine, which was successful.

Another Australian car, the Pioneer, was built in the 1890s by the Australian Horseless Carriage Syndicate of 432 Collins Street, Melbourne, on early European lines. It had a kerosene engine, a swivelling front axle, and high wheels to cut along the unkempt roads and tracks.

The first horseless carriage to reach South Africa was introduced by J. P. Hess of Pretoria in December 1896. This was a $1\frac{1}{2}$ h.p. Benz built at Mannheim, and in January 1897 it was shown to President Kruger, who awarded Mr Hess a special medal. Soon after this the first motor-cars began to appear in Cape Town and Durban. Rhodesia was to see its first petrol car in 1902, the year in which Johannesburg's first motor omnibus would operate. By 1913 some 400 cars a year would be imported into South Africa, mostly of American origin, with a market preference for the Ford, whose simple mechanism, power, and high carriage appealed to farmers who had to travel for long distances over rough tracks.

'Old Pacific', a Packard automobile, was to be the first automobile to cross the United States in 1903. The journey from San Francisco to New York was to take fifty-two days, over routes previously covered by horses, wagons, carts, carriages and coaches. Even at this time there were fewer than ten miles of

---

[1] In 1954 the Hammel completed the $56\frac{1}{2}$ miles London to Brighton run in 12 hours, 47 minutes.

concrete roads in the whole United States of America. The big revolution was yet to come.

By 1907 the *Brighton Season* would be able to report that Sunday was the great motoring day in England, 'when, weirdly masked, furred and goggled, scores if not hundreds of the Smart Set came whirling down from the metropolis to lunch perhaps at one or other of the big hotels on the front, lounge the afternoon away on the piers, sip early afternoon tea, and whizz back again to town in time for dinner'.

But even in 1913, Lady Cecil Montagu Scott would be writing in a magazine article, 'The public feeling in England at present is undoubtedly rather prejudiced against motoring'. However, Mr Lloyd George would announce in that year, at the International Road Congress, that Britain now had 220,000 licensed motor vehicles—twice as many as any Continental country, but only a third as many as the United States.

15

PUBLIC TRANSPORT

At the end of the century, when the motor-car was in its infancy, the railway was still the principal method of travelling long overland distances. In 1899 there were only four petrol 'stockists' for all the automobiles in London, and only twenty-nine in the rest of Britain, including a chemist's and a grocer's, but over the years an immensely complicated network of railway lines had been spread out over the country. The railway, the horse and the bicycle were still man's best friends if he wished to move more than a few miles.

Many towns in Britain had several railway stations and were served by more than one company, and there was considerable rivalry among the different systems. The London, Brighton and South Coast company owned two London termini, one at London Bridge and the other at Victoria. Its engines were brilliant gamboge with brass fittings, but a less decorative chocolate hue was later adopted. The London and South Western, serving the south west of England from Waterloo, painted its engines olive green and its carriages 'salmon'. The Great Eastern, based on Liverpool Street station, favoured rich blue engines with scarlet connecting rods. The Midland, from St Pancras to the north, had 'crimson lake' engines and coaches and was generally considered to be the most luxurious line in Europe. Perhaps less reputable was the South Eastern and Chatham, whose green and brass locomotives chuffed noisily out of Charing Cross and Cannon Street to serve Kent and East Sussex. This company had been formed out of the amalgamation of the South Eastern and the London, Chatham and Dover Railways—the latter being popularly known as the London, Smashem and Turnover because of its reputation for accidents.

In London the Metropolitan Railway served three lines from Baker Street with its reddish-brown engines, the Inner-Outer Circle, the Hammersmith line run jointly with the Great Western, and the Aylesbury line. From King's Cross the Great Northern sent its green locomotives peppering along towards the industrial areas to join up with the North Eastern, which too favoured green for its engines and teak for carriages. Its crack expresses included one whose name was familiar to millions who had never seen it, 'The Flying Scotsman'.

The Great Western, also using green for its engines, had chocolate and cream for its coaches and affected a handsome copper rim on the chimneys of the locomotives. This was the line to the west country, built by Isambard Kingdom Brunel, whose highly polished expresses out of Paddington for Plymouth, Bristol, Bath and Cardiff had an enviable reputation for safety, comfort and punctuality.

From Marylebone station the Great Central engines, in a rich dark green, went up the spine of England to service towns which were joined by the vast network of other companies' lines spreading out to almost every other big centre in the country. In England, you could travel up or down or across the country by many routes. At Carlisle the gleaming black engines of the London and North Western Railway from Euston joined up with the Prussian-blue locomotives of the Caledonian Railway.

London's northern suburbanites relied partly on the North London Railway, whose clanking black tank engines served Dalston and Hackney, Uxbridge Road and Gospel Oak, Kentish Town and Hampstead, Willesden Junction and Wormwood Scrubs, and carried tens of thousands of passengers daily into Broad Street. Over part of these same metals ran the London and North Western suburban line, with a terminus at Broad Street.

In 1900 London's District line was an ordinary steam-worked system, its long tunnels full of foul smoke that contributed to the winter fogs of the great metropolis. The Metropolitan line was known as the Inner or Outer Circle, according to whether one travelled east or west from Baker Street. The tickets were stamped 1 or 0 to help the inspectors.

In spite of this vast spider's web of locomotion, millions of people had never moved far from the places where they were born. Long train and boat journeys were still in 1900 rare adventures for the majority. Many provincial towns and villages were still remote from the capital. It was not until well after the First World War that the rural countryside would be fully opened up by the motor-car and the motor omnibus. Indeed, the great labouring and agricultural population continued to live much as its grandparents had done, rising early each morning and going to bed early after five o'clock teas, baking its own bread and cakes, scrimping and vainly endeavouring to save, observing family routines. For most people the only alternative to the taverns was the fireside, although many towns now had free public libraries, art galleries and public baths, and there were working mens' clubs in big industrial areas, with churches and chapels all over the country full of worshippers on Sundays.

The development of the railways between 1825 and 1860 had not only linked up the principal cities and towns, but had also cut off many of the purely rural areas, whole villages and districts being divorced from the main stream of transport and supply, so that parts of rural England, Scotland and Wales remained rustic and backward, while the large towns developed more quickly. Only with the coming of the motor-car would these villages be linked with the modern world; but by then many people were to consider that the internal combustion engine was destroying rural Britain more effectively than the railroads had done. In 1843, when the great railway mania had started, there had been fewer than 2000 miles of line in Britain. Six years later there were 5000 miles, and much of the country's railway system had been planned. By 1899 there were 21,700 miles of line open, with 1,106,681,991 passengers travelling in that year.

The end of the century saw the perfection of the steam railway as a means of transport with the use of steel rails, the block system of signalling and vast improvements in the rolling stock, including automatic braking. An English third-class corridor train of 1900 contrasted markedly with the old cattle-truck rolling stock of earlier years, whose passengers sat out in the open at the mercy of weather, smoke and steam.

'The Great Western Railway has made very material improvements in the railway service between London and Cork within the last few days,' reported *The Sphere* (June 2, 1900). 'They have built certain corridor trains with first, second and third class carriages, all of various stages of luxury. The first class carriages have a luxurious arrangement of white and gold, the second of mahogany and velvet, and the third a most effective arrangement of oak and red wool. A corridor runs right through the centre of the train from end to end. Not only can one dine, but there is a pleasant scheme by which light refreshments are supplied in every carriage by touching a button and summoning an attendant.

RAILWAY SPEEDS, 1900
THE FASTEST RUNNING TIMES WITHOUT STOPPAGES

Company	Train	From	To	Time H.M.	Distance Miles	Speed
Caledonian	9.22	Forfar	Perth	0.33	$32\frac{1}{2}$	59.09
Gt. Northern	9.12	Peterborough	Finsbury Pk	1.20	$73\frac{3}{4}$	55.31
N. Eastern	1.55	York	Darlington	0.48	$44\frac{1}{4}$	55.31
L. & N. Westn	1.28	Penrith	Preston	0.79	$79\frac{1}{4}$	54.88
Gt. Western	3.35	Paddington	Bath	2.0	107	53.5
Midland	9.42	Kettering	Kentish Tn.	1.19	$70\frac{1}{2}$	53.5
Cheshire Lns	8.59	Birkdale	Manchester	0.56	$48\frac{1}{2}$	51.96
L. & S. Westn	6.40	Salisbury	Vauxhall	1.35	$82\frac{1}{4}$	51.95
Lancashire & Yorkshire	8.13	Southport	Salford	0.39	$33\frac{1}{2}$	51.53
G. Eastern	8.51	Trowse	Ipswich	0.53	$45\frac{1}{4}$	51.23
Glasgow & S.W.	5.15	Carlisle	Dumfries	0.39	33	50.77
L., Brighton & S. Coast	11.0	Victoria	Brighton	1.0	$50\frac{3}{4}$	50.75
N. British	9.9	Haymarket	Cowlairs	0.53	$44\frac{1}{2}$	50.38
Gt. Central	10.0	Marylebone	Leicester	2.5	103	49.44
L., Chatham & Dover	5.12	St. Paul's	Margate	1.33	$74\frac{1}{2}$	48.07
S. Eastern	9.5	Cannon St	Dover Pier	1.43	$75\frac{1}{2}$	44.0

You can do the railway journey from London to New Milford in six hours.'

It was in the late 1860s that the District line in London had begun to creep round from Kensington and on towards the city. Its progress was costly, involving the rebuilding of whole streets. It was not until 1884, when to the west of London the District line had become a whole suburban network, that the two main underground systems joined to form the Inner Circle.

One of the early objections to underground railways was the smoke and steam. The use of cables, pneumatic traction, or fireless locomotives was suggested. The Victorians were never short of inventors and engineers with imagination and their condensing engines and coke fuel were an attempt to keep the air reasonably breathable. No one could claim, however, that the early underground lines were sweet places, and electric traction was a welcome innovation making possible the deep-level 'tubes', built after 1890 by new tunnelling methods which enabled workmen to dig deeper and more quickly.[1]

The City and South London electric railway had been opened in 1890, the City and Waterloo electric line was running in 1898; and now, on Wednesday June 27, 1900, the Prince of Wales opened the Central London Railway, popularly called 'the twopenny tube', an electric underground line which, it was claimed, would 'render the omnibus and the hansom cab comparatively slow, expensive and ineffectual'. A two-and-a-half-minute service of trains was provided from early in the morning until nearly midnight at a cost of twopence for the journey from the Bank of England to Shepherd's Bush, the line having cost nearly four million pounds to complete.

At the opening ceremony a descent was made by five different lifts to the platforms, where a train was waiting to take the distinguished party to Shepherd's Bush. At one end was the unfamiliar electric locomotive, decorated with flags, coupled to seven handsome carriages painted in chocolate and white, resembling the London and North Western livery. Some carriages were more luxurious than others, it having at one time been

[1] Bryan Morgan, *Down the Line*, London, 1955.

intended to run two classes. All were designed on the central corridor system and were finished inside in walnut and ash.

As the train moved swiftly along its non-stop course the Prince and his fellow-passengers experienced an odd sensation at seeing the familiar names of places on the omnibus route displayed in prominent blue and white labels on white glazed bricks at each station. Apart from the termini there were eleven stopping places, the stations being at, or close to, the General Post Office, Chancery Lane, the British Museum, Tottenham Court Road, Oxford Circus, Bond Street, Marble Arch, Lancaster Gate, Queen's Road, Notting Hill Gate and Holland Park.

LONDON'S UNDERGROUND ELECTRIC RAILWAYS: APRIL 1900

	Miles
Central London Railway (Constructing)	$6\frac{1}{2}$
City & South London Railway (Running)	$3\frac{1}{2}$
Waterloo & City Railway (Running)	$1\frac{1}{2}$
Baker Street & Waterloo Railway (Constructing)	3
Total	$14\frac{1}{2}$

Meanwhile, in New York a contract for the city's first subway was awarded to John B. McDonald, whose bids for the several sections of line totalled 35,000,000 dollars. For almost twenty miles of its length the four-track line was to be dug through solid rock. By successfully completing this giant enterprise McDonald and the banker who backed him, August Belmont, started a new era in American transportation. By 1925 nearly 600,000,000 dollars were to be spent on subways and rapid-transport lines in New York, and subways would also be adopted in Chicago and Boston.

With the expansion of the railways the canal traffic, which had for many years been the backbone of English internal trade, seriously declined. The railways had three great advantages over the canals. First, they were faster; whereas in 1823 it had been possible to carry goods by water from London to Portsmouth in four days, thirty years later the same journey was covered by train in under four hours. Second, the railways serviced many towns where there were no canals. Third, trains could carry much larger loads than barges.

Slowly the canal trade had decreased, and some great stretches of waterway and locks and tow-paths, built at the start of the century, were at the end abandoned or bankrupt or simply left to become weedy, and eventually to dry up.

On the street level in many British, American and other cities, horse tramways were still running. They had been introduced to Britain by the American G. F. Train, who established experimental tramway lines in 1861 in the London districts of Bayswater, Victoria Street, and from Westminster Bridge to Kennington Gate. He also introduced horse trams to Birkenhead—a year before London—and to Darlington, and the Potteries. Horse trams arrived in Leicester in 1874, and in Leeds they ran from the centre of the city to Kirkstall and Hunslet every ten minutes throughout the day. Until 1877 all trams were drawn by horses, but in that year a limited number of steam trams were introduced, first at Govan in Scotland. In Edinburgh, cable trams started in 1889. By the 'nineties the value of electric light and power was proved, and many towns established their own power stations to provide electric lighting for streets and houses and power for public transport.

Meanwhile hundreds of horse-drawn omnibuses caused serious traffic jams in the cities and towns. The famous 'knife-board' 'bus was out of date by 1900 but could still be seen. This gained its name from the wooden seat along the top where the passengers sat out in the open, back to back, a seat which resembled the knife-boards on which servants of the time cleaned and polished the household cutlery. The best seats on a 'knife-board', unless it was raining, were the four seats in front, in line with the driver and above the horses.

In London in 1900 there were several 'express' routes. One ran from Swiss Cottage via Oxford St and Holborn to the Bank, and cost sixpence for any distance. The changing of horses was a necessary feature of all 'bus journeys, as was the use of a 'leader' or third horse which joined the team to help the heavy load up hills.

In the big cities dozens of large and small commercial companies controlled the omnibuses, and there was strong rivalry between them. The actress Mabel Constanduros, whose grandfather was the English transport pioneer Thomas Tilling, has recalled that omnibuses played an important part in her early life.[1] The first horse trams she could remember in London were drawn by three mules abreast, the middle one having a canopy over its head hung with jingling bells. The pioneers of horse-drawn 'buses in the metropolis were Shillibeer and Tilling. The former started in 1892 with considerable capital but ended up bankrupt. Tilling, the son of a Hendon farmer, began his transport business when he was twenty with £30 capital, saved from his wages. He started by buying a grey horse and a carriage which he hired out at Walworth, then a country village. Soon he owned five horses, but they unfortunately all died in one year so he had to start again.

Early in 1850 Tilling had moved to Peckham and bought a horse omnibus, which he began to run from Rye Lane to Oxford Circus, a journey of five-and-a-half miles which took fifty minutes and cost one and sixpence. It was then the custom for 'buses to fetch many of the passengers from their homes. A business-man would send his servant to ask the 'bus to call. Because of the delays, books and newspapers were provided for the passengers, but Tilling changed the system, requiring passengers to go to the 'bus instead of it waiting on them.

'Those early 'buses were somewhat clumsy contraptions,' recalls Miss Constanturos. 'Their wheels were iron-shod—the two front ones being much smaller than those behind; and they must have been very noisy. They could carry twenty-six people, twelve inside and fourteen outside. The seats on the roof were reached by an almost perpendicular iron ladder, which was considered neither safe nor modest for ladies to mount, which is not to be wondered at, as they wore crinolines.'

The ticket system on 'buses was not introduced until 1891 and towards the end of the century the heavy old vehicles were replaced by lighter models with slatted seats of yellow wood on

[1] Noel Streatfield (ed.), *op. cit.*

the upper decks and weatherproof covers which were pulled over the knees to keep the rain off. On rainy days the conductor would ask, 'Would any gentleman oblige a lady?' seeking volunteers who would give up their warm seats and climb upstairs to sit in the rain. Miss Constanduros has recalled a music-hall song about this:

'Blige a lady, 'blige a lady, 'blige a lady, sir?
Said I, 'Old chap, she can have my lap,
But I wouldn't get drenched for 'er.'
A little fat man with a little fat voice,
From the opposite corner cried:
'If she isn't content with a full-sized lap,
Let her jolly well ride outside!'

Up to 1870 omnibuses were required to pay tolls at many of the toll gates, and also to pay the government a penny a mile, but in that year Gladstone reduced the tax to a farthing.

By 1905, sixty years after his humble start, Thomas Tilling's business was to own some seven thousand horses eating forage which cost £1000 a week. Although in 1900 all the Tilling buses were horse-drawn, in 1904 this astute business-man was to order his first double-decker motor omnibus, a Milnes-Daimler with solid rubber tyres, acetylene lighting, and curtains in the windows. By then there would be about 2500 horse buses on London's crowded streets, using about 25,000 horses, but by 1914 there would be hardly one.

The first street traction system for passengers to supersede horse-drawn vehicles was the cable-hauled tram, a simple but efficient American device which arrived in Britain in 1884. The chief cities which adopted it were Birmingham and Edinburgh. Next came the electric tram, pioneered by the Siemens company of Berlin, which opened the first regular German service in 1881 and installed the Portrush Electric Railway in Ireland in 1883. In the early 'nineties two types of electric tram, the conduit and the trolley, were adopted widely in Germany, Holland and the United States, so that by about 1897 cities such as Frankfurt, Cologne and Berlin were accustomed to swift, convenient and clean electric transport. Towards the end of the century, many corporations and private companies introduced electric tramways, at first with open tops and later with closed tops, but Manchester kept its horse trams until 1900 and London had nothing but horse-drawn vehicles on its council tramways north of the Thames until 1905.

The transition from horse bus to motor bus and from horse tram to electric tram was gradual. In 1900 there were no motor buses, and later, when they made their first appearance, they would be built like the old horse-drawn vehicles, with the engine placed directly beneath the driver, who was required to sit high up on a level with the outside passengers, as if he were a coachman. The wheels of these primitive vehicles would be iron-shod, the brakes would be of the horse-cart pattern, and there would even be a chain to lock the wheels on hills, as with the old horse buses. Meanwhile, in 1900, there were hundreds of men and boys on the streets in every big city employed at almost starvation wages to keep the roads and gutters clear of horses' droppings.

While the hansom was the most popular of private cabs, being fast, comfortable and relatively small, there were many other types of licensed carriages. On December 31, 1899 the Public Carriage Office at New Scotland Yard, London, held details of all the licensed vehicles in the metropolis:

Hansoms	7569
Clarences	3623
Omnibuses	3626
Tram-cars	1381
Hackney drivers	13,332
Stage drivers	7896
Conductors	8874

By modern standards the fares look attractive. If you hired and discharged a cab within a four-mile radius of Charing Cross you paid a shilling for the first two miles and sixpence for each extra mile or part of a mile. Outside the four-mile radius it cost a shilling for the first mile and a shilling for each extra mile or part of one. A package carried outside the cab cost twopence. If you kept a four-wheeler waiting for fifteen minutes it cost you sixpence; a two-wheeler cost eightpence, but outside the four-mile limit it cost eightpence for fifteen minutes' waiting, regardless of the number of wheels.

A favourite means of travel was by horse-brake, a heavy wagonette holding up to thirty people, drawn by a pair of horses. Outings by horse-brake were often organized by firms for their employees. Or one went by horse-brake to the races or the seaside, often accompanied by musicians or minstrels.

Public charabancs were drawn by four horses and required considerable skill to drive, for the roads at the turn of the century were congested with vehicles of all kinds. Richer folk still travelled in 'four-in-hands', private coaches with outside seats, with burnished brasses, gleaming leather, brilliantly polished varnish coachwork, and beautifully groomed horses. In London the smartest 'snob' parts, especially on Sunday, were Hyde Park Corner and Rotten Row, where gentlemen and ladies of elegance, immaculately dressed, rode on beautifully groomed horses or, dressed in finery, sought public admiration as they swept by in open carriages. St James's, Green Park and Rotten Row were the centres for people with breeding, affluence and taste—or those who claimed to have them.

In 1900 it was still possible—indeed it was comparatively easy —to travel by horse-coach from London to some centres in Britain. Black's *Guide Book to Sussex* stated:

'The coaches (fares: inside, 10s; outside 15s; box seat 20s) which from May to October have been running daily in each direction between the Hotel Victoria, Northumberland Avenue, London, and the Old Ship, Brighton, take a line a few miles to the west of the railway, for the most part passing much the same scenery. Through Surrey, indeed, the route is almost identical; but beyond Horley, where a halt is made for lunch, the road bears off to the right, entering Sussex at County Oak, a little beyond which it traverses Crawley . . . to mount a long ascent. Horses are changed at the oddly named Pease Pottage. . . .'

There was another popular, and cheap, method of getting from one place to another, and this was by bicycle. The expansion of the cycle industry had brought wealth to Midland towns whose skilled artisans had previously, during the particularly hard winters of the 'eighties, experienced great hardship. When the cycling boom began in earnest many business-men realized that there was money to be made in the cycle and pneumatic-tyre trades, the value of shares in these industries rose rapidly, and in towns and villages all over the country dealers and repair shops opened up to serve the great cycling public. A good bicycle, such as a Triumph, could be bought for ten guineas in 1900.

The 'nineties saw the hey-day of the pedal cycle and the revolutionary spectacle of men and women riding away, often over rough roads, out of town and into the country. At the Cycle Show of 1899 the motorcycle was regarded as a novelty, almost a freak. London shop-girls dressed up in men's tweed golfing suits with feathered Homburg hats and starched linen collars and accompanied their menfolk on 'bicycles built for two'. At steep hills they often dismounted and walked, and they used the new freewheeling system going downhill.

By 1894 the modern Coventry bicycles with light frames and acetylene lamps were being sold all over the world. Drop handle-bars were already fashionable. Office clerks and factory hands sped along the highways to discover new worlds of romance and enchantment at wayside public-houses or on heather commons far beyond Esher, Surbiton, Selby or Peebles. Bi-cycling brought new freedoms, fresh air, a revolutionary spirit, an expression of a changing world. Even underpaid parlour maids and 'skivvies' and grooms and stable boys and labourers could dress up and cycle along the country lanes in search of new horizons and an escape from drudgery. Never had so many people owned their own means of conveyance. They might never own horses or pony carts or broughams, and they would certainly never run one of those fantastic, expensive Panhard or Daimler motor cars that created such a dust when you got behind them, but at least they had their own bicycles, and that, in the hot, golden summer of 1900, must have seemed attractive.

16

THE END OF AN ERA

There was no doubt about the increased popularity of the Queen during her last years. Her energetic support of her armies overseas and her frequent public appearances had brought her many new friends. With some satisfaction she noted that, when she went out, the crowds welcomed her with even more enthusiasm than they showed for the Prince of Wales, who was undeniably a popular figure. The last of her many birthdays had been celebrated on May 24, 1900 with national rejoicing. She wrote in her journal:

'Again my old birthday returns, my 81st! God has been very merciful and supported me, but my trials and anxieties have been manifold and I feel tired and upset by all I have gone through this winter and spring.'

Extra men had to be rushed to Balmoral to deal with nearly four thousand telegrams of congratulation; all over the Empire flags were flown, troops paraded, bands played, and people went to their local government house or embassy to sign the visitors' book in tribute to the sovereign. At St Pancras, which was typical of many boroughs in England, an elaborate carnival paraded the streets with 300 horse-drawn decorated floats bearing military and naval displays, sections of armoured trains and guns—a kind of Lord Mayor's Show in miniature. One car, drawn by six horses and representing the Roman Hippodrome, was lent by Mr Moss of the London Hippodrome.

At South Kensington the students of the Royal Colleges of

Art, Science and Music (who owed much to the foresight of Victoria and Albert, who had planned and built the magnificent colleges and museums) had paraded London's West End dragging a tremendous triumphal car decorated with palms and flowers, in the centre of which rose a statue of the Queen modelled by the art students, and lit by acetylene lights. Behind the Queen was the model of Baden-Powell which had been carried around the town a few days earlier, on Mafeking night.

Her subjects did not know it, but the Queen was far from well. Her summer holiday in Scotland was marred by fatigue, indigestion, and evidence of old age. But by the beginning of July her busy life was in full swing again. There were visits from the Duchess of Coburg, the Connaughts, Joseph Chamberlain, the Khedive of Egypt, and members of her vast family, meetings of the Privy Council, endless studies of the casualty lists from South Africa, the daily routine of the state despatch boxes, the bestowal of nine knighthoods, the dictation or writing of countless letters and her diary, and the management of personal affairs. The 'cruel treatment' of her grand-daughter Princess Marie Louise by her husband Prince Aribert of Anhalt, after a wedding sponsored by the Kaiser, roused her to indignant action. The princess, rudely summoned from Canada to face divorce proceedings in Germany, was hastily rescued by a telegram addressed to the Governor-General from her grandmother:

'Tell my grand-daughter to come home to me.
VR.'

The disastrous marriage was annulled that December, and Princess Marie Louise was established in London with her own household, to enjoy many years of affection from the public, whom she was to serve in the best traditions of the royal family until her death in 1956.[1]

On her return from Balmoral to Windsor in November the Queen inspected a battalion of Canadian volunteers in the quadrangle of the castle and said a few words of welcome and thanks while seated in her carriage. These were her last public

[1] Elizabeth Longford, op. cit.

words. Then she went to Osborne (with its memories of her Prince Albert), never to return alive. Christmas was celebrated quietly, with the weather 'tempestuous', and she was far from well. Early on the morning of January 2nd, at the start of another century, HMS *Canada* steamed past the windows of Osborne House, bringing Field-Marshal Lord Roberts home from South Africa. He was the symbol of victory—although it was by no means yet achieved—and he was to be the army's new Commander-in-Chief.

As 'Bobs' stepped ashore at Trinity Pier, East Cowes, he was greeted with a nineteen-gun salute and every ship in the anchorage blew her whistle or rang her bell. Princess Beatrice came to welcome the hero on behalf of her mother, and the mayor read a formal address, after which Lord Roberts' staff was taken in carriages to Osborne House, passing under a triumphal arch which the household had erected. Lord Roberts was received by the little old lady who forty-two years earlier had pinned the Victoria Cross on to his tunic. She sat and talked to him and asked him about the war. Then she told him he was to be honoured with the Order of the Garter, a distinction not awarded to a victorious general since the days of Wellington. He was also to receive an earldom with remainder to his daughter, his son who would have inherited the title having been killed at Colenso. He was thus the only Briton with the Garter, the Victoria Cross, and the Order of Merit.

Next day 'Bobs', his family and staff, boarded the royal carriage in a special train. Shortly after 1 p.m. they arrived in London to find Paddington station bedecked with flowers and bunting and a stand built on Platform Nine to hold 300 privileged guests. As the band struck up *See the Conquering Hero Comes* the Prince and Princess of Wales stepped forward to greet the Field-Marshal. Their route in open carriages to Buckingham Palace followed Praed Street, Edgware Road, Marble Arch, Hyde Park Corner, Piccadilly, St James's Street and the Mall. Fourteen thousand troops lined the pavements and the cheering spectators stood six deep. Every house was decorated with flags, and across the streets coloured banners bore such slogans as 'Bravo Bobs' and 'To Bobs, the Kindest of the Kind and the Bravest of the Brave'. Parliament was to grant him £100,000 in recognition of his services and he was to settle at 47 Portland Place and to take up his duties at the war office in Pall Mall, as Commander-in-Chief.[1]

The Queen saw 'Bobs' again on January 14th, and three days earlier she gave her last audience to a minister, when Joseph Chamberlain visited her. Next day, January 15th, she took her last carriage drive beyond the gates of Osborne. Her appetite had fallen off, she had difficulty in sleeping, and her attendants had become very worried about her failing health. On the 16th a donkey chaise took her for a morning drive around the grounds, but when it returned to the door for the usual afternoon outing she was too ill to go, and it was sent away. Next day the press announced that the Queen was in need of rest, and on the following day it was known that her illness was serious. Real alarm came with an official bulletin on the 19th, announcing that the Queen's condition was causing anxiety.

The Prince of Wales was already at Osborne and other members of the family were on the way. On the evening of Tuesday January 22nd, at 6.30 p.m., she died peacefully in the presence of her nearest and dearest relatives, while the Kaiser supported her with his single strong arm, as he had done for several hours, not being able to use his other arm because it was withered, and not wishing anyone to take his place. The members of the family stood round the bed and called out their names to reassure the dying matriarch. Her last word was 'Bertie', whispered to her heir.

The Duke of Windsor has recalled the last years of his great-grandmother's life in the commentary for his film *A King's Story*: 'I was only six-and-a-half when she died, so my recollections of her are somewhat dim and hazy. She reigned for sixty-four years and my mother spent forty years of her life with Queen Victoria. I remember her at Osborne, and at Balmoral, and also a little at Windsor. It was usually out-of-doors because she liked to eat and work out-of-doors at all her three residences when-

---

[1] David James, *Lord Roberts*, London, 1954.

ever the weather permitted. She used to ride down in a little pony-carriage led by one of the retainers and would then breakfast, do her work with her secretaries, and so forth.'

The Queen's death was marked by an extraordinary outburst of national mourning. For many months black was to be the only wear for men and women. 'Victoria, the Queen, has gone and the world is poorer for her loss,' said *The Observer*. 'From savages in South Africa who say they will now look out at night for a new star in their heavens, to monarchs on their thrones who will miss the sympathy of which a modern throne needs so much, all feel they have lost a friend.'

'The golden reign is closed,' said the *Daily Telegraph* (January 23, 1901). 'The supreme woman of the world, best of the highest, greatest of the good, is gone. The Victorian age is over. Never, never was loss like this, so inward and profound that only the slow years can reveal its true reality. The Queen is dead.'

The public was aware that in her final years their sovereign had ceased to be a recluse and had unsparingly devoted herself to her 'beloved people' and the nation. When in July 1900 she had received the Christian Endeavour delegation in the quadrangle at Windsor Castle she had appeared for the first time out of mourning since her husband's death. Future generations might think of her as a widow in black, but she was dressed entirely in white; a white dress, white cashmere shawl, and a white hat trimmed with gay, white ostrich feathers.

During her reign she had seen eleven Lord Chancellors come and go, ten Prime Ministers, six Speakers of the House of Commons, at least three bishops of every see, six Archbishops of Canterbury, six Archbishops of York, and six Commanders-in-Chief. As for her family, she could look with pride on them for they filled or were about to fill the thrones of Europe, carrying a distinguished tradition to the Empires of Germany and Prussia, to the Kingdoms of Greece and Rumania, and later to Norway and Spain, as well as countless duchies and dynasties in the heart of Germany.[1] Nearly all the thrones of Europe were connected with Victoria and Albert. She left behind her forty grand-

[1] Roger Fulford, *Hanover to Windsor*, London, 1960.

children and four times the number of subjects who had paid homage to her when she came to the throne as a girl of eighteen. Her territory was thirty times the size of the United Kingdom, over three million square miles having been added to the Empire, so that on the map of the world large areas now stood out in red. The first dependency to be annexed in her reign had been Aden, in 1839; the last was the Transvaal, in 1900. In the first year of her reign the SS *Sirius* and the SS *Great Western* had crossed the Atlantic, the first steamships to connect the old world with the new. Now Britain's population was not 25,000,000 but 45,000,000, and the world was richer for many innovations and inventions, many of which had been created, discovered or developed by Victoria's subjects. They included turbine engines, railroads, ocean steamships, wireless telegraphy, improved diving apparatus, photography, cinematography, the phonograph, electric light and power, the internal combustion engine, the pneumatic rubber tyre, and the bicycle. The postal system had been improved, setting a pattern for the rest of the world, and there had been great advances in medical science. The study of aerial navigation was soon to lead to the development of the aeroplane. There had been considerable progress in education, housing and welfare services, as well as in a general appreciation of the arts, literature and music. No age had been richer in achievements.

The Queen's body was taken on the royal yacht to the mainland and was then conveyed to London and Windsor for the internment at Frogmore. Cecil Hepworth, the film pioneer, has related how he photographed the procession for the motion pictures:

'I had a wonderful position just inside the railings of Grosvenor Gardens opposite Victoria station. My camera was the coffin-like construction which had been made some time before for taking the *Phantom Rides*.[1] When it was used on the front of an engine I did not realize, or care, how much noise it made. In the great silence and hush of the most solemn funeral in history it was a

[1] Sequences of film taken in 1899 from the front of London and South Western Railway engines travelling at speed.

very different matter. That silence was a thing that closed in everything like an almost palpable curtain, not broken, but only accentuated, by the muted strains of the funeral march. Then at the moment of greatest tension I started to turn my camera, and the silence was shattered! If I could have had my deepest wish then the ground would certainly have opened at my feet and swallowed me and my beastly machine. But the noise had one curious effect. It caught the attention, as it must certainly have done, of the new King, Edward VII, and I believe that is why he halted the procession so that posterity might have the advantage of the cinematograph record.'

The King, the Kaiser and the Duke of Connaught were following on horseback close behind the gun-carriage when it turned the corner in front of the camera, so that the three figures filled the entire view. The King, hearing the whirring of the camera as the crank handle turned, suddenly held up his hand to stop the procession, and while he and his companions reined up in the centre of the picture he leaned over and talked first to one and then the other.

Mr Hepworth hurried back to his villa at Walton-on-Thames with his precious negative to develop it and start printing copies, for which he had already received orders from all over the world. He worked all through the night and the next day and following night, only to find that through some fault in the film stock all his prints had turned out milky-white. Every foot of film had to be printed again. Before the work was over, he and his assistants had worked for eight days and nights with only nine hours for food and sleep. *The Funeral of Queen Victoria* was seen by millions of people, and can still be seen, more scratched and flickering than it was originally, but a document of absorbing interest.

'Fortunately the day was dry, though cold and dreary,' wrote Prince George, the Duke of Cambridge and late Queen's cousin. 'I drove to Victoria station with Prince Edward and Dolly, now in waiting, and there joined all the Kings and royalties, whence I rode with the King and Emperor behind the hearse. The royal train with the Queen's body arrived at eleven, and then we all started. I drove in the fourth carriage with Edward Weimar and

Lady Wolseley. The crowds were very enormous, but their demeanour magnificent, solemn and silent. Got to Paddington at one and left for Windsor by train a few minutes afterwards.'

It was not only in Britain and Europe that great changes were taking place. Later in the year President Theodore Roosevelt was to move into the White House in Washington, following President McKinley's assassination, bringing with him considerable reforms, which would improve the working conditions of many wage-earners, in an effort to protect the 'common man' from exploitation. The United States was expanding so rapidly, her standards of material comfort were improving on such a vast scale, she possessed such enormous resources of wealth, that the future was bound to bring increasing problems. Already the American Federation of Labour and the Farmers' Alliance were influencing the course of government. Roosevelt was determined to work for greater social justice and a fair deal for the ordinary citizen, and in many ways he was going to succeed.

Visiting New York in December 1900, Alfred Harmsworth had been handed a message from the owner of *The World*, Joseph Pulitzer, the most powerful of New York's newspaper-owners. It invited him to take charge of *The World* for one day, remodelling it as he wished. Harmsworth was to be given complete editorial powers and was asked to produce the issue of *The World* dated January 1, 1901, the first number of the new century. He accepted the challenge and edited what he called a 'tabloid' newspaper. ('No story of more than two hundred and fifty words!' he ordered.) Subsequently a British firm of chemists issued warnings against him for his use of what they claimed was their copyright word 'tabloid', but for several days Harmsworth was a trans-continental celebrity, his name bracketed in bold type with the giants of the American press, Pulitzer, James Gordon Bennett, Frank Munsey, and William Randolph Hearst. The American war correspondent Julian Ralph said, 'Harmsworth stands out, easy, well-controlled and polished in manner, the most pre-possessing and picturesque figure in journalism on either side of the Atlantic.'

The front page of the edition bore the news that Hiram S. Maxim, the American-born inventor of 'the swiftest death-dealing machines', had been knighted by the Queen. Another headline announced that a 'roar like Niagara gone mad' had risen from City Hall Park on the stroke of midnight, the buildings being swathed in light while rockets made a brilliant canopy for the vast crowds singing *America* as the new century dawned. Harmsworth was a considerable success in New York. 'Mark Twain in great form,' he wrote in his diary. 'Went to see Edison. Spent the day with him.' At the Whitney ball at 871 Fifth Avenue ('the finest private social function ever held in New York'), the Harmsworths were announced with the Vanderbilts, the Astors, the Jays, the Harrimans, the Reids and other society families.

In recent years there has been a tendency to regard the Edwardian era as a golden age, but it is now clear that the British Empire, in spite of appearances, was past her zenith when Victoria died. Britain's commercial and industrial rivals were slowly over-taking her, particularly in the United States. In the earlier part of Victoria's reign, Britain had been not only the world's work-shop and factory but also its banker, carrier, clearing-house, insurance broker and ship-builder. Until 1870, she had produced half of the world's coal, but in 1900 her output was surpassed by that of the United States. America, Germany and Japan were the new rivals in mass production. And by the end of the Edwardian era the progress of scientific development and the industry of her competitors were seriously to undermine Britain's position as the world's workshop, and even her claim to be mistress of the seas was soon to be doubtful, while the danger of neglecting her land and naval forces in the face of growing military and maritime expansion in Germany was to be apparent.

The Edwardian age was just beginning, and for many it would be a period of splendour and prosperity. But for millions of men born only a few years before 1900 there was soon to be no further prospect, no future, nothing beyond the mud of Flanders, the beaches and trenches of the Dardanelles, or a watery grave in the Atlantic.

INDEX

247